IN THE NAME OF

ALLAH

THE ALL-COMPASSIONATE, ALL-MERCIFUL

DON'T BE SAD

BE HAPPY

Copyright ©
TX0008901934

Don't Be Sad
Be Happy

Aededan
Imam Al-Qarne

Edition 1 (1980)
Edition 4 (2011)
New Revised Edition 5 (2023)

All rights reserved. No part of this book may be reproduced or transmitted in any form or by any means, electronic or mechanical, including photocopying, recording, or by any information storage and retrieval system, without written permission from the Publisher.

Book and Cover Illustration Noaha

IIPH™

SN 0815111 SN 6602141

Table of Contents

Pronunciation and Transliteration Chart	15
About this Book	19
About the Word 'Lord'	21
Publisher's Note	23
Editor's Foreword	25
Introduction to the First Edition (Of the Arabic Version)	29
O Allah!	31
Contemplate and be thankful	33
The past is gone forever	34
Today is all you have	35
Leave the future alone until it comes	36
How to deal with bitter criticism	37
Do not expect gratitude from anyone	38
Doing good to others comforts the heart	39
Repel boredom with work	40
Don't be a mimicker	41
The pens have been lifted; the pages have dried	42
When life gives you lemons, make lemonade	44
Your home is enough for you	46
Your recompense is with Allah	47
Faith is life itself	48

Gather the honey but don't break the hive	49
Accept life as it is	52
Find consolation by remembering the afflicted	53
The prayer... the prayer	54
Patience is most fitting	57
Don't carry the weight of the world on your shoulders	58
Don't be crushed by what is insignificant	59
How wretched are the souls of such people!	60
Be content with what Allah has given you	61
Being sad is not encouraged in Islam	64
Smile	69
The blessing of pain	73
The blessing of knowledge	76
The art of happiness	78
Controlling one's emotions	81
The bliss of the Prophet's Companions	82
Eliminate boredom from your life	85
Cast off anxiety	86
Be Happy – Everything will occur according to preordainment	93
Be Happy – Wait patiently for a happy outcome	94
Be Happy – Always remember Allah	97
Be Happy – Never lose hope of Allah's mercy	99
Don't grieve over unworthy things	100

Be Happy – Repel anxiety	102
Don't grieve when others blame and disparage you	103
Don't grieve over being poor	104
Don't feel sad over fears for what may happen	104
Don't grieve over criticism from the jealous and the weak-minded	105
Be Happy – Do good to others	110
Jealousy is nothing new	113
Don't be sad for lack of ample provision	116
Appreciate that your trial is light compared to others	117
Don't mimic the personality of others	118
Isolation and its positive effects	118
Don't be shaken by hardships	121
Don't be sad – The fundamentals of happiness	122
Your best companion is a book	127
Don't grieve – There is another life to come	130
Don't feel overly stressed when work piles up	131
Don't despair when you face a difficult situation	132
Depression weakens the body and the soul	134
Depression: A cause of ulcers	134
Some other effects of depression	134
What depression and anger do	135
Hold a good opinion of your Lord	135
When your thoughts wander	136

Embrace constructive criticism	136
Most rumors are baseless	138
Gentleness averts confrontations	138
Yesterday is gone forever	139
This life does not deserve our grief	140
As long as you have faith in Allah, don't be sad	142
Don't grieve over trivialities, for the entire world is trivial	143
This is the way of the world	145
Strive to help others	145
You're not deprived as long as you have a loaf of bread	146
Blessings in disguise	146
You are unique, so be yourself	147
Much that seems harmful is in fact a blessing	149
Faith is the greatest remedy!	150
Don't lose hope	151
Don't be sad – Life is shorter than you think	152
As long as you have life's basic necessities – Don't be sad	153
Contentment repels sadness	154
If you lose a limb, you still have others to compensate for it	155
The days rotate in bringing good and bad	156
Travel throughout Allah's wide earth	157
In the last moments of life	159
Don't let calamity shake you	160

Don't grieve – This world isn't worth it	160
Don't be sad: Remember that you believe in Allah	161
Despair not - Disabilities don't prevent success	162
If you embrace Islam, there is no reason for you to be sad	163
What brings about happiness	166
The ingredients of happiness	167
You won't die before your appointed time	167
'O Allah, Who is full of majesty and honor	169
Steps to take if you fear a jealous person	173
Good manners	173
Sleepless nights	174
The evil consequences of sinning	174
Strive for your sustenance, but don't be covetous	176
The secret of guidance	177
Ten gems for a good and noble life	178
Don't be sad – Learn to deal with your reality	181
Don't be sad – Sooner or later everything in this world perishes	185
Depression leads to misery	186
Depression may lead to suicide	187
Asking Allah for forgiveness opens locked doors	191
Let others depend on you, not you on them	193
Prudence	194
Don't cling to other than Allah	196

Do those things that bring you peace	196
Preordainment	198
The sweet taste of freedom	199
Dirt was the pillow of Sufyân ath-Thawri	200
Don't pay attention to the telltale	200
The curses of the foolish are of no consequence to you	200
Appreciate the beauty of the universe	201
Avarice is of no avail	203
Bearing hardship atones for sins	204
The ingredients of happiness	205
The fatigue and stress that come with an important position	206
Come to the prayer	207
Charity brings peace to the giver	208
Don't be angry	210
Supplications of the morning	211
The Qur'an: The Blessed Book	212
Don't aspire to fame, or else you will be taxed with stress and worries	213
The good life	214
Bear trials patiently	215
Worship Allah by surrendering your will to Him	215
From governor to carpenter	216
Mixing with people of low character ruins a person's peace	217
For the calamity-stricken	218

The positive effects of having true faith in Allah alone	219
Take care of your outside as well as your inside	224
Seek refuge with Allah	226
Trust Him completely	227
They agree on three points	227
The wrongdoing of the transgressor	228
Khosrau and the old woman	229
A handicap in one area can be compensated for by excellence in another	230
A few words about the foolish	234
Faith in Allah is the way to salvation	236
Even the disbelievers are at different levels	237
An iron will	238
The inborn disposition upon which we were created	239
Whatever is written for you will unerringly come to you	240
Work hard for the fruitful end	241
Your life is full of priceless moments	245
Performing noble deeds is the way to happiness	249
Beneficial versus fruitless knowledge	249
Read more, but with understanding and contemplation	251
Take account of yourself	252
Three mistakes that are common in our everyday lives	253
Make plans and take proper precautions	253
Winning people over	254

Travel to different lands	255
Perform the late-night voluntary prayers	256
Your reward is paradise	256
True love	257
The Sharia is made easy for you	259
Tranquility and peace	260
Beware of ardent love	260
The rights of brotherhood	263
Two secrets regarding sinning (even if you know them, don't sin)	263
Seek out sustenance, but don't be covetous	264
A religion that is full of benefits	265
Stay away from these four	266
To find peace, turn to your Lord	267
Two great words of solace	268
Some positive effects of hardships	268
Knowledge	269
Happiness is a divine gift that does not distinguish between the rich	269
Being remembered after death is a second life	270
Invoke Allah with the following	270
A Lord Who wrongs not	270
Write your own history	271
Listen attentively to the words of Allah	272
Everyone is searching for happiness	273

Prepare for bad times by being thankful when all is well	274
Bliss versus the fire	275
A good life	277
What then is happiness?	278
Good words ascend to Him	280
The supplication of the wronged	284
The importance of having a good friend	284
In Islam, security is a must	285
Fleeting glory	286
Virtuous deeds are the crown on the head of a happy life	288
Everlasting life and paradise are there, not here!	290
Enemies of the divine way	291
The reality of this life	292
The key to happiness	294
How they used to live	295
What the wise say about patience	296
The importance of a positive attitude	297
A few words on patience	298
Don't grieve if you are poor	300
A word on reading	300
Don't be sad, and study Allah's signs in the creation	300
O Allah! O Allah!	304
Don't grieve, for change must take place	306

Don't give pleasure to your enemy by displaying grief	307
Optimism versus skepticism	308
O son of Adam, don't despair	310
Blessings in disguise	312
The fruits of contentment	316
Being pleased with Allah	316
For the malcontented, there is wrath	316
The benefits one reaps by being contented	317
Do not challenge your Lord	318
A just decree	318
Resentment yields no return	319
Safety is in contentment	319
Dissatisfaction is the door to doubt	320
Satisfaction is richness and safety	320
The fruit of contentment is thankfulness	321
Overlooking the faults of your brothers and sisters	323
Take advantage of health and free time	325
Allah protects those who believe	326
Signposts on the seeker's highway	328
Being blessed with honor is also a test	329
The enduring treasures	330
Determination can overcome insurmountable barriers	330
Read to gain wisdom	331

Take precautions	332
Verify the facts yourself	333
Resolve to do something, then do it	333
The life of this world	333
Hiding from evil is a temporary solution	334
Remember that you are dealing with the Most Merciful	336
Optimism	337
Life is toil	337
Treading the middle path saves you from destruction	338
You are judged by your dominant characteristics	339
It's not enough to be merely intelligent: You need true guidance as well	340
If you have inner beauty, you will discern beauty in the universe	342
Relief after hardship	343
You are above jealousy	343
Knowledge is the key to serenity and ease	345
The wrong way to go about things	345
The noblest human being	346
One step at a time	347
Whether you have a little or a lot, learn to be thankful	348
Be free from worry and fear	349
Deeds of charity	350
Recreation and relaxation	351
Contemplate the universe	355

Follow a studied plan	355
Do not be disorderly in your affairs	356
Your value is determined by your faith and character	357
The bliss of the Companions	359
The wretchedness of the disbelievers	360
Be gentle with womenfolk	361
A smile every morning	361
An obsession for revenge is poison that flows through a diseased soul	363
Do not melt into someone else's personality	364
Waiting for relief from Allah	365
Pursue work that you enjoy	366
Guidance: A natural consequence of belief	368
The middle course	369
Avoiding extremes	370
Who are the righteous ones?	371
Allah is Most Kind to His slaves	372
An early recompense	375
When you ask, ask Allah	376
Precious moments	377
Divine preordainment	378
Death	379
Allah alone is All-Powerful	380
Unexpected relief	382

Pronunciation and Transliteration Chart

Arabic script	Pronunciation	Transliterated form
ا	short 'a', as in *cat*	a
ى ــا	longer 'a', as in *cab* (not as in *cake*)	Â
ب	/b/ as in *bell*, *rubber* and *tab*	b
ت	/t/ as in *tap*, *mustard* and *sit*	t
ة	takes the sound of the preceding diacritical mark sometimes ending in h (when in pausal form): ah, ih or ooh; or atu(n), ati(n) or ata(n) when uninterrupted	h or t (when followed by another Arabic word)
ث	/th/ as in *thing*, *maths* and *wealth*	th
ج	/j/ as in *jam*, *ajar* and *age*	j
ح	a 'harsher' sound than the English initial /h/, and may occur medially and in word-final position as well	ḥ
خ	as in *Bach* (in German); may occur initially and medially as well	kh

د	/d/ as in *do*, *muddy* and *red*	d
ذ	as in *this*, *father* and *smooth*	dh
ر	/r/ as in *raw*, *arid* and *war*; may also be a rolled 'r', as pronounced in Spanish	r
ز	/z/ as in *zoo*, *easy* and *gaze*	z
س	/s/ as in *so*, *messy* and *grass*	s
ش	as in *ship*, *ashes* and *rush*	sh
ص	no close equivalent in English, but may be approximated by pronouncing it as /sw/ or /s/ farther back in the mouth	ṣ
ض	no close equivalent in English, but may be approximated by pronouncing it as /d/ farther back in the mouth	ḍ
ط	no close equivalent in English, but may be approximated by pronouncing it as /t/ farther back in the mouth	ṭ
ظ	no close equivalent in English, but may be approximated by pronouncing 'the' farther back in the mouth	<u>dh</u>
ع	no close equivalent in English: a guttural sound in the back of the throat	'
غ	no close equivalent in English, but may be closely approximated by pronouncing it like the French /r/ in 'rouge'	Gh
ف	/f/ as in *fill*, *effort* and *muff*	F
ق	no close equivalent in English, but may be approximated by pronouncing it as /k/ farther back in the mouth	Q
ك	/k/ as in *king*, *buckle* and *tack*	K

l	/l/ as in *lap, halo*; in the word Allah, it becomes velarized as in *ball*	ل
m	/m/ as in *men, simple* and *ram*	م
n	/n/ as in *net, ant* and *can*	ن
h	/h/ as in *hat*; unlike /h/ in English, in Arabic /h/ is pronounced in medial and word-final positions as well	ھ ـھـ ـھ
w	as in *wet* and *away*	و
oo	long 'u', as in *boot* and *too*	و
y	as in *yard* and *mayo*	ي
ee	long 'e', as in *eat, beef* and *see*	ي
(omitted in initial position)	glottal stop: may be closely approximated by pronouncing it like 't' in the Cockney English pronunciation of *butter*: *bu'er*, or the stop sound in *uh-oh!*	ء

Diacritical marks (*tashkeel*)

Name of mark	Pronunciation	Transliterated form
َ◌ fatḥah	very short 'a' or schwa (unstressed vowel)	A
ِ◌	shorter version of ee or schwa (unstressed vowel)	I

Kasrah		
ـُ dammah	shorter version of oo	U
ـّ shaddah	a doubled consonant is stressed in the word, and the length of the sound is also doubled	double letter
ـْ sukoon	no vowel sound between consonants or at the end of a word	absence of vowel

About this Book

This work has taken Important Points and Objectives from the Holy Qur'an. Aededan originally wrote the book and Imam and Dr. Al-Qarne summarized it further and added his invaluable comments.

This book was written for anyone who is searching for happiness or who is living through pain and grief or who has been afflicted with a hardship that results in sadness and restless nights. For the cure, we have filled the pages of this book with prescriptions taken from various sources – God's Holy Books, e.g. the Qur'an, the Torah, the Gospel, poetry, poignant anecdotes, parables, and true stories.

About the Word '*Lord*'

The word lord in English has several related meanings. The original meaning is 'master' or 'ruler', and in this sense it is often used to refer to human beings: 'the lord of the mansion' or 'Lord So-and-So' (in the United Kingdom, for example). The word *Lord* with a capital L is used in the lexicon of Islam to refer to the One and Only God — Allah. In Islam, there is no ambiguity about the meaning of this word. While it is true that one may occasionally use the word *lord* (whether capitalized or not) to refer to a human being, in Islamic discourse the reference of this term is always clear from the context. Whereas for Christians, Hindus and other polytheists, the word *Lord* with a capital L may refer to Allah, to Jesus or to some imagined deity, for Muslims, there can be no plurality of meaning. Allah alone is the Lord, and the Lord is Allah — not any other being.

The Editor

Publisher's Note

All praises and thanks belong to Allah alone, the One, the Almighty, and the All-Merciful. Blessings and peace be upon Prophet Muhammad, the last of His Messengers and Prophets, and upon his family, his Companions and all those who follow in his footsteps until the end of time.

As a publisher of Islamic books, I am inundated with a spate of books that people think should be translated and published. The process of sifting through those books and choosing the best ones is a responsibility that a publisher cannot take lightly, for those are the books upon which the English-speaking Muslims will depend to learn their religion. Making choices among those books is never easy, as there are many excellent Islamic books that have yet to be translated into English.

Be Happy, however, was an easy choice, not only because its subject matter is very relevant to our times, but also because the author deals with it very effectively. Imam Al-Qarne delves into problems that both Muslims and non-Muslims suffer from, mentioning solutions, though, from an Islamic perspective.

There are a surfeit of self-help programs and self-help books that try to deal with the ways of overcoming depression, coping with problems or calamities, or achieving happiness. Those books and programs, however, are, for the most part, feeble attempts at dealing with these problems, because they don't get to the heart of the matter: faith in

Allah. The ideas found in this book proceed from the premise that faith in Allah is necessary towards the solution of any problem.

Nevertheless, *Be Happy* is not a work that is limited to Muslims. Non-Muslims who read it with an open mind will appreciate the author's ideas, which are based on the firm footing of revealed texts, and his thoughts, which are penetrating and learned.

May Allah's peace and blessings be upon our Prophet Muhammad, his family, his Companions, and the believers.

Editor's Foreword

All praise is for Allah (Glorified and Exalted is He); may He send peace and blessings on Prophet Muhammad (blessings and peace be upon him), his family, and his Companions.

In *Be Happy*, Imam Al-Qarne offers a practical approach not only in dealing with, but also in overcoming, the various hardships and difficulties we face in life. He manages to engage the reader's attention from the very beginning of the book, answering the doubts that besiege us when we are afflicted with hardship or depression. Because Imam Al-Qarne writes from an Islamic perspective, with his advice taken from infallible sources – -the Qur'an and the Sunnah – he goes beyond other books on this topic – books that, for the most part, are full of platitudes and rhetoric and short on sound, practical advice.

Yet Imam Al-Qarne has done something in this book to which some Muslims might object: at times, he has quoted Western and Eastern philosophers. Some might argue that relying on their sayings is contrary to what an Islamic author should do, given the vast wealth of knowledge that can be found in books written and compiled by Muslim scholars. However, Imam Al-Qarne has quoted non-Muslims only when what they say is relevant to the subject matter and in agreement with the truth. Furthermore, he does not rely on those quotes to establish the principles and rules; rather, he uses them merely to add variety and flavor to the book. Wisdom is the goal of every believer; wherever one finds it, one is most deserving of it.

This book provides the reader with the Islamic approach to dealing with the trials and tribulations of life. Because change is a gradual and painstaking process, I advise you not to read this book in one sitting in an attempt to absorb everything in the span of a few hours. You should take it in doses, allowing yourself time to reflect on the seemingly simple, yet profoundly deep, wisdom written herein. At the present time, when so many of us are afflicted with the ailments described in this book – depression, grief, and spiritual malaise – -we would be wise to read *Be Happy*.

Methodology in *Be Happy*

This book is intended for all readers; however, to be fair to the English readers, Imam Al-Qarne wrote in a style that is both elegant and graceful in Arabic, but if it was translated verbatim into English, the result would be unfavorable – the style would at best seem awkward. Here I give you an outline of how I translated this work:

1. **Poetry:** I translated approximately twenty-five percent of the poems found in the original version of the book. I translated only those verses of poetry that I clearly understood and which I felt would have a positive impact on the reader. Those translated verses do not come close to their full meanings, and some of them lose the many connotations found in the precise wording of the original. Nonetheless, I translated them because their meanings contain some wisdom.

2. **Style:** The author's style, as is the style of most good Arabic writers, is very descriptive and very florid; he often uses many adjectives when attempting to give a single meaning. Because this style is not as effective in English, I had to do some pruning, striking out, and summarizing – all for the sake of conciseness. Wherever I did this, I did so in the interest of the English readers, trying to simplify and summarize sentences and paragraphs without sacrificing nuances in meaning.

3. **Islamic terms:** I loosely translated some Islamic terms that other translators often transliterate (such as *eemân*). Transliteration makes the reader pause to understand the word's meaning. In contrast, with a scholarly essay that deals with a difficult subject, a person should be able to read Bed Happy quickly, without having to stop and consider difficult terms; the reader should be able to move from one idea to the next, without being interrupted by unwelcome pauses. If the book was on Islamic jurisprudence, however, where the meanings of terms are more crucial, I would have transliterated the terms in order to preserve their complete meaning.

4. **Repetition:** The book contains a great deal of repetition; the author himself mentions this in his introduction. On some occasions, when I deemed it important to the flow of the book, I omitted some of the repetition. For the most part, though, I tried to remedy the problem by expressing an idea the second time around in a different way, changing both the wording and the style.

5. **Qur'anic verses:** Though the author did not do so, I mentioned the chapter and verse numbers of the Qur'anic text.

6. **Quotes**: The author quotes many non-Arab writers, most of whom are English thinkers or philosophers. Because he mentions the quotes in Arabic, and because of the difficulty involved in finding all the original sayings in English, I deemed it sufficient to translate the quotes back into English. Therefore, in many places, they are not the exact words of the persons being quoted.

May Allah reward the author for his efforts in writing this much-needed book. May He guide us to the Straight Path, save us from the hellfire, and admit us by His mercy into paradise.

Introduction
to the First Edition

All praise is for Allah, the Almighty. May He send peace and blessings on Muhammad (bpuh), on his family, and on his Companions. I sincerely hope that readers will benefit from this book. Before reading it, you might – after only a perfunctory glance – -pass some kind of judgment. However, let sound logic and precepts taken from revelation arbitrate that judgment. Also, bear in mind that it is indeed a culpable offence for one to judge a work before having read it thoroughly or at least hearing what it is about. Here I present to you a synopsis of this book.

This book says the following: Rejoice and be happy; remain positive and at peace. Indeed it says this as well: Live life as it should be lived – wholesomely, happily, and productively. This book diagnoses the mistakes we make that go against the intrinsic logic that we – as human beings – have been endowed with (but which we tend to forget when we do not follow correct guidance), whether those mistakes are in our thinking or in our dealings.

This book forbids you from persisting in ways that conflict with the realities of life and with what Allah, the Exalted, the All-Powerful, has preordained. It calls you not from without, but from within, from what your soul already knows – that you should trust and develop your talents, and forget the troubles and vicissitudes of life, while concentrating on the positive and the desirable destination towards which a positive attitude leads.

There are some important issues regarding this book that I now want to clarify:

1. A reminder of Allah's mercy and forgiveness, sincere faith in Him, belief in preordainment and decree, a life that is lived within the boundaries of today, and a reminder of Allah's countless favors – these are some of the more important themes of this book.
2. With its ideas and cures, this book strives to help banish worry, sadness, grief, sense of failure, and hopelessness.

3. I gleaned whatever I found to be pertinent to the topic of the book from these sources: Verses of the Qur'an, sayings of the Prophet (bpuh), stories, parables, poems, and sayings of the wise. This book is no mere sermon, idle exercise in thought, or invitation to a political ideology. Rather, this book is an earnest invitation to your happiness.

4. This book is not only for Muslims; rather, it is suitable for all readers. While writing it, I took into consideration feelings and emotions that are common to everyone. I wrote it based on the true religion (whether or not we deviate from it) that is intrinsic to us all.

5. You will find sayings of Eastern and Western writers and philosophers. I do not think I should be held blameworthy because of that, for wisdom is the goal of every believer; wherever one finds it, one is most deserving of it.

6. I did not add any footnotes to the book, thus making it easier for the reader to peruse without interruption. The source of a quote is mentioned within the text of the book.

7. Imitating those before me (Islamic writers from centuries ago), I did not mention page or volume numbers of sources, deeming this (approach) to be more beneficial for this particular book. Sometimes I directly quoted a passage; other times I summarized its main idea.

8. I did not organize this book according to chapters; rather, I varied the content, inserting topics that might not be directly related to the ones before or after them. I moved quickly from one topic to another, sometimes returning to a previous topic in order to make the perusal of this book more enjoyable.

9. I did not mention the numbers of verses, nor did I mention the sources for the Prophet's sayings. If a hadith is weak, I indicated that. If it is authentic or reliable, I either pointed that out or said nothing. All this has been done for the purpose of conciseness.

10. The reader will notice that some meanings and topics are repeated (though in varying style) throughout the book. This I have done on purpose, so that a given meaning may attach itself to the reader's mind through repetition. Whoever reflects on how recurring themes are found in the Qur'an should appreciate the benefits of following this methodology.

I do hope that you will be just in your judgment and that your bias will be towards true and correct knowledge. Finally, this book is not written for a specific group of people; rather, it is for anyone who wants to live a happy life.

Imam Al-Qarne

In the Name of Allah, the Most Beneficent, the Most Merciful

O Allah!

{Whosoever is in the heavens and on earth begs of Him. Every day He has a matter to bring forth [such as giving honor to some, disgrace to some, life to some, death to some, et cetera.]}

(Qur'an 55: 29)

$$يَسْأَلُهُۥ مَن فِى ٱلسَّمَٰوَٰتِ وَٱلْأَرْضِ ۚ كُلَّ يَوْمٍ هُوَ فِى شَأْنٍ ۝$$

When there is a violent storm and the seas are turbulent, the occupants of the boat call out, "O Allah!"

When the camel-driver and the caravan are lost in the desert, they call out, "O Allah!"

When disasters and calamities occur, the afflicted call out, "O Allah!"

When doors are shut before those who seek to enter through them and barriers are placed before those who are in need – they all cry out, "O Allah!"

When all plans end in failure, all hope is lost, and the path becomes constricted, "O Allah," is called out.

When the earth, vast and wide though it is, is straitened for you, causing your soul to feel constricted, call out, "O Allah!"

To God ascend all good words, sincere supplications, tears of the innocent, and invocations of the afflicted. Hands and eyes are extended to Him in times of hardship and misfortune. The tongue chants, cries out, and mentions His name. The heart finds peace, the soul finds rest, the nerves are relaxed, and the intellect is awakened –these are all achieved when we remember Allah, the Exalted:

{Allah is very Gracious and Kind to His slaves.}

(Qur'an 42: 19)

Allah: the most beautiful names, the truest combination of letters, and the most precious words.

{Do you know of any that is similar to Him? [There is nothing like unto Him and He is the All-Hearer, the All-Seer].}

(Qur'an 19: 65)

Allah: He is thought of when absolute richness, strength, glory and wisdom come to mind.

{Whose is the kingdom this Day? [Allah Himself will reply to His question]: It is Allah's – the one, the Irresistible!}

(Qur'an 40: 16)

Allah: He is thought of when kindness, care, relief, affection, and mercy come to mind.

{And whatever of blessings and good things you have, it is from Allah.}

(Qur'an 16: 53)

O Allah, Possessor of Majesty, Magnificence, and Might, let comfort take the place of sorrow, make happiness come after sadness, and let safety take the place of fear.

O Allah! Soothe burning hearts with the coolness of faith. O our Lord! Give peaceful slumber to the restless, and serenity to disturbed souls.

O our Lord! Guide the confused ones to your light, and those who are astray to your guidance.

O Allah! Remove evil whispers from our hearts and replace them with light, destroy falsehood with truth, and crush the evil plots of the devil with your army of angels.

O Allah! Remove from us misery, affliction, and anxiety.

We seek refuge in You from fearing anything except You, from depending upon anyone except upon You, from fully trusting anyone except You, and from invoking anyone other than You. You are the Supreme Patron and an excellent Protector.

Contemplate and be thankful

Remember the favors of Allah upon you and how they surround you from above and below – indeed, from every direction.

{And if you would count the graces of Allah, never would you be able to count them.}

(Qur'an 14: 34)

Health, safety, nourishment, clothing, air, and water – these all point to the world being yours, yet you do not realize it. You possess all that life has to offer, yet you remain ignorant.

{Do you not see that Allah has made subject to you whatever is in the heavens and whatever is in the earth and amply bestowed upon you His favors, [both] apparent and unapparent?}

(Qur'an 31: 20)

You have at your disposal two eyes, a tongue, lips, two hands, and two legs.

{Then which of the blessings of your Lord will you both [jinns and men] deny?}

(Qur'an 55: 13)

Can you picture yourself walking without feet? Should you take it lightly that you slumber soundly while misery hinders the sleep of many? Should you forget that you fill yourself with both delicious dishes and cool water while the pleasure of good food and drink is impossible for some, due to sickness and disease? Consider the faculties of hearing and seeing with which you have been endowed. Look at your healthy skin and be grateful that you have been saved from diseases that attack it. Reflect on your powers of reasoning and remember those that suffer from mental ailments.

Would you sell your ability to hear and see for the weight of Mount Uḥud in gold, or your ability to speak in exchange for huge castles? You have been given abundant favors, yet you feign ignorance. Notwithstanding warm bread, cool water, easy sleep, and good health, you remain despondent and depressed. You think about what you do not have and are ungrateful for what you have been given. You are troubled by a loss in wealth, yet you have the key to happiness and many blessings. Contemplate and be thankful.

{And also in your ownselves [are signs], will you not then see?}

(Qur'an 51: 21)

Reflect upon yourself, your family, your friends, and the entire world that is around you.

{They recognize the grace of Allah, yet they deny it.} (Qur'an 16: 83)

The past is gone forever

By brooding over the past and its tragedies, one exhibits a form of insanity – a kind of sickness that destroys one's resolve to live for the present moment. Those who have a firm purpose have filed away and forgotten the occurrences of the past; they will never again see the light of the day, since they occupy a dark place in the recesses of the mind. Episodes of the past are finished; sadness cannot retrieve them, melancholy cannot make things right, and depression will never bring the past back to life. This is because the past is non-existent.

Do not live in the nightmares of former times or under the shade of what you have missed. Save yourself from the ghostly apparition of the past. Do you think you can return the sun to its place of rising, the baby to its mother's womb, the milk to the udder, or the tears to the eye? By constantly dwelling on the past and its happenings, you place yourself in a very frightful and tragic state of mind.

Reading too much into the past is a waste of the present. When Allah mentioned the affairs of the previous nations, He, the Exalted, said:

{That was a nation who has passed away.}

(Qur'an 2: 134)

Former days are gone and done with; you benefit nothing by carrying out an autopsy over them through turning back the wheels of history.

The person who lives in the past is like someone who tries to saw sawdust. It used to be said, "Do not remove the dead from their graves."

Our tragedy is that we are incapable of dealing with the present; neglecting our beautiful castles, we wail over dilapidated buildings. If all human beings and jinn try jointly to bring back the past, they would most certainly fail. Everything on the earth marches forward, preparing for a new season – and so should you.

Today is all you have

When you wake up in the morning, do not expect to see the evening – live as though today is all you have. Yesterday has passed with its good and evil, while tomorrow has not yet arrived. Your life's span is only one day, as if you were born in it and will die at the end of it. With this attitude, you will not be caught between an obsession over the past, with all its anxieties, and the hopes of the future, with all its uncertainty. Live for today; during this day, you should pray with a wakeful heart, recite the Qur'an with understanding, and remember Allah (the Exalted) with sincerity. In this day you should be balanced in your affairs, satisfied with your allotted portion, and concerned with your appearance and health.

Organize the hours of this day, so that you make years out of minutes and months out of seconds. Seek forgiveness from your Lord, remember Him, prepare for the final parting from this world, and live today happily and at peace. Remain content with your sustenance, your spouse, your children, your work, your house and your station in life:

{So hold that which I have given you and be of the grateful.}

(Qur'an 7: 144)

Live today free from sorrow, bother, anger, jealousy, and malice.

You must engrave onto your heart one phrase: Today is my only day. If you have eaten warm, fresh bread today, what do yesterday's dry, rotten bread and tomorrow's anticipated bread matter?

If you are truthful with yourself and have a firm, solid resolve, you will undoubtedly convince yourself of the following: Today is my last day to live. When you achieve this attitude, you will profit from every moment of your day, by developing your personality, expanding your abilities, and purifying your deeds. Then you say to yourself:

Today I shall be refined in my speech and will utter neither evil speech nor obscenity. Also, I shall not backbite.

Today I shall organize my house and my office. They will not be disorderly and chaotic, but organized and neat.

Today I will be particular about my physical cleanliness and appearance. I will be meticulous in my neatness and balanced in my walk, talk, and actions.

Today I will strive to be obedient to my Lord, pray in the best manner possible, do more voluntary acts of righteousness, recite the Qur'an, and read beneficial books. I will plant goodness in my heart and extract from it the roots of evil – such as pride, jealousy, and hypocrisy.

Today I will try to help others – to visit the sick, to attend a funeral, to guide the one who is lost, and to feed the hungry. I will stand side by side with the oppressed and the weak. I will be respectful towards the scholars, merciful to the young, and reverent to the old.

O past that has departed and is gone, I will not cry over you. You will not see me remembering you, not even for a moment. This is because you have travelled away from me never to return.

O future, you are in the realm of the unseen; I will not be obsessed by your dreams. I will not be preoccupied with what is to come because tomorrow is nothing and has not yet been created.

"Today is my only day," is one of the most important statements in the dictionary of happiness, for those who desire to live life in its fullest splendour and brilliance.

Leave the future alone until it comes

{The Event [the Hour or the punishment of disbelievers and polytheists or the Islamic laws or commandments], ordained by Allah will come to pass, so seek not to hasten it.}

(Qur'an 16: 1)

Do not be hasty, rushing for things that have yet to come to pass. Do you think it is wise to pick fruits before they become ripe? Tomorrow is non-existent, having no reality today, so why should you busy yourself with it? Why should you have apprehensions about future disasters? Why should you be engrossed in thoughts about the future, especially since you do not know whether you will even see tomorrow?

The important thing to know is that tomorrow is from the world of the unseen, a bridge that we do not cross until it comes. Who knows – perhaps we might never reach the bridge, or the bridge might collapse before we reach it, or we might actually reach it and cross safely.

To be engrossed in expectations about the future is looked down upon in our religion since it leads to our having a long-term attachment to this world – this is an attachment that the good believer shuns. Many people of this world are unduly fearful of future poverty, hunger, disease, and disaster; such thinking is inspired by the devil.

{Satan threatens you with poverty and orders you to commit faḥshā [evil deeds, illegal sexual intercourse, sins et cetera.], whereas Allah promises you forgiveness from Himself and bounty...}

(Qur'an 2: 268)

Many cry because they see themselves starving tomorrow or falling sick after a month, or because they fear that the world will come to an end after a year. Those who have no clue about when they will die (which is all of us) should not busy themselves with such thoughts.

Since you are absorbed in the toils of today, leave tomorrow until it comes. Beware of becoming unduly attached to future prospects in this world.

How to deal with bitter criticism

Those who are ignorant have uttered curses at Allah, the Creator of all that exists; what treatment should we, who are full of faults, expect from people? You will always have to face criticism, which in its onslaught is like an interminable war; it shows no sign of ending. As long as you shine, give, produce, and have an effect upon others, disapproval and condemnation will be your lot in life. Until you escape from people by finding a tunnel in the ground or a ladder leading to the sky, they will not desist from censuring you or from finding fault in your character. For that reason, as long as you are among the denizens of earth, expect to be hurt, to be insulted, and to be criticized. Here is something you should contemplate: A person who is sitting on the ground does not fall, and people do not kick a dead dog. Therefore their anger toward you can be attributed to your surpassing them in righteousness, knowledge, manners, or wealth. In their eyes, you are a transgressor whose wrongs cannot be atoned for – unless you abandon your talents and strip yourself of all praiseworthy qualities, and thus become stupid, worthless, and – to them –innocuous. This result is exactly what they want for you.

So remain firm and patient when facing their insults and criticism. If you get wounded by their words and allow them to have an influence over you, you will have realized their hopes for them. Instead, forgive them by showing them the most beautiful manners. Turn away from them and do not feel distressed by their schemes. Their disapproval of you only increases you in worth and merit.

Verily, you will not be able to silence them, but you will be able to bury their criticisms by turning away from them and dismissing what they have to say.

{Say: Perish in your rage.}

(Qur'an 3: 119)

In fact, you will be able to increase their rage by increasing your merits and developing your talents.

If you desire to be accepted by all and loved by all, you desire the unattainable.

Do not expect gratitude from anyone

Allah (the Exalted) created His slaves so that they may worship and remember Him; He provided sustenance for them so that they may be grateful to Him. Nevertheless, many have worshipped other than Him, and the masses are thankful not to Him but to others. This is because the characteristic of ingratitude is widespread among human beings. Do not be dismayed when you find that others forget your favors or disregard your kind acts. Some people might even despise you and consider you to be an enemy for no reason other than the kindness you have shown them:

{And they could not find any cause to bear a grudge, except that Allah and His Messenger had enriched them of His bounty.}

(Qur'an 9: 74)

From among the ever-repeating pages of history is a story of a father and his son. The former raised him, fed him, clothed him and taught him; he would stay up nights so that his son could sleep, stay hungry so that his son could eat, and toil so that his son could be comfortable. When the son became older and stronger, he rewarded his father with disobedience, disrespect, and contempt.

So be at peace if you are requited with ungratefulness for the good you have done. Rejoice in your knowledge that you will be rewarded by the One Who has unlimited treasures at His disposal.

This is not to say that you should refrain from performing acts of kindness towards others; the point is that you should be mentally prepared for ingratitude.

Perform acts of charity seeking Allah's pleasure, because with this attitude you will assuredly be successful. The ungrateful person cannot really harm you. Praise Allah for making that person the transgressor and you the obedient servant. Also, remember that the hand that gives is better than the hand that receives.

{We feed you seeking Allah's countenance only. We wish for no reward, nor thanks from you.}
(Qur'an 76: 9)

Many people are shocked at the nature of ingratitude in others, as though they had never come across the following verse and others like it:

{And when harm touches man, he invokes Us, lying down on his side, or sitting or standing. But when We have removed his harm from him, he passes on his way as if he had never invoked Us for a harm that touched him!}
(Qur'an 10: 12)

Hence do not be in a state of agitation if you give someone a pen as a gift and he uses it to satirize you, or if you give someone a walking stick to lean upon and he strikes you with it. As I pointed out earlier, most human beings are ungrateful to their Lord, so what treatment should you and I expect?

Doing good to others comforts the heart

The first to benefit from acts of charity are the benefactors themselves. They witness a change in themselves and their manners, by finding peace, or by watching a smile form on the lips of another person.

If you find yourself in difficulty or distress, show kindness to others, and you will be the first to enjoy solace and comfort. Give to the needy, defend the oppressed, help those in distress, and visit the sick; you will find that happiness surrounds you from all directions.

An act of charity is like perfume – it benefits the user, the seller, and the buyer. Furthermore, the psychological benefits that one receives from helping others are indeed great. If you suffer from depression, an act of charity will have a more potent effect on your sickness than will the best available medicine.

Even when you smile upon meeting others, you are giving charity. The Prophet (bpuh) said:

«Do not dismiss certain acts of kindness by deeming them to be insignificant, even if (such an act) is to meet your brother with a smiling face (for that is a deed which might weigh heavily in your scale of deeds).»

On the other hand, when you frown upon meeting others, you are displaying a sign of enmity, an act that is so detrimental to brotherhood that only Allah knows the full extent of its evil effects.

The Prophet (bpuh) informed us:

«The prostitute who once gave a handful of water to a dog was rewarded for that deed with paradise, which is as wide as the heavens and the earth.»

This is because the Giver of rewards is Forgiving, Rich, and Worthy of Praise.

O you who are threatened by misery, fear and grief! Occupy yourself with the betterment of others. Help others in different ways –through charity, hospitality, sympathy, and support. In doing so, you will find all the happiness you desire.

{He who spends his wealth for increase in self-purification, and has in his mind no favor from anyone for which a reward is expected in return; except only the desire to seek the countenance of his Lord, the Most High. He surely will be pleased [when he enters paradise].}

(Qur'an 92: 18-21)

Repel boredom with work

Those who have nothing to do with their lives are the ones who spend most of their time spreading rumors and falsehood, mainly because their minds are devoid of beneficial thoughts.

{They are content to be with those [the women] who sit behind [at home]. Their hearts are sealed up [from right guidance] so they understand not.} (Qur'an 9: 87)

When you find yourself to be idle, prepare for depression and despair. This is because idleness allows your mind to wander in the past, the present, and the future, with all their difficulties. Therefore, my sincere advice to you is to perform fruitful acts instead of being idle, for idleness is a slow and veiled form of suicide.

Idleness is like 'Chinese water torture', in which prisoners are placed under a tap, from which a drop of water falls only after every hour. During the period of waiting between drops, many of them lose their minds and are driven to insanity. Being inactive means negligence of one's duties. Idleness is an expert thief, and your mind is its victim. Therefore get up now! Say a prayer or read a book; praise your Lord, study, write, organize your library, fix something in your house, or benefit others so that you can put an end to your inactivity. I say this only because I sincerely wish for your betterment.

Destroy boredom by working. When you apply this simple precept alone, you will have travelled at least fifty percent of the way towards happiness. Look at farmers, carpenters, and bread-makers, and observe how, when they are working, they recite words as melodious as the singing of birds. This is only because they are content. Afterwards, observe yourself and how you toss and turn on your bed while wiping away your tears, always miserable, always torturing yourself.

Don't be a mimicker

Don't transform yourself into someone who you are not; do not mimic others. Many forget their own voices, movements, idiosyncrasies, and habits in order to imitate others. The consequences of such behavior include artificiality, unhappiness, and a destruction of one's own entity. From Adam ('alayhi as-salâm – peace be upon him) to the last baby born, no two people are exactly the same in appearance. Why then should they be the same in mannerisms and tastes? You are unique – none have been like you in the past and none shall be like you in the future. You are totally different from X or Y, so do not force upon yourself the blind following and imitation of others. Go forth according to your own nature and disposition.

{Each [group of] people knew its own place for water.} (Qur'an 2: 60)
{For every nation there is a direction to which they face, so hasten towards all that is good.}
(Qur'an 2: 148)

Be as you were created and do not change your voice or modify your walk. Cultivate your personality by following what is found in revelation, but do not render your existence void by imitating others and by depriving yourself of your individuality.

Your tastes and preferences are specific to you, and we want you to stay as you are, especially because that is the way you were created and that is how we know you to be. The Prophet (bpuh) said:

«And let no one among you be an imitator of others.»

In terms of characteristics, people are like the world of trees and plants: sweet and sour, tall and short, and so on. Your beauty and value is in preserving your natural state. Our varied colours, languages, talents, and abilities are signs from our Creator, the Almighty, All-Glorious, so do not disbelieve in them.

The pens have been lifted; the pages have dried

{No calamity befalls on the earth or in yourselves but is inscribed in the Book of Decrees – before We bring it into existence.}

(Qur'an 57: 22)

The pens have been lifted; the pages have dried: all events that shall occur have already been decreed.

{Nothing shall ever happen to us except what Allah has ordained for us.}

(Qur'an 9: 51)

Whatever has befallen you was not meant to escape you, and whatever has escaped you was not meant to befall you. If this belief is firmly ingrained in your heart, all hardship and difficulty would turn into ease and comfort. The Prophet (bpuh) said:

«For whoever Allah wishes good, He inflicts him (with hardship).»

For this reason, do not feel overly troubled if you are afflicted with sickness, the death of a child, or a loss of wealth. Allah has decreed these matters to occur; the decisions are His, and His alone.

When we truly have this faith, we shall be rewarded well and our sins shall be atoned for.

When you are afflicted with disaster, glad tidings await you, so remain patient and happy with your Lord.

{He cannot be questioned as to what He does, while they will be questioned.}

(Qur'an 21: 23)

You will never completely feel at ease until you firmly believe that Allah has already preordained all matters. The pens have been lifted, and they have written everything that will happen to you. Therefore do not feel remorse over what is not in your hands. Do not think that you could have prevented the fence from falling, the water from flowing, the wind from blowing, or the glass from breaking. You could not have prevented these things, whether or not you wanted. All that has been preordained shall come to pass.

{Then whosoever wills, let him believe, and whosoever wills, let him disbelieve.}

(Qur'an 18: 29)

Surrender yourself; believe in preordainment, before pangs of anger and regret overwhelm you. If you have done all that was in your power, and afterwards what you had been striving against still takes place, have firm faith that it was meant to be. Do not say, "Had I done such-and-such, such-and-such would have happened." Say instead, "This is the decree of Allah, and He does what He wishes."

Verily, with hardship, there is relief

{Verily, with hardship, there is relief.}

(Qur'an 94: 6)

Eating follows hunger, drinking follows thirst, sleep comes after restlessness, and health takes the place of sickness. The lost will find their way, the ones in difficulty will find relief, and the day will follow the night.

{Perhaps Allah may bring a victory or a decision according to His will.}

(Qur'an 5: 52)

Inform the night of a coming morning, the light of which will permeate the mountains and valleys. To the afflicted, give tidings of a sudden relief that will reach them with the speed of light in the blink of an eye.

If you see that the desert extends for miles and miles, then know that beyond that distance are green meadows with plentiful shade. If you see the rope tighten and tighten, know that it will snap.

Tears are followed by a smile, fear is replaced by comfort, and anxiety is overthrown by serenity. When the fire was set for him, Prophet Abraham (pbuh) did not feel its heat because of the help he received from his Lord.

{We [Allah] said: O fire! Be you coolness and safety for Abraham!}

(Qur'an 21: 69)

The sea would not drown Prophet Moses (pbuh), because he uttered in a confident, strong, and truthful manner:

{Nay, verily! With me is my Lord, He will guide me.}

(Qur'an 26: 62)

Prophet Muhammad (bpuh) told Abu Bakr (radiya Allâhu 'anhu - may Allah be pleased with him) in the cave that Allah was with them -then peace and tranquility descended upon them.

Those who are slaves of the moment see only misery. This is because they look only at the wall and door of the room, whereas they should look beyond such barriers as are set before them.

Therefore do not be in despair; it is impossible for things to remain the same. The days and years rotate, the future is unseen, and every day Allah has matters to bring forth. You know it not, but it may be that Allah will afterwards bring some new thing to pass. Verily, with hardship there is relief.

When life gives you lemons, make lemonade

An intelligent and skillful person transforms losses into profits, whereas an unskilled person aggravates his or her own predicament, often making two disasters out of one.

The Prophet (bpuh) was compelled to leave Makkah, but rather than quit his mission, he continued it in Madinah – the city that took its place in history with lightning speed.

Imam Ahmad ibn Hanbal was severely tortured and flogged, yet he emerged triumphant from that ordeal, becoming the Imam of the Sunnah. Imam Ibn Taymiyah was put into prison; he later came out an even more accomplished scholar than he was before. Imam as-Sarakhsi was held as a prisoner, kept at the bottom of an unused well; he managed therein to produce twenty volumes on Islamic jurisprudence. Ibn Atheer became crippled, after which he wrote Jamay' al-Uṣool and an-Nihâyah, two of the most famous books in the Science of Hadith. Imam Ibn al-Jawzi was banished from Baghdad. Then, through his travels, he became proficient in the seven recitations of the Qur'an. Mâlik ibn ar-Rayb was on his deathbed when he recited his most famous and beautiful poem, which is appreciated until this day. When Abi Dhu'ayb al-Hadhali's children died before him, he eulogized them with a poem that the world listened to and admired.

Therefore, if you are afflicted with a misfortune, look on the bright side. If someone hands you a glass full of squeezed lemons, add to it a handful of sugar. If someone gives you a snake as a gift, keep its precious skin and leave the rest.

{And it may be that you dislike a thing that is good for you...}

(Qur'an 2: 216)

Before its violent revolution, France imprisoned two brilliant poets: one an optimist and the other a pessimist. They both squeezed their heads through the bars of their cell windows. The optimist then stared at the stars and laughed, while the pessimist looked at the dirt of a neighboring road and wept. Look at the other side of a tragedy – a circumstance of pure evil does not exist, and in all situations one can find goodness and profit and reward from Allah.

Is He [not best] Who responds to the desperate one?

{Is He [not best] Who responds to the desperate one when he calls upon Him...?}

(Qur'an 27: 62)

From Whom do the weak and the oppressed seek victory? Whom does everyone beseech? He is Allah. None has the right to be worshipped except Him. Therefore it is most advisable for you and I to invoke Him both in times of hardship and ease, to seek shelter with Him in difficult times, and to plead at His doorstep with tears of repentance; then will His help and relief quickly arrive.

{Is He [not best] Who responds to the desperate one when he calls upon Him...?}

(Qur'an 27: 62)

He saves the one who is drowning, gives victory to the oppressed, guides the misguided, cures the sick, and provides relief to the afflicted.

{And when they embark on a ship, they invoke Allah, making their faith pure for Him only...}

(Qur'an 29: 65)

As for the various supplications one makes to remove hardship, I refer you to the books of the Sunnah. In them, you will learn prophetic supplications with which you can call to Allah (the Exalted), supplicate to Him, and seek His aid. If you have found Him, then you have found everything, but if you lose your faith in Him, then you have lost everything. By supplicating to Him, you are performing one of the highest forms of worship. If you are persistent and sincere in your supplication, you will achieve freedom from worry and anxiety. All ropes are cut loose save His, and all doors are shut save His. He is near; He, the Most Merciful, hears all and answers those who supplicate to Him.

{...Invoke Me [and ask Me for anything], I will respond to your [invocation].}

(Qur'an 40: 60)

If you are living through affliction and pain, remember Allah, call out His name, and ask Him for help. Place your forehead on the ground and mention His praises, so that you can obtain true freedom. Raise your hands in supplication, and ask of Him constantly. Cling to His door, have good thoughts about Him, and wait for His help – you will then find true happiness and success.

Your home is enough for you

The words 'isolation' and 'seclusion' have a special meaning in our religion: to stay away from evil and its perpetrators, and to keep those who are foolish at a distance. When you seclude yourself from evil in this manner, you will have an opportunity to reflect, to think, to graze in the meadows of enlightenment.

When you isolate yourself from things that divert you from Allah's obedience, you are giving yourself a dose of medicine, one that doctors of the heart have found to be a most potent cure. When you seclude yourself from evil and idleness, your brain is stimulated into action. The result is an increase in faith, repentance, and remembrance of Allah, the Almighty, All-Compassionate.

However, some gatherings are not only recommended, but necessary: the congregational prayer, circles of learning, and all gatherings of righteousness. As for gatherings wherein frivolity and shallowness prevail, be wary of them. Take flight from such gatherings, weep over your wrongdoing, hold your tongue, and be content within the boundaries of your home. By mixing with others based on foolish motives, you endanger the stability and soundness of your mind, for the people you indiscriminately mix with are likely to be experts at wasting time, masters at spreading lies, and skilled in spreading both trouble and mischief.

{Had they marched out with you, they would have added to you nothing except disorder, and they would have hurried about in your midst [spreading corruption] and sowing sedition among you...}
(Qur'an 9: 47)

I advise you to fortify yourself in accordance with your purpose and to isolate yourself in your room, except when you leave it to speak well or to do well. When you apply this advice, you will find that your heart has returned to you. So use your time well and save your life from being wasted. Hold your tongue from backbiting, free your heart from anxiety, and preserve your ears from profanity.

Your recompense is with Allah

When Allah (the Exalted) takes something away from you, He compensates you with something better, but only if you are patient and seek your reward from Him. The Prophet (bpuh) said:

«Whoever has his eyesight taken away from him and is (then) patient, he will be compensated for it with paradise.»

The Prophet (bpuh) said in another hadith:

«Whoever loses a loved one from the people of this world and then seeks his recompense with his Lord, he will be compensated with paradise.»

So do not feel excessive sorrow over some misfortune, because the One Who decreed it has with Him paradise: recompense and a great reward. Those who are afflicted in this world and are close to Allah will be praised in the highest part of heaven:

{Peace be upon you, because you persevered in patience! Excellent indeed is the final home!}
(Qur'an 13: 24)

We must contemplate the reward one receives for forbearing hardship.

{They are those on whom are the blessings [that is, who are blessed and will be forgiven] from their Lord, and they are those who receive His mercy. And it is they who are the guided ones.}

(Qur'an 2: 157)

Truly, the life of this world is short, and its treasures are few. The hereafter is better and everlasting; those who are afflicted here shall find their reward there, and those who work hard here shall find ease there. As for those who cling to this world, who are attached to it, and who are in love with it, the hardest thing for them to bear would be to lose the world's comforts and riches; they desire to enjoy this life alone. Because of this desire, they don't react to misfortune as well as others do. What they perceive around them is this life alone; they are blind to its impermanence and insignificance.

O afflicted ones, if you are patient you lose nothing; and though you may not perceive it, you are profiting. The person who is afflicted with hardship should reflect upon the outcome in the hereafter, the outcome for those who are patient.

{So a wall will be put up between them, with a gate therein. Inside it will be mercy, and outside it will be torment.}

(Qur'an 57: 13)

Faith is life itself

Those who are wretched in the full sense of the word are those who are bereft of the treasures of faith. They are always in a state of misery and anger.

{But whosoever turns away from My Reminder [that is, neither believes in this Qur'an nor acts on its orders, et cetera] verily, for him is a life of hardship...}

(Qur'an 20: 124)

The only means of purifying the heart and of removing anxieties and worries from it is to have complete faith in Allah, Lord of all that exists. In fact, there can be no true meaning to life when one has no faith.

How base and mean is a life without faith! How eternally accursed is the existence enveloping those who are outside of the boundaries set down by Allah (the Exalted)!

{And We shall turn their hearts and their eyes away [from guidance], as they refused to believe therein for the first time, and We shall leave them in their trespass to wander blindly.}

(Qur'an 6: 110)

Has not the time come when the world should have an unquestioning faith – that none has the right to be worshipped except Allah (the Exalted)? After centuries of experience, should not humankind be led to the realization that having faith in a statue is ludicrous, that atheism is absurd, that the Prophets were truthful, and that to Allah alone belongs the dominion of the heavens and earth? All praise is due to Allah, and He is capable of all things. You will be happy and at peace in proportion to the level of your faith -strong or weak, firm or wavering.

{Whoever works righteousness, whether male or female, while he is a true believer; verily, to him We will give a good life [in this world with respect, contentment, and lawful provision]. And We shall pay them certainly a reward in proportion to the best of what they used to do [that is, paradise in the hereafter].}

(Qur'an 16: 97)

The 'good life' that is mentioned in this verse refers to having a firm faith in the promise of our Lord and a steady heart that loves Him. People who lead this 'good life' will also have calm nerves when afflicted with hardship; they will be satisfied with everything that befalls them, because it was written for them, and because they are pleased with Allah as their Lord, with Islam as their religion, and with Muhammad as their Prophet and Messenger.

Gather the honey but don't break the hive

Everything that has gentleness in it is beautified, and whatever lacks it is spoiled. When you meet someone, giving him or her a bright smile and a kind word, you are displaying a characteristic of the truly successful person, a characteristic that even a bee exhibits. When a bee lands on a flower (doing so for a practical purpose) it does not destroy it, because Allah rewards gentleness with that which He does not give for harshness. There are certain people whose personalities are like magnets, attracting everyone who is nearby, simply because they are loved for their gentle talk, their good manners, and their noble deeds. Winning the friendship of others is an art that is mastered by those who are noble and pious; a circle of people constantly surrounds them. Their mere presence in a gathering is a blessing, and when they are absent they are missed and asked about. These blessed people have a code of conduct entitled:

{Repel [the evil] with one which is better [that is, Allah ordered the faithful believers to be patient at the time of anger, and to excuse those who treat them badly], then verily! He, between whom and you there was enmity, [will become] as though he was a close friend.}

(Qur'an 41: 34)

They suck out malice from others with their sincerity, forgiveness, and gentleness. They forget evil that was enacted upon them and preserve the memory of kindnesses received. Biting, harsh words may be aimed at them, but such words pass by their ears without entering and continue on their path without ever returning.

They are in a state of calmness. People in general, and Muslims in particular, are safe from suffering any harm at their hands. The Prophet (bpuh) said:

«The Muslim is the person whose tongue and hand do not harm other Muslims, and the believer is he whom others trust, with their blood and wealth.»

He also said:

«Verily, Allah ordered me to keep relations with those who cut me off, to forgive the one who does an injustice to me, and to give to those who withhold from me.»

{Those who repress anger, and who pardon men; verily, Allah loves the good-doers.}

(Qur'an 3: 134)

Give to such people glad tidings of an imminent reward in this world, in terms of peace and tranquility.

Also give glad tidings to them of a great reward in the hereafter, of paradise, wherein they will be in close proximity to their forgiving Lord.

Verily, in the remembrance of Allah do hearts find rest

{Verily, in the remembrance of Allah do hearts find rest.}

(Qur'an 13: 28)

Truthfulness is beloved by Allah and is like a purifying soap for the heart. There is no deed that gives such pleasure to the heart, or has greater reward, than the remembrance of Allah.

{Therefore remember Me, and I will remember you...} (Qur'an 2: 152)

Remembrance of Allah is His paradise on earth, and whoever does not enter it will not enter the paradise of the hereafter. Remembrance is not only a safe haven from the problems and worries of this world, but it is also the short and easy path to achieving ultimate success. Read the various revealed texts that refer to the remembrance of Allah, and you will appreciate its benefits.

When you remember Allah, clouds of worry and fear are driven away, and the mountains that make up your problems are blown away.

We should not be surprised when we hear that people who remember Allah are at peace. What is truly surprising is how the negligent and unmindful survive without remembering Him.

{[They are] dead, lifeless, and they know not when they will be raised up.}

(Qur'an 16: 21)

O whosoever complains of sleepless nights and is in shock over a misfortune, call out His holy name.

{Do you know of any that is similar to Him? [There is nothing like unto Him and He is the All-Hearer, the All-Seer].}

(Qur'an 19: 65)

To the degree that you remember Allah, your heart will be calm and cheerful. His remembrance carries with it the meaning of total dependence upon Him, of turning to Him for aid, of having good thoughts about Him, and of waiting for victory from Him. Truly, He is near when supplicated, He hears when He is called and He answers when He is invoked, so humble yourself before Him and ask of Him sincerely. Repeat His beautiful blessed name, and mention Him as being alone worthy of worship. Mention His praises, supplicate to Him, and ask forgiveness from Him; you will then find -by the will of Allah -happiness, peace, and illumination.

{So Allah gave them the reward of this world, and the excellent reward of the hereafter.}

(Qur'an 3: 148)

Or do they envy men for what Allah has given them of His bounty?

{Or do they envy men for what Allah has given them of His bounty?}

(Qur'an 4: 54)

Jealousy is a disease that wreaks havoc not only on the mind, but also on the body. It is said that there is no repose for the jealous one and that he or she is an enemy wearing the garb of a friend. In doing justice to the disease of jealousy, one can say that it is at least fair, for it begins with its bearer, killing him first.

I forbid both you and myself from jealousy, because before we can show mercy to others we must first show it to ourselves. By being jealous of others, we are feeding misery with our flesh and blood, and we are giving our sound sleep to others.

The jealous person lights a fire and then jumps into it. Jealousy begets grief, pain, and suffering, thus destroying what was once a calm and virtuous life.

The curse of the jealous ones is that they contest fate and contend that their Creator is unjust.

How like a disease is jealousy, yet unlike other diseases in that the one afflicted by it receives no reward in the hereafter. Those who are jealous shall remain in fury until the day they die, or until the good fortune of others departs from them. Everyone can be reconciled except the jealous, because reconciliation with them requires that the blessings of Allah are removed from you or that you give up your talents and good qualities. If you were to do this, then perhaps they would become happy despite themselves. We seek refuge in Allah from the evil of the jealous one, a person who becomes like a black poisonous snake, finding no repose until it releases its venom into an innocent body.

So stay far away from jealousy and seek refuge in Allah from jealous people, because they are constantly watching you.

Accept life as it is

The pleasures of life are short-lived, and more often than not, they are followed by sorrow. Life means responsibility, a journey wherein change is constant and difficulties are relentless in their onslaught.

You will not find a father, a wife, or a friend who is free from problems. Allah has willed for this world to be filled with pairs of opposites: good and evil, righteousness and corruption, happiness and misery. Thus goodness, uprightness, and happiness are for paradise; evil, corruption, and misery are for the fire. The Prophet (bpuh) said:

> «This world is cursed along with all that is in it, except for these: the remembrance of Allah, what follows it (such as good deeds and whatever Allah loves), the scholar, and the student.»

So live according to your reality without always envisioning the ideal life, one that is free from worry and toil. Accept life as it is, and adapt accordingly to all circumstances. You will not find in this world such things as the flawless companion or the perfect situation, because flawlessness and perfection are qualities that are foreign to this life. It is necessary for us to make amends; to take what is easy and leave what is difficult; and very frequently, to overlook the faults and mistakes of others.

Find consolation by remembering the afflicted

Look around you, to the right and to the left. Do you not see the afflicted and the unfortunate? In every house there is mourning, and upon every cheek run tears.

How many tribulations and how many people persevere with patience? You are not alone in your troubles, which are few when compared to those of others. How many sick people remain bedridden for years while suffering from unspeakable pain?

How many have not seen the light of the sun for years due to their imprisonment, having knowledge of nothing but the four corners of their cell?

How many men and women have lost their dear children in the prime of youth?

How many people are troubled or tormented?

Find consolation with those who are worse off than you; know that this life is like a prison for the believer, an abode of grief and sadness. In the morning, castles are bustling with inhabitants; then in an instant, disaster occurs, and they are empty and desolate. Life can be peaceful, the body in good health, wealth abundant, and children healthy; yet in only a matter of days, poverty, death, separation, and sickness can all take their place.

{And you dwelt in the dwellings of men who wronged themselves, and it was clear to you how We had dealt with them. And We put forth [many] parables for you.}

(Qur'an 14: 45)

You must adapt like the experienced camel, which manages, when necessary, to kneel upon a rock. You must also compare your difficulties with the difficulties of those around you, and with those who have come before you. You should realize that you are in good shape relative to them, and that you have merely been pricked by tiny difficulties. So praise Allah for His kindness, be thankful for what He has left for you, seek recompense from Him for what He has taken, and seek consolation with those who are afflicted.

You have a perfect example in the Prophet (bpuh). The entrails of a camel were placed upon his head; his feet bled; his face was fractured; he was besieged in a mountain pass until he was forced to eat tree leaves; he was driven out of Makkah; his front tooth was broken in battle; his innocent wife was accused of wrongdoing; seventy of his Companions were killed; he was bereaved of his son and of most of his daughters; he would tie a stone around his stomach to lessen the pangs of hunger; and he was accused of being a poet, a magician, a soothsayer, a madman, and a liar – all at the same time. Yet Allah protected him throughout these severe trials and tribulations. Prophet Zachariah was killed, Prophet John was slaughtered, Prophet Moses was afflicted with great trials, Prophet Abraham was thrown in the fire (may peace be upon them all), and the Imams of righteousness followed them upon this path. 'Umar was assassinated, as were 'Uthmân and 'Ali (may Allah be pleased with them all). Many scholars of the past have been flogged, imprisoned, or tortured.

{Or think you that you will enter paradise without such [trials] as came to those who passed away before you? They were afflicted with severe poverty, ailments and were shaken.}

(Qur'an 2: 214)

The prayer... the prayer

{O you who believe! Seek help in patience and the prayer.}

(Qur'an 2: 153)

If you are beset with fear and anxieties, stand up right now and pray; your soul will find comfort and solace. The prayer – as long as you perform it sincerely with a wakeful heart – is guaranteed to have this effect for you.

Whenever the Prophet (asa) was afflicted with hardship, he would say:

«O Bilâl! Give us comfort and call for the prayer.»

The prayer was his joy and pleasure; it was the delight of his eye.

I have read biographies of many righteous people who would always turn to prayer when they were surrounded by difficulties and hardship, people who would pray until their strength, will, and resolution returned to them.

The prayer of fear (which is performed during battle) was prescribed in situations wherein limbs are severed, skulls fly, and souls depart from their bodies – a time when strength and resolution can only be derived from heartfelt prayer.

This generation, which is consumed by psychological sicknesses, must return to the mosque, going there to perform prostration and to seek Allah's pleasure. If we do not do this, tears will burn our eyes and grief will destroy our nerves.

By earnestly performing the five daily prayers, we achieve the greatest of blessings: atonement for our sins and an increase in rank with our Lord. Prayer is also a potent remedy for our sicknesses, for it instills faith in our souls. As for those who stay away from the mosque and away from prayer, for them are unhappiness, wretchedness, and an embittered life.

{For them is destruction, and Allah will make their deeds vain.}

(Qur'an 47: 8)

Allah is sufficient for us, and He is the best Disposer of our affairs

{Allah [alone] is sufficient for us, and He is the best Disposer of affairs [for us].}

(Qur'an 3: 173)

By leaving your affairs to Allah, the Almighty, All-Merciful, by depending upon Him, by trusting in His promise, by being pleased with His decree, by thinking favorably of Him, and by waiting patiently for His help, you reap some of the greater fruits of faith and display the more prominent characteristics of the believer. When you incorporate these qualities into your character, you will be at peace concerning the future, because you will depend on your Lord for everything. As a result, you will find care, help, protection, and victory.

When Prophet Abraham was placed in the fire, he said:

{Allah [alone] is sufficient for us, and He is the best Disposer of affairs [for us].}

(Qur'an 3: 173)

Thereupon, Allah caused the fire to be cool, safe, and peaceful for Abraham. When the Prophet Muhammad (bpuh) and his Companions were threatened by the impending attack of the enemy, they said words that are related in the first part of this verse:

{Allah [alone] is Sufficient for us, and He is the Best Disposer of affairs [for us]. So they returned with grace and bounty from Allah. No harm touched them; and they followed the good pleasure of Allah. And Allah is the Owner of great bounty.}

(Qur'an 3: 173-174)

No person alone is capable of fighting against the current of misfortune, nor can he or she fend off the blows of disaster when they strike. This is because the human being was created weak and fragile. In times of difficulty, the believers place their dependency and trust with their Lord, knowing that all difficulties can be overcome.

{And put your trust in Allah if you are believers indeed.}

(Qur'an 5: 23)

O you who wish to be sincere to yourselves: depend upon the Almighty, All-Rich to save you from calamity and disaster. Live your lives according to this precept: Allah alone is sufficient for us, and He is the best Disposer of our affairs. If you have meager means, if you are deep in debt, or if you are in any kind of worldly difficulty, call out, "Allah alone is sufficient for us, and He is the best Disposer of our affairs."

If you face your enemy and are alarmed, or if you fear the misdeeds of the oppressor, say aloud, "Allah alone is sufficient for us, and He is the best Disposer of our affairs."

{But Sufficient is your Lord as a Guide and Helper.} (Qur'an 25: 31)

Travel in the land

{Say [O Muhammad]: Travel in the land...}

(Qur'an 6: 11)

There is one activity worthy of mention here, because it both gives pleasure and removes dark clouds that may hang over you: namely, for you to travel through the lands, observe the open book of creation, and appreciate all of its wonders. During your journeys, you can see gardens of splendor and beautiful green meadows. Leave your home and contemplate that which surrounds you.

Hike up mountains, traverse valleys, climb trees, and drink sweet, pure spring water. Thereupon, you will find your soul to be free like the bird that sings and swims in the sky in perfect rapture. Leave your home and remove the black blindfold from your eyes, and then travel through the spacious lands of Allah, remembering and glorifying Him.

To isolate yourself in the confines of your own room, while passing the hours away with lethal idleness, is a certain path to self-destruction. Your room is not the only place in the world, and you are not the sole inhabitant of it. Then why do you surrender yourself to misery and solitude? Call out with your eyes, ears, and heart:

{March forth, whether you are light [being healthy, young and wealthy] or heavy [being ill, old and poor].}

(Qur'an 9: 41)

Come, recite the Qur'an beside a mountain brook or among the birds as they sing.

Traveling to different lands is an activity which doctors recommend, especially for those who are feeling downcast, constricted by the narrowness of their own rooms. Therefore go forth and find delight in traveling.

{And they think deeply about the creation of the heavens and the earth, [saying]: Our Lord! You have not created [all] this without purpose, glory to You!}

(Qur'an 3: 191)

Patience is most fitting

Those who meet hardship with a strong bearing and a patient countenance are in the minority. But we must consider this, though it may seem obvious: if you or I will not be patient, then what else is there for us to do? Do you have an alternative solution? Do you know of any provision that is better than patience?

Those that achieve greatness have to surmount an ocean of difficulties and hardships before finally achieving success. Know that each time you escape a difficulty, you will have to face another. Through this constant conflict, you must arm yourself with patience and a strong trust in Allah.

This is the way of the noble-minded: they face difficulties with firm resolution, and they wrestle hardship to the ground.

Therefore be patient and know that your patience is only through Allah. Have patience like those who are confident of forthcoming ease, those who know that there will be a good ending, and those who seek reward from their Lord, hoping that, by facing difficulties, they will find expiation for their sins. Have patience, no matter what the difficulty and no matter how dark the road ahead seems. For truly, with patience comes victory, and with difficulty, relief follows close behind.

After having read biographies of some successful people from the past, I became amazed at the amount of patience they displayed, at their ability to bear heavy burdens only to emerge as stronger human beings. Hardship fell upon their heads like the lashing of freezing rain, yet they were as firm as mountains. Then, after a short time had passed, they were rewarded for their patience with success.

Don't carry the weight of the world on your shoulders

In a certain class of people there rages an internal war, which takes place not on the battlefield but in their own bedrooms, offices and homes. It is a war that results in ulcers or an increase in blood pressure. Everything frustrates these people; they become angry at inflation, furious because the rains came late, and exasperated when the value of their currency falls. They are forever perturbed and vexed, no matter what the reason.

{They think that every cry is against them.}

(Qur'an 63: 4)

My advice to you is this: do not carry the weight of the world on your shoulders. Let the ground carry the burden of those things that happen. Some people have hearts that are like sponges, absorbing all kinds of fallacies and misconceptions. This type of heart is troubled by the most insignificant of matters; it is the kind of heart that is sure to destroy its possessor.

Those who are principled and are upon the true path are not shaken by hardship; instead, hardship helps to strengthen their resolve and faith. But the reverse is true for the weak-hearted: when they face adversity or trouble, it is only their level of fear that increases. At a time of calamity, there is nothing more beneficial to you than having a brave heart.

The one who has such a heart is self-possessed – having firm faith and cool nerves. Cowards, on the other hand, during the course of any given day, slaughter themselves many times with apprehensions and presentiments of impending doom. Therefore, if you desire for yourself a stable life, face all situations with bravery and perseverance.

{And let not those who have no certainty of faith discourage you...}   (Qur'an 30: 60)

Be more resolute than your circumstances and more ferocious than the winds of calamity. May mercy descend upon the weak-hearted, for how often it is that they are shaken by the smallest of tremors.

{And verily, you will find them the greediest of humankind for life...}

(Qur'an 2: 96)

As for those who are resolute, they receive help from their Lord and are confident of His promise.

{He sent down calmness and tranquility upon them...}   (Qur'an 48: 18)

Don't be crushed by what is insignificant

Many are those who are distressed not by pressing matters of great import, but by minor trifles. Observe the hypocrites and how weak they are in their resolution. The Qur'an relates to us some of their sayings:

{Those who stayed away [from the Tabuk expedition] rejoiced in their staying behind the Messenger of Allah; they hated to strive and fight with their properties and their lives in the cause of Allah, and they said: March not forth in the heat.}

(Qur'an 9: 81)

{Grant me leave [to be exempted from jihad] and put me not into trial.}

(Qur'an 9: 49)

{And a band of them ask for permission of the Prophet [Muhammad] saying: Truly, our homes lie open [to the enemy]. And they lay not open. They but wished to flee.}

(Qur'an 33: 13)

{We fear lest some misfortune of a disaster may befall us.}

(Qur'an 5: 52)

{And when the hypocrites and those in whose hearts is a disease said: Allah and His Messenger promised us nothing but delusions!}

(Qur'an 33: 12)

How wretched are the souls of such people!

Their principal concerns are for their stomachs, cars, houses, and castles. They never once raise their eyes to a life of ideals and virtues; the extent of their knowledge is their cars, clothes, shoes, and food.

Some people are distressed day and night, because of a disagreement with a spouse, son, or relative, or because they have been subjected to criticism, or because of some other trivial event. Such are the calamities of these people. They have no aspiration to higher principles or goals to keep them busy, and they have no noble ambition in their lives for which they can strive day and night. It has been said, "When water leaves a container, the container is then filled with air." Therefore reflect on what gives you cause for concern or anxiety, and ask yourself this: does it merit your energies and toils? This is an indispensable question, because whatever it is that causes your anxiety, you are, with mind, flesh, and blood, giving it energy and time. If it does not merit your energy and time, you will have squandered a great deal of your most precious resources. Psychologists say that you should judge everything in proportion to its true value and then put it in its proper place. More truthful than this is the saying of Allah (the Exalted):

{Indeed Allah has set a measure for all things.}

(Qur'an 65: 3)

So give to each situation according to its size, weight, measure, and importance. Stay away from immoderation or from exceeding the proper bounds.

Learn from the example of the Prophet's Companions, when their sole concern was to give their pledge of allegiance under the tree and thus obtain the pleasure of Allah. With them was a man whose concern was focused on a missing camel, a preoccupation that caused him to miss the pledge of allegiance – and consequently, he was deprived of the rewards that were reaped by the others.

Therefore do not be preoccupied with matters that are insignificant. If you follow this advice, you will find that most of your worries will have left you.

Be content with what Allah has given you, and you will be the richest of people

Wealth, appearance, children, house, and talents – you must be content with your share in these things:

{So hold that which I have given you and be of the grateful.}

(Qur'an 7: 144)

Most Islamic scholars and pious Muslims of the early generations of Islam were poor; needless to say, they did not have beautiful houses or nice cars. Yet, despite these disadvantages, they led fruitful lives, and they benefited humankind, not by some miracle, but because they used all that they were given, and spent their time in the correct way. Hence they were blessed in their lives, their time, and their talents.

On the contrary, there are many people who have been bestowed with wealth, children, and all forms of blessings, yet these blessings have been the very reason for their misery and ruin. They deviated from what their inborn instincts were telling them, namely, that material things are not everything. Look at those who have obtained degrees from world – renowned universities, yet they are paragons of obscurity. Their talents and abilities remain unused. Meanwhile, others who are limited in the scope of their knowledge have managed to make mountains out of what they have been given, benefiting both themselves and society.

If you are a seeker of happiness, be satisfied with the looks Allah has favored you with, with your family situation, with the sound of your voice, with the level of your understanding, and with the amount of your salary. Certain educators go further than this by saying that you should imagine being contented with even less than you actually have now.

Here for you is a list of those who have shone from our Islamic heritage despite each being challenged by various disadvantages:

'Aṭâ' ibn Rabaḥ was a world-renowned scholar of his time. He was not only a freed slave, but he was also paralyzed.

Al-Aḥnaf ibn Qays was famous among the Arabs for his singular level of patience. He achieved that fame despite being emaciated and humpbacked, with crooked legs and a fragile frame.

Al-A'mash was among the most famous scholars of Hadith in his time. He was a freed slave, he had bad eyesight, and he was poor. His clothes were ripped, his appearance was disheveled, and he lived in straitened circumstances.

In fact, every prophet was, at one time or another, a shepherd. David (pbuh) was a blacksmith, Zachariah (pbuh) a carpenter, and Enoch a tailor; yet they were the best of humankind.

Your value is in your abilities, good deeds, manners, and contributions to society. Do not feel grief, then, over what has passed you by in life in terms of good looks, wealth, or family; be content with what Allah (the Exalted) has allotted for you.

{It is We Who portion out between them their livelihood in this world.}

(Qur'an 43: 32)

Remind yourself of paradise, which is as wide as are the heavens and the Earth.

If you are hungry in this world, if you are sad, ill or oppressed, remember the eternal bliss of paradise. If you do this, then your losses are really profits, and the hardships you face are really gifts. The most wise of people are those who work for the hereafter, because it is better and everlasting. The most foolish are those who see this world as their eternal abode – in it reside all of their hopes. You will find such people to be the most grief-stricken of all when faced with calamity. They will be the most affected by worldly loss, simply because they see nothing beyond the insignificant lives that they lead. They see and think only of this impermanent life. They wish for nothing to spoil their state of happiness. Were they to remove the veil of ignorance from their eyes, they would commune with themselves about the eternal abode – its bliss, pleasures, and castles. They would listen attentively when they were informed through the Qur'an and the Sunnah about its description. Indeed, that is the abode that deserves our attention and merits our striving and our toiling, so that we may achieve the best of it.

Have we reflected at length about the description of the inhabitants of paradise? Illness does not befall them, grief does not come near them, they die not, they remain young, and their attire remains both perfect and clean. They are in a beautiful home. In paradise is found that which no eye has seen, no ear has heard, and no human mind has imagined. The rider travels under a tree in paradise for one hundred years and yet he still does not reach its end. The length of a tent in paradise is sixty miles. Its rivers are constant, its castles are lofty, and its fruits are not only close by but are also easily picked.

{Therein will be a running spring. Therein will be thrones raised high, and cups set at hand, and cushions set in rows, and rich carpets [all] spread out.} (Qur'an 88: 12-16)

The happiness of paradise will be absolute. So why do we not contemplate this fact?

If paradise is our final destination — and we ask Allah (the Exalted) for paradise — then the hardships of this world are less heavy than they may seem, so let the hearts of the afflicted ones find solace.

O you who live in poverty, or are afflicted with calamity, work righteous deeds so that you shall live in Allah's paradise.

{Peace be upon you, because you persevered in patience! Excellent indeed is the final home!}
(Qur'an 13: 24)

Thus We have made you a just nation

{Thus We have made you a just nation.} (Qur'an 2: 143)

Both your conscience and your religion demand that you be just, which means that you should neither exaggerate nor understate, neither go into excess nor do too little. Those who seek happiness should be just, regardless of whether they are in an angry, a sad, or a joyful mood. Exaggeration in our dealings with others is unacceptable. The best course is the middle course. Those who follow their desires will likely magnify the importance of any given situation, always making a big deal out of nothing. They will feel jealousy and malice toward others. Since they live in a world of exaggeration and imagination, they will envisage everyone else to be against them, even to the extent that they perceive others to be always conspiring to destroy them. Because of this, they live under a dark cloud, constantly overcome by fear and apprehension.

Living according to hearsay and superstition is prohibited in our religion.

{They think that every cry is against them.}
(Qur'an 63: 4)

More often than not, what you fear will happen in the future does not end up taking place. Here is something you should try: when you fear something, imagine that the worst possible outcome takes place, and then train yourself to feel prepared and contented with that outcome. If you do this, you will find that you have saved yourself from apprehensions and superstitions that would otherwise have caused you much grief.

Lend your attention to each matter in proportion to its importance. In any given situation, do not make mountains out of molehills; rather, keep in mind your objectivity and fairness. Do not follow false suspicion or the deceitful illusion of the mirage; be balanced. Listen to the balance of love and hate as explained by the Prophet (bpuh):

> «Love the one who is beloved to you in due moderation, for perhaps the day will come when you will abhor him. And hate the one whom you detest in due moderation, for perhaps the day will arrive when you will come to love him.»

{Perhaps Allah will make friendship between you and those whom you hold as enemies. And Allah has power [over all things], and Allah is Oft-Forgiving, Most Merciful.}

(Qur'an 60: 7)

Being happy is encouraged in Islam

{Do not become weak [against your enemy], nor be sad...}

(Qur'an 3: 139)

{And grieve not over them, and be not distressed because of what they plot.}

(Qur'an 16: 127)

{Be not sad, surely Allah is with us.}

(Qur'an 9: 40)

Referring to true believers, Allah informs us that:

{...upon such shall come no fear, nor shall they grieve.}

(Qur'an 2: 38)

Sadness enervates the soul's will to act and paralyzes the body into inactivity. Sadness prevents one from taking action instead of compelling one towards it. The heart benefits nothing through grief. The most beloved thing to the devil is to make the worshippers sad in order to prevent them from continuing on their path. Allah (the Exalted) says:

{Secret counsels [conspiracies] are only from Satan, in order that he may cause grief to the believers.}

(Qur'an 58: 10)

In the following hadith, the Prophet (bpuh) said:

«In a company of three, it is forbidden for two to hold secret counsel to the exclusion of the third, since doing so will be a cause of sadness for him.»

Contrary to what some (those who have an extreme ascetic bent) believe, the believer should not seek out sadness, because sadness is a harmful condition that afflicts the soul. The Muslim must repel sadness and fight it in any way that is permissible in our religion.

There is no real benefit to sadness; the Prophet (bpuh) sought refuge from it in the following supplication:

«O Allah, I seek refuge in you from anxiety and grief.»

Grief is coupled with anxiety in this hadith. The difference between the two is that if a bad feeling is related to what is going to happen in the future, then one is feeling anxiety, but if the cause of this feeling concerns the past, then one is feeling grief. Both of them weaken the heart, causing inactivity and a decrease in willpower.

Despite what has been mentioned above, grief may sometimes be both inevitable and necessary. When they enter paradise, its dwellers will say:

{All the praises and thanks be to Allah, Who has removed from us [all] grief.}

(Qur'an 35: 34)

This verse implies that they were afflicted with grief in this life, just as they were afflicted with other forms of hardship, both of which were out of their control. So whenever one is overcome by grief and there is no way to avoid it, one is rewarded, because grief is a form of hardship, and the believer is rewarded for going through hardship. Nonetheless, the believer must ward off grief with supplication and other practical means. As for the saying of Allah (the Exalted):

{Nor [is there blame] on those who came to you to be provided with mounts, and when you said: can find no mounts for you, they turned back, while their eyes overflowed with tears of grief that they could not find anything to spend.}

(Qur'an 9: 92)

They were not praised for their grief in itself, but for what that grief indicated and pointed to – namely, strong faith. This occurred when they remained behind during one of the Prophet's expeditions, due to their inability to find the resources needed to make the trip. The verse also exposed the hypocrites, because they did not feel grief when they remained behind.

Therefore the good kind of grief is that which stems from missing out an opportunity to do a good deed or from performing a sin. When you feel sad because you were negligent in fulfilling the rights of Allah, you show a characteristic of a person who is on the right path. As for the hadith:

«Whatever befalls the believer in terms of anxiety, hardship or grief, Allah will make it an atonement for (some of) his sins»

- it indicates that grief is a trial with which the believers are afflicted, and through which some of their sins are atoned for. However, it does not indicate that grief is something to be sought after; the believers should not seek out means of finding grief, thinking that they are performing an act of worship. If this were the case, then the Prophet (bpuh) would have been the first to apply this principle. But he didn't seek out misery; on the contrary, his face was always smiling, his heart was content, and he was continually joyful.

As for the narration of Hind, "He was continually sorrowful," it is considered to be unsubstantiated by scholars of Hadith, because among its narrators is someone who is unknown. Not only is the hadith weak because of its chain of narrators; it is also weak because it is contrary to how the Prophet (bpuh) really was.

How could he have been continually in grief when Allah had informed him that he was forgiven for everything (guaranteeing his entry into paradise) and had protected him from feeling grief over matters pertaining to this life? For example, Allah forbade him from feeling grief over the actions of the disbelievers. How could he have felt grief when all the time his heart was filled with the remembrance of Allah, and when he was at peace with Allah's promise? In fact, he was always pleasant, and his teeth were always visible due to his constant smiles. Whoever delves deeply into his life will know that he came to remove falsehood and to eradicate anxiety, confusion, and grief. He came to free our souls from the tyranny of doubt, disbelief, confusion, and disorder. He came to save our souls from destruction. So many indeed are the favors that were bestowed upon humankind through him.

As for the alleged hadith, "Verily, Allah loves all sad hearts," the chain of its narrators is unknown, so it is not an authentic hadith, especially in view of the fact that it is contrary to the basic principles of our religion. Even if we were to suppose the hadith to be authentic, then its meaning would be that sadness is one of the hardships of life imposed upon the worshippers as a form of trial. If the worshippers persevere through patience, then Allah loves them. As for those who have praised melancholy and have lauded its many virtues (while claiming that our religion encourages it), they are very mistaken. In fact, every text from revelation that touches upon sadness forbids it and orders its opposite: namely, that we should be content with the mercy and blessings of Allah, and happy with that which has been sent with the Messenger of Allah (bpuh).

Those who incline towards extremes in asceticism also relate the following narration, "If Allah loves one of his slaves, He makes that slave's heart that of a weeper. And if he hates one of his slaves, then he places a flute in his heart (thus making him constantly light and happy)."

First, we must note that this is an Israelite tradition, which is claimed to be found in the Torah. Nevertheless, it does have a correct meaning since, truly, the believer feels grief due to his sins and the evildoer is ever playful and frivolous, light and joyful. So if the hearts of the faithful grieve, then it is only due to opportunities lost in terms of righteous deeds or because of sins committed. This is contrary to the sadness of the evildoers, whose grief is caused by losing out on physical pleasure or worldly benefit. Their yearnings, anxieties, and sadness are always for these ends and for nothing else.

In this verse, Allah (the Exalted) says of his Prophet Jacob (pbuh):

{And he lost his sight because of the sorrow that he was suppressing.}

(Qur'an 12: 84)

Here we are informed of his grief over losing his beloved son. Simply informing about something does not in itself signify either approval or disapproval of that thing. The fact is that we have been ordered to seek refuge from sadness, as it is a heavy cloud that hangs above its victim, and is a barrier that prevents one from advancing to higher aims.

There is no doubt that sadness is a trial and a hardship, and is in some ways similar to sickness. However, it is not a stage, level, or condition that the pious should actively seek out.

You are required to seek the means of happiness and peace, to ask Allah to grant you a good life, one that gives you a clear conscience and peace of mind. The achievement of this is an early reward, a point that is underscored by the saying of some, "In this world is a paradise, and whoever does not enter it shall not enter the paradise of the hereafter."

We ask Allah to open our hearts to the light of faith, to guide our hearts to His straight path, and to save us from a miserable life.

Take a moment to reflect

Let us make these supplications, their purpose being to eliminate hardship, anxiety and grief:

«There is none worthy of worship except Allah, the Ever-Forbearing, the Most Great. There is none worthy of worship except Allah, the Lord of the tremendous throne. There is none worthy of worship except Allah, the Lord of the heavens, the Lord of the earth, and the Lord of the noble throne. O Ever-Living, and O One Who sustains and protects all that exists, there is none worthy of worship except You, and by Your mercy do we seek Your aid.»

«O Allah, Your mercy do I hope for; so do not leave me to myself, not even for the blink of an eye. And make well for me all of my affairs. There is none worthy of worship except You.»

«I seek forgiveness from Allah; none is worthy of worship except Him. He is the Ever-Living and the One who sustains and protects all that exists, and I turn to Him in repentance.»

«There is none worthy of worship except You, and how perfect you are; verily, I was among the wrongdoers.»

«O Allah, verily I am Your slave, the son of Your slaves; my forelock is in Your Hand, Your order concerning me will be executed, and just is Your judgment upon me. I ask You by all of Your names that you have named Yourself with, have revealed in Your book, have taught to one of Your creation, or that are in Your knowledge only (from the matters of the unseen) – make the Qur'an the spring of my heart, the light of my chest, the remover of my sadness, and the purger of my anxiety.»

«O Allah, I seek refuge in you from anxiety and grief, from inability and laziness, from avarice and cowardice, from being engrossed by debt, and from being overpowered by men.»

«Allah (alone) is Sufficient for us, and He is the best Disposer of affairs (for us).»

Smile

Laughing moderately can act as a cure or as therapy for depression and sadness. It has a strong influence on keeping the soul light and the heart clear. Abu ad-Dardâ' (may Allah be pleased with him) said:

> «I make it a practice to laugh in order to give rest and comfort to my heart. And the noblest of people, Muhammad (bpuh), would laugh, sometimes until his molars became visible.»

Laughing is an efficacious way to achieve comfort and light-heartedness, but keep in mind that, as in other things, you should not be immoderate. The Prophet (bpuh) said:

> «Do not laugh excessively, for verily, excessive laughter kills the heart.»

What is called for is moderation.

> «And if you smile in the face of your brother, then that is a form of charity.»

> {So he, Solomon, smiled, amused by her speech.}
>
> *(Qur'an 27: 19)*

Also, when you laugh, you should not do so in a mocking or jeering fashion:

> {But when he came to them with Our Âyât [proofs, evidences, verses, lessons, signs, revelations, et cetera] behold! They laughed at them.}
>
> *(Qur'an 43: 47)*

Among the pleasures of paradise will be laughter:

> {But this Day [the Day of Resurrection] those who believe will laugh at the disbelievers.}
>
> *(Qur'an 83: 34)*

The Arabs would hold in high esteem a person who was known for his smile and laughter. They believed this to be a sign of a generous personality and of a person who has a noble disposition and a clear mind.

The truth is that the principles of Islam are based on moderation and on good measure, whether it is in matters of belief, worship, manners, or conduct. Islam does not condone a rigid, frowning expression, nor does it condone a constant playful giddiness; what it does promote is seriousness when it is called for, and a reasonable level of light-heartedness when it is called for.

A gloomy expression and a frowning countenance are marks of a lowly character, a troubled nature, and hot-headedness.

{Then he frowned and he looked in a bad tempered way...}

(Qur'an 74: 22)

The Prophet (bpuh) said:

«Do not disparage (underestimate) any good deed (no matter how small it is), even if that deed was to meet your brother with a friendly countenance.»

Ahmed Ameen said in his book Fayḍ al-Khâṭir:

People who are always smiling not only make their own lives more joyful, but what's more, they are more productive people in their work and have a greater ability to live up to their responsibilities. They are more prepared to face difficulties and to find expedient solutions for them. They are prolific workers who benefit themselves and others.

If I were given a choice between having both status in society and plentiful money, or having a happy, radiant, smiling self, I would choose the latter. For what is great wealth if it begets misery? And what is high position if what comes with it is constant gloominess? And what good is the most beautiful wife if she transforms her house into a living hell? Much better than her – a thousand times at least – is a wife who has not reached such a pinnacle of beauty, but nonetheless has made her house a kind of paradise.

Consider this imagery: In a sense, the rose is smiling and so is the forest. The oceans, rivers, sky, stars and birds are all smiling. Similarly, the human being by nature is a smiling entity, were it not for those things that counteract this natural disposition, such as greed and selfishness, evils that contribute to frowning. This is an anomaly and at odds with the natural harmony of all that surrounds a person; therefore, one whose heart is sullied cannot see things as they truly are. We all see the world through ourselves – through our actions, thoughts, and motives. So if our actions are noble, if our thoughts are pure, and if our motives are honorable, then the spectacles through which we see the world will be clean, and the world will be seen by us as it really is – a beautiful creation. If the spectacles become dirty, and their lenses stained, then everything will seem to be black and morbid.

There are those souls who are able to turn everything into misery, while there are others who are able to derive happiness from the most difficult of circumstances. There is the woman whose eyes fall upon nothing but mistakes. Today is black because a piece of fine china broke or because the cook put too much salt in the food. Then she flares up and curses, and no one in the house escapes from her curses. Then there is the man who brings misery upon his own self and, through his disposition, heaps the same upon others. Any word that he hears, he interprets in the worst possible way. He is affected gravely by the most insignificant of things that occur to him, or that have occurred to him through his actions. He is drawn into misery by profits lost, by profits expected that went unrealized, and so on. The whole world from his perspective is black, and so he blackens it for those around him. Such people have an extraordinary ability to exaggerate the trifles that occur to them. Thus they make mountains out of molehills. Their ability to do well is negligent, and they are never happy or content with that which they have, even if what they have is plenty. No matter how great their possessions, they will never feel any blessings from what they have.

Life is like an art or a science: it needs to be learned and cultivated. It is much better for a person to plant love in his life than to glorify money, using all his might to help it ease its way into his pocket or into his account. What is life when all its energies are exploited and used for the sole purpose of accumulating wealth, with no energy directed towards the cultivation of beauty, splendor, and love?

Most people do not open their eyes to the beauty of life, but open them only to gold or silver. They pass by a lush and luxuriant garden, a beautiful bed of roses, a flowing river, or a group of singing birds, yet they are unmoved by such scenes. All that moves them is the coming and going of money into or out of their pockets. Money is but a means to a happy life. They have reversed this fact, having sold their happy existence and made money an end in itself. Our body has been equipped with eyes to see beauty with, yet we have trained them to look at nothing but money.

Nothing causes the soul or the face to frown more often and with more intensity than despondency. If you want to be a smiling person, wage war against despondency and hopelessness. The door to opportunity is always open to you and to others, and so is the door to success. So indoctrinate your mind with hopes of prosperity in the future.

If you believe that you are inconsequential and have been created for things of only minor importance, then your achievement in life will never surpass this initial goal. On the other hand, if you believe that your calling in life is to achieve extraordinary feats, you will feel a determination that can destroy all kinds of barriers. This can be exemplified as follows. Whoever enters a 100m race will feel tired the moment it is completed, whereas one who enters a 400m race will not feel fatigue after passing the 100m or 200m mark. Therefore the soul gives resolution and willpower in proportion to your goal. Hence you must identify your goal, and let it be high and difficult to achieve. Never feel despondency as long as every day you are taking a new step in its direction. What blocks the soul, making it frown and placing it in a dark prison? The answer is despondency, hopelessness, seeing everything as being evil, searching for faults in others, and constantly speaking about the evilness of the world.

Blessed are those who have teachers who help them to develop their natural abilities and broaden their horizons. The best teachers are those who instill kindness and generosity in their pupils, teaching that the noblest of pursuits that one can strive for is to be a source of goodness to others, in accordance with one's abilities. The soul should be like the sun, radiating light and hope. The heart should be filled with tenderness, virtue, benevolence, and a genuine love for spreading goodness to all those connected to it.

The smiling soul sees difficulties, and it loves to surmount them. When it sees problems, it smiles, reveling in the opportunity to solve and overcome them. The frowning soul, when faced with a problem, magnifies it and belittles its own determination, while spending all its time justifying. It loves success in life but is not willing to pay its price. On every path, it sees a grinning lion. It waits only for gold to shower down upon it, or to chance upon some treasure in the ground.

Difficult things in life are only relative, for everything is difficult for the ordinary person, while there is no great difficulty for the remarkable person. While the remarkable person increases in worthiness by overcoming obstacles, the weak person increases in meanness by running away from them. Problems are comparable to a vicious dog. When it sees you scared or running away, it barks and follows in pursuit. However, when it sees your scorn or your lack of concern, and when you shine your eyes in its direction, it gives way and draws back.

Furthermore, there is nothing more deadly than a feeling of inferiority, a feeling that makes its holders lose all faith in their adequacy. When they embark upon a project, they are immediately doubtful of its completion or success, and they act accordingly by gratifying these doubts; thus they fail. Self-confidence is a noble virtue and a pillar of success in life. It is important to note, though, that there is a vast difference between conceit and confidence. Conceit means to rely upon a deceitful imagination and false pride. Confidence means to rely upon true abilities; it means fulfilling responsibilities, developing talents and organizational skills.

Indeed, how much we are in need of a smile, a friendly face, easygoing manners, and a gentle, generous soul. The Prophet (bpuh) said:

> «Verily, Allah has revealed to me that you should be humble, so that none of you should transgress upon another, and so that none of you should be arrogant and proud to another.»

Smile – Pause to reflect

When you experienced sadness yesterday, your situation didn't get any better by your being sad. Your son failed in school, and you became depressed, yet did your depression change the fact that he failed? Your father passed away, and you became downhearted, yet did that bring him back to life? You lost your business, and you became saddened. Did this change your situation by transforming losses into profits?

Don't be sad: You became despondent due to a calamity, and by doing so, created additional calamities. You became depressed because of poverty, and this only increased the bitterness of your situation. You became gloomy because of what your enemies said to you; by entering into that mental state, you unwittingly helped them in their attack against you. You became sullen because you expected a particular misfortune, and yet it never came to pass.

Don't be sad: Truly a large mansion will not protect you from the effects of depression; neither will a beautiful wife, abundant wealth, a high position, or brilliant children.

Don't be sad: Sadness causes you to imagine poison when you are really looking at pure water, to see a cactus when you are looking at a rose, to see a barren desert when you are looking at a lush garden, and to feel that you are in an unbearable prison when you are living on a vast and spacious earth.

Don't be sad: You have two eyes, two ears, lips, two hands, two legs, a tongue, a heart, peace, safety, and a healthy body.

{Then which of the blessings of your Lord will you deny?}

(Qur'an 55: 13)

Don't be sad: You have the true religion to live by, a house to live in, bread to eat, water to drink, clothes to wear, a spouse to find comfort with; why then the melancholy?

The blessing of pain

Pain is not always a negative force, and it is not something that you should always hate. At times a person benefits from feeling pain.

You might recall that at times when you felt a lot of pain, you sincerely supplicated and remembered Allah. While studying, students often feel the pangs of heavy burdens, sometimes perhaps the burden of monotony, yet they eventually leave this stage of life as scholars. They felt burdened with pain at the beginning but shone at the end. The aches and pangs of passion, the poverty and the scorn of others, the frustration and anger at injustices – these all cause the poets to write flowing and captivating verses. This is because they themselves feel pain in their hearts, in their nerves, and in their blood, and as a result, they are able to infuse the same emotions, via their poetry, into the hearts of others. How many painful experiences did the best writers have to undergo, experiences that inspired brilliant works which we continue to enjoy and benefit from today.

The student who lives the life of comfort and repose, who is not stung by hardships and has never been afflicted with calamity, will be an unproductive, lazy, and lethargic person.

Indeed, the poets who know no pain and who have never tasted bitter disappointment will invariably produce heaps upon heaps of cheap words. This is because the words pour forth from their tongues and not from their feelings or emotions; though they may comprehend what they have written, their hearts and bodies have not lived the experience.

More worthy and relevant to the aforementioned examples are the lives of the early believers, who lived during the period of revelation and who took part in the most important religious revolution that the world has ever seen. Indeed, they had greater faith, nobler hearts, more truthful tongues, and deeper knowledge than those who came after them; they had all of these because they lived through pain and suffering, both of which are necessary concomitants to great revolutions. They felt the pains of hunger, of poverty, of rejection, of abuse, of banishment from home and country, of abandonment of all pleasures, of wounds, and of death and torture. They were in truth chosen ones, the elite of mankind. They were models of purity, nobleness, and sacrifice.

{That is because they suffer neither thirst nor fatigue, nor hunger in the cause of Allah, nor they take any step to raise the anger of disbelievers nor inflict any injury upon an enemy, but is written to their credit as a deed of righteousness. Surely, Allah wastes not the reward of the doers of good.}

(Qur'an 9: 120)

In the history of the world, there are those who have produced their greatest works due to the pain and the suffering that they experienced. Al-Mutanabbi wrote some of his best poetry when afflicted with a severe fever. After an-Nu'mân ibn Mundhir threatened an-Nâbighah with death, the latter produced some of his best poetry. The well-known line he spoke, roughly translated, is:

Verily, you are the sun, and the other kings are the stars,

For when the sun rises, no star in the sky is visible.

In fact, there are many examples of those who prospered and achieved as a result of the suffering they experienced.

Therefore, do not become excessively anxious when you think of pain, and do not fear suffering. It might well be that through pain and suffering, you will become stronger. Moreover, for you to live with a burning and passionate heart that has been stung is purer and nobler than to live the apathetic existence of a person who has a cold heart and a shortsighted outlook.

{But Allah was averse to their being sent forth, so He made them lag behind, and it was said [to them]: Sit you among those who sit [at home].}

(Qur'an 9: 46)

The words of a passionate sermon can reach the innermost depths of the heart and penetrate the deepest regions of the soul, usually because the one who gives such sermons has himself experienced pain and suffering.

{He knew what was in their hearts, and He sent down as-Sakeenah [calmness and tranquility] upon them, and He rewarded them with a near victory.}

(Qur'an 48: 18)

I have read many books of poetry, and a high percentage of them are passionless, without life or soul. This is because their authors never endured hardship, and because they were composed among surroundings of comfort. Hence the works of such authors were cold, like blocks of ice.

I have read books filled with sermons that do not shake a hair on the body of the listener and that lack an atom's weight of impact. The orator (whose sermons were put to print) is not speaking with feeling and sentiment, or in other words, pain and suffering.

{They say with their mouths, that which is not in their hearts.} (Qur'an 3: 167)

If you wish to affect and influence others, whether it is with your speech or poetry, or even with your actions, you must first feel the passion inside of you. You must be moved yourself by the meanings of what you are trying to convey. Then, and then only, you will come to realize that you have an influence upon others.

{But when We send down water [rain] on it, it is stirred [to life], it swells and puts forth every lovely kind [of growth].}

(Qur'an 22: 5)

The blessing of knowledge

{And Allah taught you that which you knew not. And Ever-Great is the grace of Allah unto you [O Muhammad].}

(Qur'an 4: 113)

Ignorance kills one's conscience and soul.

{I admonish you, lest you be one of the ignorant.}

(Qur'an 11: 46)

Knowledge is a light that leads to wisdom. It is life for one's soul and fuel for one's character.

{Is he who was dead [without faith by ignorance and disbelief] and We gave him life [by knowledge and faith] and set for him a light [of belief] whereby he can walk amongst men, like him who is in the darkness [of disbelief, polytheism and hypocrisy] from which he can never come out?}

(Qur'an 6: 122)

Happiness and high spirits come with enlightenment, because through knowledge, we may fulfill our goals and discover what was previously hidden from us. The soul, by its very nature, longs for the acquisition of new knowledge to stimulate it and the mind.

Ignorance is boredom and grief, because the ignorant person leads a life that never offers anything new or thought-provoking. Yesterday is like today, which in turn is like tomorrow.

If you desire happiness, then seek out knowledge and enlightenment, and you will find that anxiety, depression, and grief will leave you:

{And say: My Lord! Increase me in knowledge.}

(Qur'an 20: 114)

{Read! In the name of your Lord, Who has created [all that exists].}

(Qur'an 96: 1)

The Prophet (bpuh) said:

«If Allah wishes good for someone, He gives him an understanding of the religion.»

Therefore if someone is ignorant, let him not be proud of either his wealth or his status in society; his life is lacking in meaning, and his achievements are woefully incomplete.

{Shall he then who knows that what has been revealed unto you [O Muhammad] from your Lord is the truth be like him who is blind?}

(Qur'an 13: 19)

Az-Zamakhshari, the well-known commentator of the Qur'an, said in verse form:

The sleepless nights I spend in learning the sciences are more beloved to me than the company or caresses of the enchanting woman.

My rapturous exhilaration when understanding a difficult concept is more delicious to me than the most exotic drink. More delightful to me than the sound of a woman's hand on the drum are my hands on my papers in order to remove dust.

O he who tries to attain my level by wishful thinking, how much difference there is between the one who finds the pain of climbing to be too much and the one who climbs and reaches the summit.

Do I toil through the night, while you sleep through it, yet you hope to surpass me?

How noble is enlightenment! And through it, how happy is the soul!

{Is he who is on a clear proof from his Lord, like those for whom their evil deeds that they do are beautified for them, while they follow their own lusts [evil desires]?}

(Qur'an 47: 14)

The art of happiness

Among the greatest of blessings is to have a calm, stable, and happy heart. For in happiness the mind is clear, enabling one to be a productive person. It has been said that happiness is an art that needs to be learned, and if you learn it, you will be blessed in this life. But how does one learn it? A basic principle of achieving happiness is having an ability to endure and to cope with any situation. Therefore you should neither be swayed nor governed by difficult circumstances, nor should you be annoyed by insignificant trifles. Based on the purity of the heart and its ability to endure, a person will shine. When you train yourself to be patient and forbearing, then hardship and calamity will be easy for you to bear.

The opposite of being content is being shortsighted, being concerned for no one but one's own self and forgetting about the world and all that is in it. Allah described his enemies as follows:

{Thinking about themselves [as in how to save their ownselves, ignoring the others and the Prophet]...}

(Qur'an 3: 154)

It is as if such people see themselves as being the whole universe, or at least at the center of it. They think not of others, nor do they live for anyone but themselves. It is incumbent upon you and I to take time out to be preoccupied with more than just us, and to sometimes distance ourselves from our own problems in order to forget our wounds and hurts. By doing this, we gain two things: we make ourselves happy, and we bring joy to others.

Basic to the art of happiness is to bridle our thoughts and to restrain them, not allowing them to wander, stray, escape, or go wild. If you leave your thoughts to wander as they wish, then they will run wild and control you. They will open the catalogue of your past woes. They will remind you of the history of your misfortunes, beginning from the day that your mother gave birth to you. If your thoughts are left to roam, then they will bring to you images of past difficulties and images of a future that is frightening. These thoughts will shake your very being and will cause your feelings to flare. Therefore bridle them, and restrain them by directing them to the concentrated application of the kind of serious thought that begets fruitful and beneficial work:

{And put your trust in the Ever-Living One Who dies not.}

(Qur'an 25: 58)

Also among the principles of the art of happiness is to value life on this earth according to its true merit and worth. This life is frivolous and does not warrant anything from you except that you turn away from it. This life is filled with calamities, aches, and wounds. If that is the description of this life, then how can we be unduly affected by its minor calamities, and how can we grieve over such material things as have passed us by? The best moments of life are tainted, its future promises are mere mirages, the successful ones in it are envied, the one who is blessed is constantly threatened, and lovers are struck down by some unexpected misfortune.

And in a hadith:

«Verily, knowledge is only acquired by the practice of learning, and tolerance is acquired by the practice of tolerating.»

If we were to attempt to apply the meaning of this hadith to the topic under discussion, then we could go one step further and say that happiness is acquired by assuming it. It is acquired by constantly smiling, by hunting for the reasons that make us happy, and even by forcing it onto ourselves, however awkward that may seem. We do all of these things until happiness becomes second nature.

The truth of the matter is that you cannot remove from yourself all remnants of grief. The reason for this is that life was created as a test:

{Verily, We have created man in toil.}

(Qur'an 90: 4)

{That He might try you, which of you is the best in deeds.}

(Qur'an 11: 7)

But the message I wish to convey to you is that you should, as much as is possible, reduce the amount and intensity of your grief. As for being completely free from grief, this is for the inhabitants of paradise in the hereafter. This is why the dwellers of paradise will say:

{All the praises and thanks be to Allah, Who has removed from us [all] grief.}

(Qur'an 35: 34)

This is considered to be a proof that grief will not be removed from them except in paradise. Likewise, grudges and bitterness will not be completely removed except in paradise.

{And We shall remove from their breasts any sense of injury [that they may have]...}

(Qur'an 15: 47)

So when we know the nature of this world and its qualities, we come to realize that it is dry, deceitful, and unworthy; we come to fully understand that that is its nature and its description. An Arab poet said:

> You have taken an oath not to betray us in our pacts,
>
> And it is as if you have vowed that in the end,
>
> you shall deceive us.

If this world is as I have described it to be, then it is worthy of the intelligent person not to help it in its onslaught, nor to surrender to depression and anxiety. What we should do is defend ourselves from all feelings that may spoil our lives, in a war that we must wage with all the strength that we have been endowed with.

{And make ready against them all you can of power, including steeds of war to threaten the enemy of Allah and your enemy...}

(Qur'an 8: 60)

{But they never lost heart for that which did befall them in Allah's way, nor did they weaken nor degrade themselves.}

(Qur'an 3: 146)

The art of happiness – Pause to reflect

Don't be sad. If you are poor, then someone else is immersed in debt. If you do not own your own means of transportation, then someone else has been deprived of his legs. If you have reason to complain concerning the pains of sickness, then someone else has been bedridden for years. If you have lost a child, then someone else has lost many children, for instance, in a single car accident.

Don't be sad. You are a Muslim who believes in Allah, His Messengers, His angels, the hereafter, and preordainment -both the good and the bad of it. While you are blessed with this faith, which is the greatest of blessings, others disbelieve in Allah, discredit the Messengers, differ among themselves concerning the Book, deny the hereafter, and deviate in their understanding of divine preordainment. Don't be sad, because if you are, you disturb your soul and heart, and you prevent yourself from sleeping. One of the Arab poets said:

How often is the young man overcome with despair when afflicted, and with Allah is the way out.

The situation becomes unbearable, and when its rope tightens, it snaps, and throughout, he never thought that he would be saved.

Controlling one's emotions

Emotions flare up for two reasons: either because of joy or inner pain. In a hadith, the Prophet (bpuh) said:

«Verily, I have been prohibited from emitting two foolish and wicked sounds: one that is emitted when something favorable happens, and the other that is expressed when calamity strikes.»

{In order that you may not be sad over matters that you fail to get, nor rejoice because of that which has been given to you.}

(Qur'an 57: 23)

For this reason, the Prophet (bpuh) said:

«Verily, true patience is that which is displayed during the initial shock.»

Therefore, when we contain our emotions upon both the joyful and the calamitous occasions, we are likely to achieve peace and tranquility, happiness and comfort, and the taste of triumph over our ownselves. Allah described human beings as being exultant and boastful, irritable, discontented when evil touches them, and niggardly when good touches them. The exceptions, Allah informed us, are those who remain constant in prayer, for they are on a middle path in times of both joy and sorrow. They are thankful during times of ease and patient during times of hardship.

Unbridled emotions can greatly wear people out, causing pain and loss of sleep. When such persons become angry, they flare up, threaten others, lose all self-control, and surpass the boundaries of justice and balance. In contrast, if they become happy, they are in a state of rapture and wildness. In the intoxication of joy, they forget themselves and surpass the bounds of modesty. When they renounce and relinquish the company of others, they disparage them, forgetting their virtues while stamping out their good qualities.

On the other hand, if they love others, then they spare no pains in according them all forms of veneration and honor, portraying them as being the pinnacles of perfection.

The Prophet (bpuh) said:

«Love the one who is beloved to you in due moderation, for perhaps the day will come when you will abhor him. And hate the one whom you detest in due moderation, for perhaps the day will arrive when you will come to love him.»

In another hadith, the Prophet (bpuh) said:

«I ask you (O Allah) to make me just, both while being in a state of anger and while being in a state of joy.»

So when we curb our emotions, control our minds, and give to each matter according to the weight of its importance, we will have taken a step towards wisdom and true understanding.

{Indeed We have sent Our Messengers with clear proofs, and revealed with them the scripture and the balance [justice] that humankind may keep up justice.} (Qur'an 57: 25)

Indeed, Islam came as much with its balance in morals, manners, and dealings as it did with its straightforward, holy, and truthful way of life.

{Thus We have made you a just [and the best] nation.} (Qur'an 2: 143)

Being just is an end that is called for both in our manners and in matters of jurisprudence. In fact, Islam is founded on truth and justice – truthfulness in all that we learn from revealed texts, and justice in rulings, sayings, actions, and manners.

{And the word of your Lord has been fulfilled in truth and in justice.} (Qur'an 6: 115)

The bliss of the Prophet's Companions

Our Prophet Muhammad (bpuh) came to all people with a heavenly message. He was not driven by worldly ambition; he had no treasure from which to spend, no splendid gardens from which to eat, and no castle in which to live. Despite all this, his loving followers pledged allegiance to him and remained steadfast, enduring a hard life full of difficulties. They were few and weak, always in fear of being uprooted by those surrounding them, and yet they loved the Prophet (bpuh) wholly and completely.

They were besieged in a mountain pass, and during that time, they had little or no food. Their reputations were attacked, their own relatives waged war against them, and yet their love for him was perfect.

Some of them were dragged over the hot sands of the desert, some were imprisoned, and others were subjected to inventive and innovative ways of punishment -all of which the disbelievers inflicted upon them. Despite having to endure all of that, they still loved him unreservedly with heart and soul.

They were deprived of home, country, family, and wealth. They were driven out from the playing fields of their childhood and from the homes in which they were raised. Despite all this suffering, they loved him unequivocally.

The believers faced trials because of his message. The very ground under them was shaken violently, and yet their love for him continued to grow.

The best among their youth constantly had swords hanging menacingly over their heads.

Their men moved forward lightly across the battlefield, advancing to death as if they were upon an excursion or a holiday, for the simple reason that they loved him unconditionally.

One of them was charged with the duty of carrying the Prophet's message to a king in a foreign land, and that person knew that it was a mission from which he would not return. Yet he went and fulfilled his duty. One of them was sent on another mission, knowing that it would be the cause of his death, and he went happily, for he loved the Prophet (bpuh) with unmitigated love.

But why did they love him, and why were they so happy with his message and content with his example? Why did they forget the pain, the suffering, and the hardship that resulted from following him?

To put it simply, he epitomized benevolence and righteousness. They perceived in him all the signs of truth and purity. He was a symbol for those who sought out higher things. With his tenderness, he cooled the rancor in the hearts of people, with words of truth he soothed their chests, and with his message he filled their souls with peace.

He poured happiness into their hearts, until the pain that they endured from being at his side was made to seem insignificant. He instilled into their souls a belief that made them forget every injury and every adversity that they had to endure.

He polished their insides with his guidance, and he illuminated their eyes with his brilliance. He removed from them the burdens of ignorance, the depravities of idolatry, and the evil consequences of polytheism. He extinguished the fires of malice and animosity from their souls, and he poured the water of faith into their hearts. Thus, their minds and bodies became tranquil, and their hearts found peace.

They tasted the beauty of life with him, and they knew delight in his company. They found happiness at his side, safety and salvation in following him, and an inner richness in emulating him:

{And we have sent you [O Muhammad] not but as a mercy for all that exists.}

(Qur'an 21: 107)

{And verily, you [O Muhammad] are indeed guiding [humankind] to the straight path.}

(Qur'an 42: 52)

{And he brings them out of darkness [by Allah's will] unto light...}

(Qur'an 5: 16)

{He it is Who sent among the unlettered ones a Messenger [Muhammad] from among themselves, reciting to them His verses, purifying them [from the filth of disbelief and polytheism], and teaching them the Book and al-Ḥikmah [as-Sunnah: legal ways, orders, acts of worship, et cetera of Prophet Muhammad]. And verily, they had been before in manifest error.}

(Qur'an 62: 2)

{He releases them from their heavy burdens and from the fetters [bindings] that were upon them.}

(Qur'an 7: 157)

{Answer Allah [by obeying him] and [His] Messenger when he calls you to that which will give you life.}

(Qur'an 8: 24)

{And you were on the brink of a pit of fire, and He saved you from it.}

(Qur'an 3: 103)

They were truly happy with their leader, and so they rightly deserved to be.

O Allah, send prayers and peace upon Muhammad, the liberator of minds from the shackles of deviation and the rescuer of souls from the curses of falsehood, and be pleased with his noble Companions as a recompense for their striving and for their efforts.

Eliminate boredom from your life

One who lives a life of repetition and routine will almost inevitably become a victim of boredom, especially since human beings, by their very nature, tire from a lack of change. For this reason, Allah (the Exalted) gave us variety in times and places, in food and drink – diversity in the many forms of creation: night and day, valley and mountain, white and black, hot and cold, shade and sun, sweet and sour. Allah (the Exalted) mentioned this diversity in His book:

{There comes forth from their bellies, a drink of varying color.}

(Qur'an 16: 69)

{...And date-palms, growing out two or three from a single stem root, or otherwise [one stem root for every palm]...}

(Qur'an 13: 4)

{And crops of different shape and taste [its fruits and its seeds] and olives, and pomegranates, similar [in kind] and different [in taste].}

(Qur'an 6: 141)

{...And among the mountains are streaks white and red, of varying colors...}

(Qur'an 35: 27)

{And so are the days [good and not so good]. We give to men by turns...}

(Qur'an 3: 140)

The children of Israel tired of eating the one kind of food they were given – even though it was the best of foods – simply because it was all that they ate:
{We cannot endure one kind of food.}

(Qur'an 2: 61)

Al-Ma'moon would alternate between reading, standing, sitting, and lying down, and he said, "The soul is ever so prone to boredom."

{Those who remember Allah [always, and in prayers] standing, sitting and lying down on their sides...}

(Qur'an 3: 191)

You should contemplate the many forms of worship that are legislated in Islam. There are deeds of the heart, of the tongue, of the limbs, and of wealth, by spending it for a good cause. The prayer, alms giving, fasting, pilgrimages to Makkah, fighting in the way of Allah – these are only some examples of worship. The prayer involves standing, bowing, prostrating, and sitting. If you desire relaxation, vitality, and continued productivity, then bring diversity into your work, your reading, and your daily life. In terms of reading, for example, read a broad range of topics: the Qur'an, its explanation, the biography of the Prophet (bpuh) and his Companions, hadiths, Islamic jurisprudence, history, literature, books of general knowledge, and so forth. Distribute your time between worship and enjoying what is lawful, from visiting friends, entertaining guests, playing sports, or going on excursions. You will find yourself to be a lively and bright person, because the soul delights in variety and things that are new.

Cast off anxiety

Don't be sad, for your Lord says:

{Have We not opened your breast for you [O Muhammad]?}

(Qur'an 94: 1)

The message of this verse embraces all those who carry the truth, who see the light, and who tread the path of guidance.

{Is he whose breast Allah has opened to Islam, so that he is in light from His Lord [as he who is non-Muslim]? So, woe to those whose hearts are hardened against the remembrance of Allah!}

(Qur'an 39: 22)

Therefore there is a truth that causes the heart to be opened and a falsehood that causes it to harden.

{And whosoever Allah wills to guide, He opens his breast to Islam.}

(Qur'an 6: 125)

So the acceptance of and adherence to this religion is a goal that cannot be achieved except by the one who is blessed.

{Be not sad [or afraid], surely Allah is with us.}

(Qur'an 9: 40)

All those who have faith in Allah's care, guardianship, and mercy speak the words that are related in this verse.

{Those [that is, believers] unto whom the people [hypocrites] said: Verily, the people [pagans] have gathered against you [a great army], therefore, fear them. But it [only] increased them in faith, and they said: Allah [alone] is Sufficient for us, and He is the Best Disposer of affairs [for us].}

(Qur'an 3: 173)

His being Sufficient for us frees us from dependence upon others, and His Guardianship protects us.

{O Prophet [Muhammad]! Allah is Sufficient for you and for the believers who follow you.}

(Qur'an 8: 64)

{And put your trust in the Ever-Living One Who dies not...}

(Qur'an 25: 58)

{And endure you patiently [O Muhammad], your patience is not but from Allah. And grieve not over them [polytheists and pagans, et cetera.], and be not distressed because of what they plot. Truly, Allah is with those who fear Him [keep their duty unto Him] and those who are good-doers.}

(Qur'an 16: 127-128)

Allah being with them in this verse refers to a special blessing for his obedient worshippers, in terms of protection, care, support, and guardianship. This is in proportion to the level of their faith, actions, and efforts.

{So do not become weak [against your enemy], nor be sad, and you will be superior [in victory] if you are indeed [true] believers.} (Qur'an 3: 139)

{They will do you no harm, barring a trifling annoyance; and if they fight against you, they will show you their backs, and they will not be helped.} (Qur'an 3: 111)

Be Happy

{Allah has decreed: Verily! It is I and My Messengers who shall be the victorious. Verily, Allah is All-Powerful, All-Mighty.}

(Qur'an 58: 21)

{Verily, We will indeed make victorious Our Messengers and those who believe [in the Oneness of Allah -Islamic monotheism] in this world's life and on the Day when the witnesses will stand forth [that is, Day of Resurrection].}

(Qur'an 40: 51)

{And my affair I leave it to Allah. Verily, Allah is the All-Seer of [His] slaves. So Allah saved him from the evils that they plotted [against him]...}

(Qur'an 40: 44-45)

{And in Allah should the believers put their trust.}

(Qur'an 3: 122)

Don't be sad: live today as if it were the last day of your life. With this frame of mind and outlook towards life, you have no reason to allow sadness or anger to steal the little time you have. The Prophet (bpuh) said:

«When the morning comes, do not expect to see the evening, and when the evening comes, do not expect to see the morning.»

In other words, live with heart, body, and soul for today only, without dwelling upon the past and without being anxious about the future. An Arab poet said:

The past is lost forever,

And that which is hoped for is from the unseen,

So all that you have is the present hour.

Being preoccupied with the past and dragging past woes into the present – these are the signs of an unstable and unsound mind. A Chinese proverb reads:

Don't cross the bridge until you reach it.

In other words, be anxious over events only when they come to pass. One of our pious predecessors said:

O son of Adam, verily, you have only three days:

Yesterday, and it has forsaken you;

Tomorrow, and it has yet to arrive;

And today, so fear Allah and obey Him in it.

How can they truly live who carry with them the concerns of the past, the present, and the future? How can they find peace while constantly recollecting that which has already occurred? Such individuals play past events back in their minds and feel the pain, yet they gain nothing from the process.

The meaning of: «When the morning comes, do not expect to see the evening, and when the evening comes, do not expect to see the morning,» is that we should not have lofty or long-term hopes for this world. Expect death, and do your best in doing good deeds. Do not let your concerns and ambitions surpass the limit of that day in which you live; this is a code that will allow you to concentrate and spend all of your energies on being productive each day. Use time efficiently and concentrate all of your efforts on achieving something today, by improving your manners, taking care of your health, and improving your relations with others.

Cast off anxiety – Pause to reflect

Don't be sad, for that which has been preordained has already been decided upon and will take place, though you may not like it. The pens have been lifted, the scrolls have been rolled up, and every affair is firmly established. Therefore your sadness will not change your reality in the least.

Don't be sad, because with your sadness, you desire the suspension of time: for the sun to stop in its place, for the hands of the clock to stand still, for your feet to move backwards, and for the river to flow back to its source.

Don't be sad, because sadness is like a hurricane that violently tosses the waves, changing the atmosphere and destroying the blooming flowers of the luxuriant garden.

Don't be sad, because the one who is sad is like a person who pours water into a bucket that has a hole in it, or like a writer who uses his or her finger to write on water.

Don't be sad, because the true span of life is measured by the number of days in which you are content. Do not then spend your days in grief, do not waste your nights in sorrow, and do not be extravagant in squandering your time; for truly, Allah loves not those who are extravagant and wasteful.

Don't be sad, for in truth, your Lord forgives sins and accepts repentance.

When you read the following verse, don't you feel that your heart is peaceful, your worries are driven away, and happiness permeates your whole being?

{Say: O My slaves who have transgressed against themselves [by committing evil deeds and sins]! Despair not of the mercy of Allah, verily Allah forgives all sins. Truly, He is Oft-Forgiving, Most Merciful.}

(Qur'an 39: 53)

He addressed them with, {O My slaves}, to tame their hearts and souls. He specifically mentioned those who transgress, since they are more disposed than others to perpetrate evil deeds on a continual basis. How much greater then will His mercy be for others! Thus He forbade them from despairing and from losing hope of attaining forgiveness. He informed them that He forgives all sins of the one who repents, whether they are big or small, important or unimportant. Do you not then rejoice upon reading the following verses?

{And those who, when they have committed Faḥshâ [illegal sexual intercourse et cetera] or wronged themselves with evil, remember Allah and ask forgiveness for their sins – and none can forgive sins but Allah – And do not persist in what [wrong] they have done, while they know.}

(Qur'an 3: 135)

{And whoever does evil or wrongs himself but afterwards seeks Allah's Forgiveness, he will find Allah Oft-Forgiving, Most Merciful.}

(Qur'an 4: 110)

{If you avoid the great sins which you are forbidden to do, We shall remit from you your [small] sins, and admit you to a noble entrance [that is, into paradise].}

(Qur'an 4: 31)

{If they [hypocrites], when they had been unjust to themselves, had come to you [Muhammad] and begged Allah's forgiveness, and the Messenger had begged forgiveness for them: indeed, they would have found Allah All-Forgiving [One Who accepts repentance], Most Merciful.}

(Qur'an 4: 64)

{And verily, I am indeed forgiving to him who repents, believes [in My Oneness, and associates none in worship with Me] and does righteous good deeds, and then remains constant in doing them [until his death].}

(Qur'an 20: 82)

When Prophet Moses (pbuh) killed a man, he said, "O my Lord, forgive me," and He forgave him. When Prophet David (pbuh) repented, Allah (the Exalted) said:

{So We forgave him that, and verily, for him is a near access to Us, and a good place of [final] return [paradise].}

(Qur'an 38: 25)

How perfect, merciful, and generous is Allah! He even proffered His mercy and forgiveness for those who believe in the trinity – that is, if they repent:

{Surely, disbelievers are those who said: Allah is the third of the three [in a trinity]. But there is no Ilah [god] [none who has the right to be worshipped] but One Ilah [God-Allah]. And if they cease not from what they say, verily, a painful torment will befall the disbelievers among them. Will they not repent to Allah and ask His forgiveness? For Allah is Oft-Forgiving, Most Merciful.}

(Qur'an 5: 73-74)

In an authentic hadith, the Prophet (bpuh) told us that Allah (the Exalted) says:

«O son of Adam, indeed, you will not supplicate to Me and hope from Me except that I will forgive you, in proportion to what came from you (meaning the level of sincerity), and I won't mind.

O son of Adam, if your sins were to reach in magnitude the height of the heavens, and then you were to ask Me for forgiveness, I would forgive you, and I won't mind.

O son of Adam, were you to come to Me with sins that (in their size) almost fill the earth, and you met Me without ascribing to Me any partners, I would come to you with its size in forgiveness.»

Bukhari related that the Prophet (bpuh) said:

«Indeed, Allah extends His Hand in the night to forgive the one who sins in the day, and He extends His Hand in the day to forgive the one who sins at night, and this continues until the sun rises from the west.»

In another hadith, the Prophet (bpuh) relates that Allah (the Exalted) said:

«O my slaves, verily you sin by day and night, and I forgive all sins; so seek forgiveness from Me, and I will forgive you.»

In another authentic hadith, the Prophet (bpuh) said:

«By the One Who has my soul in His Hand, if you were not to sin, then Allah would remove you, and would bring another nation who sins, and who then seek forgiveness from Allah; and He would forgive them.»

The Prophet (bpuh) also said:

«By the One Who has my soul in His Hand, if you were not to sin, then I would fear for you that which is more severe than sin, and that is self-conceit.»

In another authentic narration, the Prophet (bpuh) said:

«Every one of you is constantly doing wrong, and the best of those who constantly do wrong are the ones who are constantly making repentance.»

He also said in this authentic hadith:

«Truly, Allah is happier with the repentance of His slave than one of you who is on his mount, and upon his mount is his drink and food; then he loses his mount in the desert, and he searches for it until he loses hope; so he sleeps and then wakes up to find that his mount is beside him, and he says: O Allah, you are my slave and I am your Lord. He pronounced this mistake as a result of his extreme happiness.»

He is also authentically reported to have said:

«Verily, a slave (of Allah) commits a sin and then he says: O Allah, forgive me my sin, for indeed, none forgives sins except You. Then he commits another sin, and he says afterwards: O Allah, forgive me my sin, for indeed, none forgives sins except You. Then he commits another sin, and he afterwards says: O Allah, forgive me my sin, for indeed, none forgives sins except You. Then Allah says: My slave knows that he has a Lord Who takes one to account for sins and Who also forgives sins, so let my slave do as he wishes.»

The meaning of this is that as long as Allah's slave is contrite and repentant, then Allah will forgive him.

Be Happy – Everything will occur according to preordainment

Everything occurs according to preordainment and according to what has been decreed. Such is the belief of Muslims, the followers of Muhammad (bpuh). Nothing happens in the universe except through Allah's knowledge, permission, and divine plan.

{No calamity befalls on the earth or in yourselves but is inscribed in the Book of Decrees, before We bring it into existence. Verily, that is easy for Allah.}

(Qur'an 57: 22)

{Verily, We have created all things with Qadr [divine preordainments of all things before their creation, as written in the Book of Decrees].}

(Qur'an 54: 49)

{And certainly, We shall test you with something of fear, hunger, loss of wealth, lives and fruits, but give glad tidings to the patient ones.}

(Qur'an 2: 155)

The Prophet (bpuh) said:

«Wonderful is the affair of the believer! His affairs in their entirety are good for him: if good befalls him, he is thankful, and that is good for him. If harm befalls him, he is patient, and that is good for him. And this (prosperous state of being) is only for the believer.»

In an authentic hadith, the Prophet (bpuh) said:

«If you ask, then ask of Allah, and if you seek help, then seek it from Allah. And know that if the whole of the nation were to rally together in order to bring benefit to you in anything, they would not benefit you except with what Allah has written for you. And if they were to gather together in order to inflict harm upon you with something, they would not harm you except with what Allah has written for you. The pens have been raised and the pages have dried.»

The Prophet (bpuh) also said:

«And know that what has befallen you was not going to miss you, and that which missed you was not meant to befall you.»

In another authentic hadith, the Prophet (bpuh) said:

«Strive for what will benefit you, seek help from Allah, do not be weak, and do not say: If I had done such and such, the situation would be such and such. But say: Allah has decreed, and what He wishes, He does.»

In yet another authentic hadith, the Prophet (bpuh) said:

«Every matter that Allah decrees for His slave is better for him.»

Shaykh al-Islam Ibn Taymiyah was asked whether sin could be good for someone. He said:

Yes, with the condition that it is followed by being remorseful and repentant, by seeking forgiveness, and by being sincerely moved (to submission) on the inside.

Allah (the Exalted) says:

{And it may be that you dislike a thing that is good for you, and that you like a thing that is bad for you. Allah knows, but you do not know.}

(Qur'an 2: 216)

Be Happy – Wait patiently for a happy outcome

The following hadith is found in the book of Tirmidhi:

«The best form of worship is to wait (patiently) for a happy outcome.»

{Is not the morning near?}

(Qur'an 11: 81)

The morning of the afflicted is looming, so watch for it. An Arab proverb says, "If the rope becomes too tight, it will snap."

In other words, if a situation reaches the level of crisis, then expect a light and an opening to appear. Allah (the Exalted) says:

{And whosoever fears Allah and keeps his duty to Him, He will remit his sins from him, and will enlarge his reward.} *(Qur'an 65: 5)*
{And whosoever fears Allah and keeps his duty to Him, He will make his matter easy for him.}

(Qur'an 65: 4)

In an authentic hadith, the Prophet (bpuh) relates this saying from Allah (the Exalted):

«I am with the thoughts of My slave towards Me, so let him think of Me as he pleases.»

Allah (the Exalted) says:

{[They were reprieved] until, when the Messengers gave up hope and thought that they were denied [by their people], then came to them Our help, and whosoever We willed were delivered.}

(Qur'an 12: 110)

Know that, truly, with hardship there is relief. Some commentators of the Qur'an said (considering it to be a hadith) that:

"One hardship cannot overcome two reliefs."

The Prophet (bpuh) said in an authentic hadith:

«And know that victory comes with patience, and that relief comes with hardship.»

An Arab poet said:

Some eyes are restless while others are in sleep,

In meditating about what may or may not occur.

So leave worrying as much as possible,

As carrying the burdens of anxiety is madness.

There is your Lord, who provided you with solutions to yesterday,

And He will similarly provide for what is to come tomorrow.

Another said:

Let events flow in their predestined path,

And do not sleep except with a clear mind.

Between the period of the blinking of the eye and its opening,

Allah changes things from one state to another.

Wait patiently for a happy outcome – Pause to reflect

Don't worry about your wealth that is stored in vaults. Unless you have faith in Allah, your high castles and your green gardens will only bring you worry, grief, and hopelessness.

Don't be sad: even the diagnosis of the doctor and his medicine cannot make you happy if you have allowed sadness to dwell in your heart, letting it permeate your emotions and your existence.

Don't be sad: you have the ability to supplicate to Allah and thus excel at humbling yourself at the doorstep of the King of kings. You have the blessed last third of the night to invoke Allah and to rub your head upon the ground in prostration.

Don't be sad: Allah has created for you the earth and what is in it. He has caused gardens of beauty to grow, filling them with many kinds of plants and flowers in pairs, both male and female. He has made tall palm trees, shining stars, forests, rivers and streams – yet you are sad!

Don't be sad: you drink water that is pure, you breathe fresh air, you walk upon your two feet in health, and you sleep in the evenings in peace.

Be Happy: Seek forgiveness from Allah often, for your Lord is Oft-Forgiving

{I [Noah] said [to them]: Ask forgiveness from your Lord; verily, He is Oft-Forgiving. He will send rain to you in abundance; and give you increase in wealth and children; and bestow on you gardens; and bestow on you rivers.}   (Qur'an 71: 10-12)

So seek forgiveness from Allah more often, and you will reap the benefits of doing so: peace of mind, lawful provisions, righteous offspring, and plentiful rain.

{And [commanding you]: Seek the forgiveness of your Lord, and turn to Him in repentance, that He may grant you good enjoyment, for a term appointed. And that He may bestow His abounding grace to every owner of grace [that is, the one who helps and serves the needy and deserving, physically and with his wealth, and even with good words].}

(Qur'an 11: 3)

The Prophet (bpuh) said:

«Whosoever seeks forgiveness (from Allah) often, then Allah makes for him a good ending for every matter of concern and provides for him a way out of every tight situation.»

Related in Bukhari is a hadith that is known as the chief of al-istighfâr [the supplications with which one asks Allah (the Exalted) for forgiveness]:

«O Allah, You are my Lord, and none has the right to be worshipped except You. You have created me and I am your slave; I am upon your covenant and promise as much as I am able to be. I seek refuge in You from the evil that I have perpetrated. I confess to You Your favor upon me, and I confess to You my sin, so forgive me; for verily, none forgives sins except You.»

Be Happy – Always remember Allah

Concerning His remembrance, Allah, the All-Glorious, says:

{Verily, in the remembrance of Allah do hearts find rest.}

(Qur'an 13: 28)

{Therefore remember Me [by praying, glorifying Me, and so on] and I will remember you...}

(Qur'an 2: 152)

{And the men and the women who remember Allah much with their hearts and tongues, Allah has prepared for them forgiveness and a great reward [that is, paradise].}

(Qur'an 33: 35)

{O you who believe! Remember Allah with much remembrance. And glorify His praises morning and afternoon [the dawn and afternoon prayers].}

(Qur'an 33: 41-42)

{O you who believe! Let not your properties or your children divert you from the remembrance of Allah.} *(Qur'an 63: 9)*

{And remember your Lord when you forget...}

(Qur'an 18: 24)

{And glorify the praises of your Lord when you get up from sleep. And in the night-time also, glorify His praises – and at the setting of the stars.}

(Qur'an 52: 48-49)

{O you who believe! When you meet [an enemy] force, take a firm stand against them and remember the name of Allah much [both with tongue and mind], so that you may be successful.}

(Qur'an 8: 45)

In an authentic hadith, the Prophet (bpuh) said:

«The example of one who remembers his Lord in relation to one who does not remember his Lord is that of the living and the dead.»

«The Prophet (bpuh) also said: The mufarridoon outstrip others.

His Companions asked: Who are the mufarridoon, O Messenger of Allah?

He replied: The men who remember Allah often and the women who remember Allah often.»

In another authentic hadith:

«The Prophet (bpuh) said: Shall I not inform you of the best of deeds, and the purest of them with your Lord? The deed which is better for you than spending gold and silver (for a good cause), and which is better for you than to meet your enemy, and you cut their throats and they cut yours?

They said: Yes, O Messenger of Allah.

He said: The remembrance of Allah.»

The following is an authentic hadith:

«A man came to the Prophet (bpuh) and said: O Messenger of Allah, the commandments of Islam have become too much for me, and I am old; so inform of something that I can adhere to.

He said: That your tongue (continually) remains moist with the remembrance of Allah.»

Be Happy – Never lose hope of Allah's mercy

{Certainly noone despairs of Allah's mercy, except the people who disbelieve.}

(Qur'an 12: 87)

{[They were reprieved] until, when the Messengers gave up hope and thought that they were denied [by their people], then came to them Our help...}

(Qur'an 12: 110)

{And We delivered him from the distress. And thus We do deliver the believers.}

(Qur'an 21: 88)

{And you were harboring doubts about Allah. There, the believers were tried and shaken with a mighty shaking.}

(Qur'an 33: 10-11)

Don't grieve over the hurt that is inflicted upon you by others, and forgive those who have ill-treated you.

The price of jealousy and rancor is enormous; it is the price that the revengeful person pays in exchange for his malice towards others. He pays with his heart, flesh, and blood. His peace, his relaxation, and his happiness – these he forsakes because he desires the sweetness of revenge and because he resents others.

Jealousy and rancor are illnesses for which Allah has given the cure and remedy:

{[Those] who repress anger, and who pardon men...}

(Qur'an 3: 134)

{Show forgiveness, enjoin what is good, and turn away from the foolish [that is, don't punish them].}

(Qur'an 7: 199)

{Repel [the evil] with one which is better [that is, Allah ordered the faithful believers to be patient at the time of anger, and to excuse those who treat them badly], then verily! He, between whom and you there was enmity, [will become] as though he was a close friend.}

(Qur'an 41: 34)

Do not grieve over what has passed you by in life, for indeed you have been blessed with much.

Contemplate the many favors and gifts that Allah (the Exalted) has bestowed upon you and be thankful to Him for them. Remind yourself of Allah's many blessings, for He, the Exalted, the Almighty, said:

{And if you would count the graces of Allah, never would you be able to count them.}

(Qur'an 16: 18)

{Do you not see that Allah has made subject to you whatever is in the heavens and whatever is in the earth and amply bestowed upon you His favors, [both] apparent and unapparent?}

(Qur'an 31: 20)

{And whatever of blessings and good things you have, it is from Allah. Then, when harm touches you, unto Him you cry aloud for help.}

(Qur'an 16: 53)

Allah (the Exalted) said, establishing His favors upon man:

{Have We not made for him a pair of eyes; and a tongue and a pair of lips? And shown him the two ways [good and evil]?}

(Qur'an 90: 8-10)

Life, health, the faculties of hearing and seeing, two hands and two legs, water, air, food - these are some of the more visible blessings in this world, while the greatest of all blessings is that of Islam and correct guidance. What would you say to someone who offered you large sums of money in return for your eyes, your ears, your legs, your hands, or your heart? How great is your wealth in reality? By not being thankful, you do not render justice to Allah's countless favors.

Don't grieve over unworthy things

By being unconcerned over trivial matters, you display a virtue that will bring you happiness, for those who are lofty in their aims are engrossed only with concern for the hereafter.

One of our pious predecessors advised one of his brothers with the following words:

Be concerned about this only: about meeting Allah, about standing in front of Him, and about the hereafter.

{That day shall you be brought to judgment, not a secret of yours will be hidden.}

(Qur'an 69: 18)

There is not a single worry or concern whose significance is not diminished when it is compared to the concerns of the hereafter. What are the worries of this life? They are status, prestige, fame, income, wealth, mansions, and children. They are all nothing when compared to the accountability before Allah! Allah (the Exalted) described His enemies, the hypocrites, by saying:

{While another party was thinking about themselves [as to how to save their ownselves, ignoring the others and the Prophet] and thought wrongly of Allah...}

(Qur'an 3: 154)

Their concerns are for themselves, their stomachs, and their lusts; they know nothing of higher motives.

While the people pledged allegiance to the Prophet of Allah (bpuh) under the tree, one of the hypocrites left hastily in search of his red camel, which had strayed. He said, "For me to find my camel is more beloved to me than your ceremony of pledging allegiance."

In relation to this incident, the Prophet (bpuh) said:

«All of you have been forgiven, except for the owner of the red camel.»

One of the hypocrites, who was worried only about himself, said to his companions concerning the expedition to Tabuk, "Do not march forth in the heat." Allah (the Exalted) said:

{Say: The fire of hell is more intense in heat...}

(Qur'an 9: 81)

Another one of them said:

{Grant me leave [to be exempted from jihad] and put me not into trial}

(Qur'an 9: 49)

And Allah (the Exalted) said:

{Surely, they have fallen into trial.}

(Qur'an 9:49)

Yet others were troubled and concerned only for their wealth and their families:

{Our possessions and our families occupied us, so ask forgiveness for us.}

(Qur'an 48: 11)

These concerns are trifles that none should be preoccupied with –except for those who are themselves trifling and insignificant. As for the noble Companions, they desired the favors of Allah (the Exalted) and they longed for His pleasure.

Don't be sad – Repel anxiety

Idleness is destructive, and most people who suffer from worries and anxieties are the same people who are idle and inactive. Rumors and gossip are the only dividends for those who are bankrupt in regard to meaningful and fruitful work.

Apply yourself to something and work hard at it. Read, recite, and glorify your Lord with praises. Write, visit friends, and benefit from your time. In short, do not give a single minute away to idleness. The day that you do that will be the day that anxieties and worries will find their way into your life. Superstition and evil whispers will enter your mind, allowing you to become a playground for the games of the devil.

Don't grieve over the person who forgets or denies the favors you once gave to him, for your desire should be solely for the reward of Allah.

Perform righteous deeds purely and sincerely for the pleasure of Allah, and don't expect either congratulations or gratitude from any person. Do not take it to heart if you confer a favor upon someone who then turns out to be ungrateful, showing no sign of appreciation for what you have done. Seek your reward from Allah.

Allah (the Exalted) says of His righteous slaves:

{They seek bounties from Allah and His pleasure.}

(Qur'an 59: 8)

{Say: No reward do I ask of you for this...}

(Qur'an 25: 57)

{And have in his mind no favor from anyone for which a reward is expected in return.}

(Qur'an 92: 19)

{[Saying]: We feed you seeking Allah's countenance only. We wish for no reward, nor thanks from you.}

(Qur'an 76: 9)

So make your dealings with Allah alone, as He, the Almighty, All-Compassionate is the One Who rewards people for good deeds. He gives and He bestows, or He punishes and He takes to account, being pleased with those who do well and angry with those who do evil. Martyrs were killed in Qandahar, and 'Umar (may Allah be pleased with him) asked the Companions, "Who was killed?" They mentioned some names to him, and then they said, "And people whom you do not know." 'Umar's eyes filled with tears and he said, "But Allah knows them."

A pious person fed the best and finest of food to a blind man. His family said to him, "This blind man does not know what he is eating (so give him something of lower quality)." He replied, "But Allah knows!"

Since Allah knows your deeds, knows the good you do and the help you give to others, remain carefree and untroubled about what people think.

Don't grieve when others blame and disparage you

{They will do you no harm, barring a trifling annoyance...}

(Qur'an 3: 111)

{...and be not distressed because of what they plot.}

(Qur'an 16: 127)

{...and harm them not. And put your trust in Allah...}

(Qur'an 33: 48)

{...but Allah cleared him [Moses] of that which they alleged...}

(Qur'an 33: 69)

An Arab poet said:

The vast ocean feels no harm

When the boy pitches into it a rock.

In a reliable hadith, the Prophet (bpuh) said:

«Do not speak ill to me of my Companions, for verily, I would love to leave you with a sound breast.»

Don't grieve over being poor

The more the body enjoys, the more the soul becomes sullied, and there is safety in having little. Taking only that which you need from this world is an early comfort that Allah (bpuh) bestows upon whomsoever He pleases among His slaves.

{Verily! We will inherit the earth and whatsoever is thereon.}

(Qur'an 19: 40)

One poet said:

Water, bread, and shade,

These form a most worthy bliss,

I have denied the favors of my Lord,

If I said that I had too little.

What in this world is truly important other than cold water, warm bread, and plentiful shade!

Don't feel sad over fears for what may happen

In the Torah, the following has been related: Most of what is feared to occur, never happens! This means that most apprehensions and fears of impending difficulty fail to take shape in reality. Conjectures of the mind are far greater in number and in scope than the things that actually happen in life. An Arab poet said:

I said to my heart when it was attacked by a fit of anxiety,

Be happy, because most fears are false.

This implies that if you hear of an impending calamity, or hear of oncoming disaster, you should not be overly alarmed, especially since the majority of predictions about impending harm are false.

{...And my affair I leave it to Allah. Verily, Allah is the All-Seer of [His] slaves. So Allah saved him from the evils that they plotted [against him]...}

(Qur'an 40: 44-45)

Don't grieve over criticism from the jealous and the weak-minded

You will be rewarded if you show forbearance concerning their criticism and their impertinent remarks. The more they criticize you, the more you are increased in worth, because only someone who is unaccomplished has no one who is jealous of him or her. According to the Arab saying, "People do not kick a dead dog." One poet said:

They are jealous of he who has surpassed them,

People show him enmity and opposition,

Just like spiteful women, who speak of the fair maiden,

With jealousy and malice – that she is of a low and base character.

Zuhayr said:

They are jealous of that with which he has been blessed,

Allah will not take away from him the cause of their resentment.

Another said:

They will envy my death, what wretchedness is this,

Even in my death, I am not spared from their jealousy.

Another poet said:

I complained about the injustice of gossipmongers, and you will not find,

The honorable and successful person who has escaped from jealousy,

You remain, O honorable and worthy friend, the victim of it,

Yet no one begrudges the one who is miserable and wretched.

In another poem:

If a person reaches the sky with his nobleness,

Then his enemies will be the numbers of the stars in the sky,

They shoot at him using a bow with every kind of persecution,

Yet their abuses will never bring them to the level of his nobility.

Prophet Moses (pbuh) asked his Lord to prevent people from abusing him with their tongues. Allah (the Exalted) said, "O Moses, I have not done so for Myself. I have created them and provided for them, and they blaspheme and curse Me!"

It has been authentically narrated that the Prophet (bpuh) related that Allah (the Exalted) says:

«The son of Adam curses Me and blasphemes Me, and he has no right to do so. As for his cursing Me, he curses the time, and I am the time: I alternate the day and night as I please. As for their blaspheming Me, they say that I have a wife and a child, and I have neither a wife nor a child.»

You may not be able to prevent people from attacking your honor, but you are able to do well, and ultimately, to ignore and turn away from their criticism and scorn. Another poet said:

I move past the fool who curses me,

And I continue on my previous course saying:

He does not refer to me!

And yet another said:

When the fool speaks, do not respond to him,

For better than to answer him is silence.

Idiots and fools clearly feel insulted by those who shine, those who are noble, and those who display genius.

If the strengths and good points that I possess,

Were my sins, then pray tell me, how can I make amends?

{Woe to every slanderer and backbiter who has gathered wealth and counted it. He thinks that this wealth will make him last forever! Nay! Verily, he will be thrown into the crushing fire.}

(Qur'an 104: 1-4)

A well-known Western writer said, "Do what is right, and then turn your back on every vulgar criticism."

Do not respond to an injurious statement that is made about you. Forbearance buries faults, tolerance is superior, silence conquers the enemy, and forgiveness is honor for which you shall be rewarded. If defamatory remarks are printed about you, know that half of those who read such things quickly forget them, while the other half are uninterested in the first place. So do not create further noise and fuss by refuting what has been said. A wise person said, "People are oblivious of you and me, and are busily striving for their bread. And if one of them is thirsty, he will forget my death and yours."

A poet said:

Do not broadcast your affairs to your sitting companions,

Because they are jealous and will rejoice at your misfortune.

A house that has within it serenity and bread is better than a house that is replete with many kinds of expensive foods, yet is a place of trouble and unrest.

Stop to reflect

Don't be sad, for sickness is a transient state of being, the sin can be forgiven, the debt will be repaid, the captive will be released, the beloved one who is abroad will return, the sinner will repent, and the poor will be increased in their wealth.

Don't be sad, for do you not see how the black clouds disperse and the violent winds subside? Your hardships will be followed by comfort, and your future is bright.

Don't be sad, for the blaze of the sun is extinguished by luxurious shade, the thirst of noon is refreshed by fresh water, the pangs of hunger find relief in warm bread, the anxiety of sleeplessness is followed by calm repose, and the pains of sickness are soon forgotten after the return of health. It is only upon you to forbear for a short time and to be patient for a few moments.

Don't be sad, for even doctors, wise persons, scholars, and poets are weak and unable to defy or change that which has been decreed. 'Ali ibn Jabla said:

Perhaps a way out will come, perhaps,

We comfort ourselves with perhaps,

So do not despair when you meet

With affliction that weakens your spirit,

Since the closest one comes

To relief is when he loses all hope.

Don't be sad; select for yourself what Allah has chosen for you.

Stand if He causes you to stand, and sit if He orders you to sit. Show patience if He has made you poor, and be thankful if He makes you rich. These points are understood from the statement, "I am pleased with Allah as my Lord, with Islam as a religion, and with Muhammad as a Messenger."

An Arab poet said:

Do not weave a plan for yourself,

The people of plotting are destroyed,

Be contented with our decree,

We are worthier to plan for you than you yourself.

Don't be sad; overlook the actions of others. They can lay no claim on giving benefit or harm, death or life, reward or punishment. Ibraheem ibn Adham said, "We live such a life (of amazing pleasure in the worship of Allah) that if the kings knew about it, they would fight us over it with swords."

Ibn Taymiyah said, "Sometimes the heart is in such a state that I say: If the people of paradise experience this, then they indeed have a wonderful life.

He said on another occasion, "The heart sometimes dances rapturously, from the happiness of remembering Allah and of feeling close to Him."

Upon entering prison, as the guards were closing the doors upon him, he recited:

﴾So a wall will be put up between them, with a gate therein. Inside it will be mercy, and outside it will be torment.﴿

(Qur'an 57: 13)

He said while he was in prison:

What can my enemies do to me? My garden and my paradise are in my breast; wherever I go, they are with me. If my enemies kill me, I become a martyr; if they banish me from my country, I go abroad as a tourist; and by imprisoning me, they allow me to have solitude (so that I can worship Allah).

A wise person once said:

What has he found who has lost Allah, and what has he discovered who has found Allah? They can never be equal: the one who has found Allah has found everything, and the one who has lost Him has lost everything.

Don't blindly feel grief; instead, make sure you know the value of the thing over which you feel sad.

The Prophet (bpuh) said:

«For me to say: How perfect is Allah, All praise is for Him, there is none worthy of worship except Him, and Allah is the greatest – this is more beloved to me than all that the sun rises upon.»

Of rich people, their castles, houses, and wealth, one of our pious predecessors said:

We eat and they eat. We drink and they drink. We see and they see. We will not be called to account, and they will be held accountable (for their wealth, how it was acquired and how it was spent).

In the words of a poet:

> The first night in the grave causes one to forget,
>
> The castles of Khosrau and the treasures of Caesar.

Allah (the Exalted) said:

{And truly you have come unto Us alone [without wealth, companions or anything else] as We created you the first time.} (Qur'an 6: 94)

The believers say:

{This is what Allah and His Messenger [Muhammad] had promised us, and Allah and His Messenger had spoken the truth.} (Qur'an 33: 22)

And the hypocrites say:

{Allah and his Messenger promised us nothing but delusions!} (Qur'an 33: 12)

Your life is the product of your thoughts. The thoughts that you invest in will have an indelible effect upon your life, regardless of whether they are happy thoughts or miserable thoughts. A poet said:

> Fear does not fill my heart before the occurrence of that which is feared,
>
> And I don't become overly distressed if that event does occur.

Don't be sad – Do good to others

Being of service to others leads to happiness. In an authentic hadith, the Prophet (bpuh) said:

> «Verily, Allah will say to His slave as He is taking account of him on the Day of Judgment: O son of Adam, I was hungry and you did not feed Me. He will answer: How can I feed You and You are the Lord of the worlds! He will say: Did you not know that My slave So-and-so, who is the son of So-and-so, felt hunger, and you did not feed him? Alas! Had you fed him, you would have found that (reward) with Me. O son of Adam, I was thirsty and you gave Me nothing to drink. He will say: How can I give You drink, and You are the Lord of the worlds! He will say: Did you not know that My slave So-and-so, the son of So-and--so, felt thirsty, and you did not give him drink? Alas! If you had given him, you would have found that (reward) with Me.

> O son of Adam, I became sick and you did not visit Me. He will say: How can I visit You, and You are the Lord of the worlds! He will say: Did you not know that My slave So-and-so, the son of So-and-so, became sick and you did not visit him. Alas! Had you visited him, you would have found Me with him.»

Here is an interesting point; in the last third of the hadith are the words:

> «...you would have found Me with him.»

This is unlike the first two parts of the hadith:

> «You would have found that (the reward for feeding and giving drink) with Me.»

The reason for the difference is that Allah, the All-Merciful, is with those whose hearts are troubled, as is the case with the person who is sick. And in another hadith, the Prophet (bpuh) said:

> «There is reward in each moist liver (meaning that service to any living creature will be rewarded).»

Allah admitted the prostitute from the children of Israel into paradise because she gave a drink to a dog that was thirsty, so what will be the case for the one who feeds other people, giving them drink and removing from them hardships?

In an authentic hadith, the Prophet (bpuh) said:

> «Whoever has extra provision should give from it to the one who has no provision, and whoever has an extra mount should give this extra to the one who has no mount.»

Commanding his servant to search for guests, Ḥâtim said in some of his more beautiful verses:

> Burn the coals, for truly, the night is chilly,
>
> If you bring me a guest, then I have set you free.

And he said to his wife:

> Whenever you make food, then search
>
> For he who is hungry, as I do not eat alone.

Ibn Mubârak's neighbor was a Jew. He would always feed him before feeding his own children and would provide clothing for him first and then for his children. Some people said to the Jew, "Sell us your house." He answered, "My house is for two thousand dinars. One thousand is for the price of the house, and one thousand is for having Ibn Mubârak as a neighbor!" Ibn Mubârak heard of this and he exclaimed, "O Allah, guide him to Islam." Then, by the permission of Allah, he accepted Islam.

On another occasion, Ibn Mubârak passed by a caravan of people who were traveling to make the pilgrimage to Makkah, and he was on his way to do the same. He saw one of the women from the caravan take a dead crow from a cesspit. He sent his servant to inquire about this; when he asked her, she replied, "We have had nothing for three days except what finds its way into it." When Ibn Mubârak heard of this, his eyes swelled with tears. He ordered that all of his provisions be distributed among the members of the caravan; having nothing left with which to continue the journey, he gave up the idea of making the pilgrimage that year and returned to his home. Later, he saw someone in a dream saying, "Your pilgrimage has been accepted, as have your rites, and your sins have been forgiven.'" Allah (the Exalted) says:

{And give them preference over themselves, even though they were in need of that themselves.}

(Qur'an 59: 9)

One poet said:

Even if I am a person who is far

From his friend in terms of distance,

I offer him my help and wish to alleviate his difficulties,

And I answer his invitation and his call to me for help,

And if he dons a wonderful new outfit I will not say,

Alas, were I to be blessed with the clothes that he wears.

By Allah, how wonderful are good manners and a generous soul!

No one regrets having done well, even if he or she was extravagant in doing so. Regret is only for the mistake or for the wrong done, even when that wrong is a minor one.

Jealousy is nothing new

If you hear the beating of resentful words in your ears, don't worry – jealousy is nothing new. As a poet said:

> Devote yourself to the gathering of virtues, and work,
>
> And turn your back on someone who cools his jealousy by giving you censure,
>
> Know that your life's span is the season of good deeds,
>
> In it, they may be accepted, and after is death, when all jealousy ceases.

A wise person said, "When facing criticism or the unjust rebuke, those who have sensitive feelings must pour a certain amount of coolness into their nerves by force."

Another said, "The coward dies many deaths, and the brave man dies one."

If Allah wishes good for one of His slaves, He covers him with slumber as a security, as occurred to Talḥah (may Allah be pleased with him) before the battle of Uḥud. A short time before the battle, while the disbelievers waited in nervous apprehension, he was overtaken by a slumber that made him, on a few occasions, drop his sword, so serene and calm did he feel. Allah (the Exalted) said:

{Say: Do you wait for us [anything] except one of the two best things [martyrdom or victory]; while we await for you either that Allah will afflict you with a punishment from Himself or at our hands. So wait, we too are waiting with you.}

(Qur'an 9: 52)

{And no person can ever die except by Allah's leave and at an appointed term.}

(Qur'an 3: 145)

'Ali (may Allah be pleased with him) said:

> Which of the two days of death do I fear? The day in which it was not decreed for me to die or the day in which death was preordained for me. As for the former, I fear it not. And as for the latter, it is destined to happen, and even cautious ones cannot be saved on that day.

Abu Bakr (may Allah be pleased with him) said, "Seek out death (by being brave), and you shall be granted life."

Stop to reflect

Do not be sad, for Allah defends you and the angels ask forgiveness for you, the believers share with you their supplications in every prayer, the Prophet (bpuh) will intercede for the believers, the Qur'an is replete with good promises, and above all is the mercy of He Who is the Most Merciful.

Don't be sad: the good deed is increased so that its value is multiplied tenfold or seven hundred fold or even much, much more. Meanwhile, the evil deed is valued without increase or multiplication, and your Lord can forgive even that. How many times do we witness Allah's generosity, a generosity that is unmatched by any! And benevolence from anyone else cannot reach even near His benevolence.

If you do not associate partners with Allah, if you believe in the true religion, and if you love Allah and His Messenger (bpuh), don't feel sad. If you feel regret for your bad deeds and you rejoice when you do a worthy act, don't feel sad. You have much good with you that you do not perceive.

If, in your life, you are able to establish the state of balanced harmony that is referred to in the following hadith, don't feel sad:

> «How wonderful is the state of the believer. All of his affairs are good for him! And that is not so, except for the believer. If he has cause to be happy, he is thankful, and that is good for him. If he is afflicted with hardship, he is patient, and that is good for him.»

Don't be sad: forbearance in times of distress is the path to both success and happiness.

{And endure patiently, and your patience is not but from Allah.}

(Qur'an 16: 127)

{So [for me] patience is most fitting. And it is Allah [alone] Whose help can be sought against that which you assert.}

(Qur'an 12: 18)

{So be patient, with a good patience.}

(Qur'an 70: 5)

{Peace be upon you for that you persevered in patience!}

(Qur'an 13: 24)

{And bear with patience whatever befalls you.}

(Qur'an 31: 17)

{Endure and be more patient [than your enemy], and guard your territory by stationing army units permanently at the places from where the enemy can attack you...}

(Qur'an 3: 200)

'Umar (may Allah be pleased with him) said, "Through patience we have now achieved a good life."

For the people of the Sunnah, there are three things that they resort to when faced with calamity: patience, supplication, and waiting with expectation for a good outcome.

A poet said:

We have poured them a glass,

And they have similarly poured one for us (alluding to the blood that enemies draw from each other in battle),

But in the face of death, we were the more patient.

In an authentic hadith, the Prophet (bpuh) said:

«There is none who is more patient when he hears something offensive than Allah. They claim that He has a child and a wife, yet He gives them health and provision.»

The Prophet (bpuh) also said:

«May Allah have mercy on Moses (pbuh). He was tested with more than this (than what I have been tested with), and he was still patient.»

And he said:

«Whoever is patient, Allah will give him further strength to continue to be patient.»

A poet said:

I have crawled my way to distinction, and those who have striven have reached it,

With the toil of labor, and the sparing of no small effort,

Many have tried to reach it, and most became bored or tired during their journey,

> And they embrace distinction, who remain true and are patient,
>
> Do not consider distinction to be an apple that you eat,
>
> You will not achieve distinction until you overcome hardship with your patience.

Higher goals are not achieved through dreaming or fantasizing; they can only be reached through dedication and commitment.

Do not grieve over how people treat you, and learn this lesson by observing how they behave with Allah.

Imam Aḥmad reported a hadith in the book of Zuhd, in which the Prophet (bpuh) relates the following saying from Allah:

> «Strange are you, O son of Adam! I have created you, and you worship other than Me. I have provided for you, and you thank those besides Me. I show you love by giving you blessings, and I do not need you, while you show Me animosity through your sins, and you are to Me poor. My good is descending to you, and your evil is rising to Me.»

It is related that Prophet Jesus (pbuh) by the permission of Allah, healed thirty sick people and cured many who were afflicted with blindness. Afterwards they turned on him as enemies.

Don't be sad for lack of ample provision

Verily, the One Who provides sustenance is Allah. He has made it binding upon Himself that whatever provision He has written for His slaves will reach them.

{And in the heaven is your provision, and that which you are promised.}

(Qur'an 51: 22)

If Allah is the One Who provides for the creation, why curry favor with people? And why should you degrade yourselves in front of another person in the hope of procuring from that person your sustenance? Allah (the Exalted) said:

{And no living creature is there on earth but its provision is due from Allah.}

(Qur'an 11: 6)

{Whatever of mercy, Allah may grant to humankind, none can withhold it, and whatever He may withhold, none can grant it thereafter.}

(Qur'an 35: 2)

Don't be sad, for there are means of making it easier to bear calamity. Among them are the following:

1. Expecting reward and recompense from Allah (the Exalted):

   {Only those who are patient shall receive their rewards in full, without reckoning.}

   (Qur'an 39: 10)

2. Visiting those who are afflicted and seeking comfort in the knowledge that you are better off than many others. A poet said:

   If not for the many mourners around me,

   Who weep for their brothers,

   I would have taken my own life.

So look at those who surround you. There will not be one who has not been touched by hardship or affliction.

Appreciate that your trial is light compared to others

If you know that your trial is not in your religion, but it is in worldly matters, then be content.

Know that no trick or artifice can be used to undo what has already taken place. A poet said:

Do not use trickery to change the circumstance,

For the only trick is in leaving all trickery.

Appreciate that the choice of what is good for you or not good for you belongs only with Allah (the Exalted):

{...And it may be that you dislike a thing which is good for you.}

(Qur'an 2: 216)

Don't mimic the personality of others

{For every nation there is a direction to which they face. So hasten towards all that is good.}

(Qur'an 2: 148)

{And it is He Who has made you generations coming after generations, replacing each other on the earth. And he has raised you in ranks, some above others...}

(Qur'an 6: 165)

{Each [group of] people knew its own place for water.}

(Qur'an 2: 60)

Every person has a unique set of talents, abilities, skills, and preferences. One aspect of the Prophet's character was his ability to lead; he employed his Companions each in accordance with his or her talent and expertise. 'Ali (may Allah be pleased with him) was both just and wise, so the Prophet (bpuh) appointed him to be a judge. The Prophet (bpuh) used Mu'âdh for his knowledge; Ubayy for the Qur'an; Zayd for rulings in matters of inheritance; Khâlid for jihad; Ḥassân for poetry; and Qays ibn Thâbit for public speeches (may Allah be pleased with them all).

To melt into the personality of another, for whatever reason, is akin to suicide, and to imitate the natural traits of others is to deliver a deathblow to one's own self. Among Allah's signs that one should marvel at are the diverse characteristics of people – such as their talents, the different languages they speak, and their different colors. Abu Bakr (may Allah be pleased with him), for example, through his gentleness and tenderness, greatly benefited Islam and this nation. 'Umar, on the other hand, helped Islam and its adherents to be victorious through his stern demeanor and austerity. Therefore, be comfortable with your inherent talents and abilities. Develop them, expand them, and benefit from them.

{Allah burdens not a person beyond his scope.}

(Qur'an 2: 286)

Isolation and its positive effects

If applied with a correct understanding, isolation can be most beneficial. Ibn Taymiyah said:

At times, it is necessary for the worshipper to be isolated from others in order to pray, remember Allah, recite the Qur'an, and evaluate himself and his deeds. Also, isolation allows one to supplicate, seek forgiveness, stay away from evil, and so on.

Ibn al-Jawzi dedicated three chapters of his well-known book Ṣayd al-Khâṭir to this topic. He said:

> I have not seen or heard of anything that brings repose, honor, and dignity as much as seclusion does. It helps one to stay away from evil, it protects one's honor, and it saves time. It keeps one away from the jealous minded and those who take pleasure in your affliction. It promotes the remembrance of the hereafter, and it allows one to reflect on his meeting with Allah. In times of seclusion, one's thoughts may roam in that which is beneficial, in that which contains wisdom...

Only Allah (the Exalted) knows the full benefits of seclusion, for in seclusion, one's mind develops, views are ripened, the heart finds repose, and one finds oneself to be in an ideal atmosphere for worship. By remaining isolated at times, one distances oneself from trials, from flattering the person who deserves no praise, and from the eyes of jealous and envious persons. One is saved from the haughtiness of the proud and the follies of the foolish. In isolation, one's faults, deeds, and sayings are all secluded behind a veil.

During periods of isolation, one is able to delve deep into a sea of ideas and concepts. In such a state, the mind is free to form its opinions. Isolated from the company of others, the soul is free to achieve a state of rapture and to hunt for the stimulating thought. When alone, an individual does nothing for show or ostentation, since none but Allah sees and hears him or her.

Every person who was a genius, a mental giant, or a great contributor to the human race watered the seeds of his or her greatness from the well of isolation, until the seed became a plant and then finally a formidable tree.

Al-Qâdi 'Ali ibn 'Abdul 'Aziz al-Jurjani said:

> I never tasted the sweetness of life until,
>
> I became a companion of home and book.
>
> There is nothing more honorable than knowledge,
>
> So I seek in no other an associate.
>
> Truly, the only degradation is in mixing with people;

Be Happy

Therefore leave them and live in a noble and stately manner.

Another said:

I found company in my solitude and I remained fervently in my home,

So felicity was perpetual for me and my happiness grew,

I have severed human relations and I couldn't care,

Whether the army has gone forth or the president has given us a visit!

Aḥmad ibn Khaleel al-Ḥanbali said:

Whoever strives for dignity and comfort

From a long and tedious anxiety,

Let him be one of the people,

And be contented with a little.

As long as one lives unwholesomely,

How can he find pleasure in life?

Between being poked by the deceitful

And giving flattery to the conceited,

Between tolerating the jealous

And forbearing the stingy,

Woe to becoming acquainted with

People, and with all of their ways and follies.

Another poet said:

Meeting with people brings about no benefit,

Except with the increase of, 'it has been said', and, 'he said,'

So spend less time in conversing with others, though barring,

The acquirement of knowledge or the improvement of one's condition.

Ibn Fâris said:

They asked how I was, and I said, well, and thank you,

A need is fulfilled and another is neglected,

When distress is such that my heart becomes constricted,

I say that perhaps one day will bring with it some aid,

My comrade is my cat and my soul's companions are my books,

And the object of my love is my night-lantern.

Don't be shaken by hardships

Hardship strengthens your heart, atones for your sins, and helps to suppress an inclination towards pride and haughtiness. You might remember that in times of hardship you abandoned senseless folly and you remembered Allah. When you were afflicted, others extended brotherly compassion to you, and you became the fortunate recipient of the supplications of the righteous. At such times, you wilfully and humbly surrendered yourself to Allah's will and resigned yourself to His decree. Affliction begets circumspection and provides the afflicted with an early warning against following the path of evil. Those upon whom calamity has fallen can display courage with patience; their circumstances, unlike those who are drunk with worldly pleasures, permit them to solemnly prepare for a meeting with their Lord. They are able to pass judgment on this world with an impartial ruling, and thus they will come to know it as something that is not worth pining for. Other points associated with the wisdom and benefits of sometimes facing hardship, though they might escape our comprehension, are definitely present and known to the Lord of all that exists.

Pause to think about hardships

Don't be sad, for sadness will weaken your determination and the quality of your worship. One of the offshoots of depression is that it often causes one to be pessimistic, to find blame in everyone, including – and we seek refuge in Allah (the Exalted) – Allah Himself.

Don't be sad, for sadness, grief, and anxiety are the roots of mental problems, the sources of stress.

Don't be sad, for you have with you the Qur'an, supplication, remembrance, and prayer. You can lighten the load of your anxiety by giving to others, doing well, and being productive.

Don't be sad, and do not surrender to sadness by taking the easy path of idleness and inactivity, but pray, glorify your Lord, read, write, work, visit relatives and friends, and reflect.

{Invoke Me [ask me for anything]. I will respond to your [invocation].}

(Qur'an 40: 60)

{Invoke your Lord with humility and in secret. He likes not the aggressors.}

(Qur'an 7: 55)

{So, call you [O Muhammad and the believers] upon [or invoke] Allah making [your] worship pure for Him [alone] [by worshipping none but Him and by doing religious deeds sincerely for Allah's sake only and not to show off and not to set up rivals with Him in worship].}

(Qur'an 40: 14)

{Say [O Muhammad]: Invoke Allah or invoke the Most Beneficent [Allah], by whatever name you invoke Him [it is the same], for to Him belong the best names.}

(Qur'an 17: 110)

Don't be sad – The fundamentals of happiness

1. Know that if you do not live within the scope of today, your thoughts will be scattered, your affairs will become confused, and your worrying will increase – these realities explain the hadith:

   «When the morning comes, do not expect to see the evening, and when the evening comes, do not expect to see the morning.»

2. Forget the past and all that it contained. Being absorbed in things that are gone is sheer lunacy.

3. Don't be preoccupied with the future. The future is in the world of the unseen; do not let it bother you until it comes.

4. Don't be shaken by criticism; instead, be firm. Know that the level of people's criticism rises in proportion to your worth.

5. Faith in Allah and good deeds are the ingredients that make up a good and happy life.

6. Whoever desires peace, tranquility, and comfort can find it all in the remembrance of Allah.

7. You should know with certainty that everything that happens occurs in accordance with a divine decree.

8. Don't expect gratitude from anyone.

9. Train yourself to be ready and prepared for the worst eventuality.

10. Perhaps what has happened is in your best interest (though you may not comprehend how that is so).

11. Everything that is decreed for the Muslim is best for him or her.

12. Enumerate the blessings of Allah (the Exalted), and be thankful for them.

13. You are better off than many others.

14. Relief comes from one hour to the next.

15. In both times of hardship and ease, one should turn to supplication and prayer.

16. Calamities should strengthen your heart and reshape your outlook in a positive sense.

17. Indeed, with each difficulty there is relief.

18. Do not let trivial matters be the cause of your destruction.

19. Indeed, your Lord is Oft-Forgiving.

20. Don't be angry... Don't be angry... Don't be angry.

21. Life is bread, water, and shade, so do not be perturbed by a lack of any other material thing.

{And in the heaven is your provision, and that which you are promised.}

(Qur'an 51: 22)

22. Most of the evil that is supposed to happen never occurs.

23. Look at those who are afflicted, and be thankful.

24. When Allah loves a people, He makes them endure trials.

25. You should constantly repeat those supplications that the Prophet (bpuh) taught us to say during times of hardship.

26. Work hard at something that is productive, and cast off idleness.

27. Don't spread rumors, and don't listen to them. If you hear a rumor inadvertently, then don't believe it.

28. Your malice and your striving to seek revenge are much more harmful to your own health than they are to your antagonist.

29. The hardships that befall you atone for your sins.

Why grieve when you have the six ingredients?

The author of Ease After Difficulty mentioned the story of a wise person who was afflicted by calamity. His brothers went to him and tried to console him over his loss. He answered, "I have put together a remedy that is composed of six ingredients." They asked him what those ingredients were, and he answered:

The first is to have a firm trust in Allah, the Almighty.

The second is resigning oneself to the inescapable fact that everything that is decreed will happen and will follow its unalterable course.

The third is that patience has no substitute for the positive effect it has on the afflicted.

The fourth is an unwavering belief in the implications of this phrase, "Without showing forbearance, what will I accomplish?"

The fifth is to ask oneself, "Why should I be a willful party to my own destruction?"

The sixth is knowing that from one hour to the next, circumstances are transformed and difficulties vanish.

Do not grieve if others inflict upon you harm or pain, or if you are oppressed or are the subject of envy. Shaykh al-Islam (Ibn Taymiyah) said, "The believer does not seek quarrel or revenge; nor does he find blame or fault in others."

Do not despair if you face obstacles or problems; rather, forbear and be patient.

O time, if you have any of that left over,

From which you bring down the worthy, then let me have it.

Patience, as opposed to anxiety, bears the fruit of comfort; and those who do not voluntarily show patience will have it forced upon them by circumstances. Al-Mutanabbi said:

Time has showered me with trouble until

The arrows on my heart have formed a cover,

That now when I am struck with an arrow,

The blade of it strikes into the shaft of another,

Now I live without a care for troubles,

Since I have not profited by caring.

Don't be distressed if someone refuses you a favor, or if you are frowned upon, or if the miserly person refuses you.

If, by refraining from asking others, you prevent the sweat of humiliation from pouring down your face, then a wooden hut or a tent of cloth is better for you than a spacious house and a beautiful garden – material things that will only bring you worry and disquiet.

Tribulation is similar to sickness; it must run its course before it goes away, and those who are hasty in attempting to remove it often cause it to increase. It is imperative that those who are afflicted be patient; they must wait with hope for relief, and they must be persistent in their prayers.

The fundamentals of happiness – - Verses to reflect on

{And never give up hope of Allah's mercy. Certainly no one despairs of Allah's mercy, except the people who disbelieve.}

(Qur'an 12: 87)

{And who despairs of the mercy of his Lord except those who are astray?}

(Qur'an 15: 56)

{Surely, Allah's mercy is [ever] near unto the good-doers.}

(Qur'an 7: 56)

{You know not, it may be that Allah will afterward bring some new thing to pass.}

(Qur'an 65: 1)

{It may be that you dislike a thing which is good for you and that you like a thing which is bad for you. Allah knows but you do not know.}

(Qur'an 2: 216)

{Allah is very Gracious and Kind to His slaves.}

(Qur'an 42: 19)

{...And My mercy embraces all things.}

(Qur'an 7: 156)

{Be not sad [or afraid], surely Allah is with us.}

(Qur'an 9: 40)

{[Remember] when you sought help from your Lord and He answered you.}

(Qur'an 8: 9)

{And He it is Who sends down the rain after they have despaired, and spreads abroad His mercy.}

(Qur'an 42: 28)

{And they used to call on Us with hope and fear, and used to humble themselves before Us.}

(Qur'an 21: 90)

Your best companion is a book

An activity that brings about joy is for you to read a book and develop your mind through the acquisition of knowledge. Al-Jâhidh, an Arab writer from centuries ago, advised one to repel anxiety through the reading of books:

> The book is a companion that does not praise you and does not entice you to evil. It is a friend that does not bore you, and it is a neighbor that causes you no harm. It is an acquaintance that desires not to extract from you favors through flattery, and it does not deceive you with duplicity and lies. When you are poring through the pages of a book, your senses are stimulated and your intellect sharpens... Through reading the biographies of others, you gain an appreciation of common people while learning the ways of kings. It can even be said that you sometimes learn from the pages of a book in a month, that which you do not learn from the tongues of men in a century. All this benefit, yet no loss in wealth and no need to stand at the door of the teacher who is waiting for his fees or to learn from someone who is lower than you in manners. The book obeys you by night as it does by day, both when you are traveling and when you are at home. A book is not impaired by sleep nor does it tire in the late hours of the night. It is the teacher who is there for you whenever you are in need of it, and it is the teacher who, if you refuse to give to it, does not refuse to give to you. If you abandon it, it does not decrease in obedience. And when all turn against you, showing you enmity, it remains by your side. As long as you are remotely attached to a book, it suffices you from having to keep company with those that are idle. It prevents you from sitting on your doorstep and watching those who pass by. It saves you from mixing with those that are frivolous in their character, foul in their speech, and woeful in their ignorance. If the only benefit of a book was that it keeps you from foolish daydreaming and prevents you from frivolity, it would certainly be considered a true friend who has given you a great favor.

Sayings about the virtues of books

Abu 'Ubaydah said:

> Al-Muhallab gave his son the following advice: O son, do not linger in the marketplace unless you are visiting the maker of armor or the bookseller.

Ḥasan al-Lulu'ee said, "Forty years have passed, and I have not dozed off in the day or in the night... except that a book was resting on my chest."

Ibn al-Jahm said:

If I feel drowsy when it is time to sleep -and wasteful is the sleep that exceeds one's needs – I take up a book from the books of wisdom and I find bliss in coming across a pearl (of wisdom)…I am more alert when I am happily engaged in reading and learning than I am when I hear the braying of the donkey or the shrill noise of something breaking.

He also said:

If I find a book to be agreeable and enjoyable, and if I deem it to be beneficial, you will see me hour after hour checking how many pages are left, from fear of being close to the end. And if it is many volumes with a great number of pages, my life and my happiness are complete.

And the best, highest, and worthiest of books is:

{[This is the] Book [the Qur'an] sent down unto you [O Muhammad], so let not your breast be narrow therefrom, that you warn thereby, and a reminder unto the believers.}

(Qur'an 7: 2)

The benefits of reading

1. Reading repels anxiety and grief.

2. While busy reading, one is prevented from delving into falsehood.

3. Habitual reading makes one too busy to keep company with the idle and the inactive.

4. By reading often, one develops eloquence and clarity in speech.

5. Reading helps to develop the mind and purify its thoughts.

6. Reading increases one in knowledge and improves both memory and understanding.

7. By reading, one benefits from the experiences of others: the wisdom of the wise and the understanding of scholars.

8. By reading often, one develops the ability to both acquire and process knowledge and to learn about the different fields of knowledge and their applications to life.

9. One's faith will increase when one reads beneficial books, especially books written by practicing Muslim writers. The book is the best giver of sermons, and it has a forceful effect in guiding one towards goodness and away from evil.
10. Reading helps to relax one's mind from distraction and to save one's time from being wasted.
11. By reading often, one gains a mastery over many words and learns the different constructions of sentences; moreover, one improves his or her ability to grasp concepts and to understand what is written 'between the lines'.

Nourishment of the soul is in concepts and meanings,

And not in food and drink.

Pause to reflect

'Umar (may Allah be pleased with him) said, "We have found that the best life is that which is accompanied by patience."

He also said, "The best life that we have experienced is that of patience, and if patience were a man, he would be most generous."

'Ali (may Allah be pleased with him) said, "Truly, patience is to faith as the head is to the body. If the head is severed, the body becomes wasted."

Then he raised his voice and said, "Verily, there is no faith in the man who has no patience." He also said, "Patience is a mount that does not stumble or trip."

Ḥasan said:

Patience is a treasure from the treasures of goodness, a treasure that Allah does not give away except to a slave (of His) whom He regards as being worthy.

'Umar ibn 'Abdul 'Aziz said:

Whenever Allah gives a blessing to one of His slaves and then removes it from him and supplants it with patience, then that which replaces is invariably better than that which is being replaced.

Sulaymân ibn al-Qâsim said, "The reward for every deed other than patience is known."

Allah (the Exalted) said:

{Only those who are patient shall receive their rewards in full, without reckoning.}

(Qur'an 39: 10)

Don't grieve – There is another life to come

The day will come when Allah will gather together the first of the creation and the last of it. The knowledge of this occurrence alone should reassure you of Allah's justice. So whoever's money is usurped here shall find it there, whoever is oppressed here shall find justice carried out there, and whoever oppresses here shall find punishment there. Immanuel Kant, the German philosopher, said:

> The drama of this life is not complete; there must be a second scene to it, for we see the tyrant and his victims without seeing justice being executed. We see the conqueror and the subjugated, without the latter finding any revenge. Therefore there must be another world, where justice will be carried out.

Shaykh 'Ali aṭ-Ṭanṭawi, commenting on this, said, "This statement suggests a confession from this foreigner (to Islam), of the existence of a hereafter where judgment will take place."

An Arab poet said:

> If the minister and his delegates rule despotically,
>
> And the judge on earth is unjust in his judgments,
>
> Then woe, followed by woe after woe
>
> Upon the judge of the earth from the judge Who is above.

{This Day shall every person be recompensed for what he earned. No injustice [shall be done to anybody]. Truly, Allah is Swift in reckoning.}

(Qur'an 40: 17)

Don't feel overly stressed when work piles up

Robert Louis Stevenson said:

> Every person is capable of performing his daily tasks, no matter how difficult they are, and every person is capable of living happily during his day until the sun sets: and this is the meaning of life.

Stephen Leacock wrote:

The child says, 'when I am a big boy'. But what is that? The big boy says, 'when I grow up'. And then, grown up, he says, 'when I get married'. But to be married, what is that after all? The thoughts change to, 'when I retire'. And then when retirement comes, he looks back over the landscape traversed; a cold wind seems to sweep over it; somehow he has missed it all, and it is gone. Life, we learn too late, is in the living, in the tissue of every day and hour.

Such is the state of those who put off repenting for their sins.

One of our pious predecessors said:

> I warn you of delaying and saying that I will do it later, for this is a phrase that prevents one from doing good and causes one to fall behind in deeds of righteousness.

﴾Leave them to eat and enjoy, and let them be preoccupied with [false] hope. They will come to know!﴿

(Qur'an 15: 3)

The French philosopher, Montaigne, said, "My life was filled with bad luck that never showed mercy."

I assert that despite their knowledge and intelligence, many famous thinkers knew nothing of the wisdom behind their own creation. They were not guided by the teachings that Allah sent through His Messenger, Muhammad (bpuh).

﴾And he for whom Allah has not appointed light, for him there is no light.﴿

(Qur'an 24: 40)

﴾Verily, We showed him the way, whether he be grateful or ungrateful.﴿

(Qur'an 76: 3)

Dante said, "Consider that this day will not occur again."

Better and more beautiful and complete is the hadith:

«Pray as if it is your farewell prayer.»

Whoever puts it into their mind that today is their last day, will make a fresh repentance, will do good deeds, and will strive to be obedient to their Lord, the Almighty, and His Messenger (bpuh).

Don't grieve, and ask yourself these questions

1. Do I put off living in the present because of fears and apprehensions about the future or because of hopes of the magical garden beyond the horizon?
2. Do I embitter my present life by mulling over events that occurred in the past?
3. Do I wake up in the morning with an intention of spending my day usefully?
4. Do I find that I am benefiting from my life when I try to concentrate on a present situation or task?
5. When will I begin to live in the present moment, without worrying too much about the past and future? Next week? Tomorrow? Or today?

Don't despair when you face a difficult situation

If you find yourself in a tough situation, do the following:

1. Ask yourself: what is the worst that can happen?
2. Prepare yourself to cope and deal with that worst-case scenario.
3. If something bad does occur, meet it with calm nerves in order to deal with the situation better.

{Those [that is, believers] unto whom the people [hypocrites] said: Verily, the people [pagans] have gathered against you [a great army], therefore, fear them. But it [only] increased them in faith, and they said: Allah [alone] is Sufficient for us, and He is the Best Disposer of affairs [for us].} (Qur'an 3: 173)

Contemplate these verses

{And whosoever fears Allah and keeps his duty to Him, He will make a way for him to get out [from every difficulty]. And He will provide for him from [sources] he never could imagine. And whosoever puts his trust in Allah, then He will suffice him.}

(Qur'an 65: 2-3)

{Allah will grant after hardship, ease.}

(Qur'an 65: 7)

The Prophet (bpuh) said:

«And know that victory comes with patience, and with hardship there is a way out, and with difficulty comes ease.»

In another hadith, the Prophet (bpuh) related that Allah (pbuh) said:

«I am with my slave's thoughts about Me, so let him think of Me as he chooses.»

{Allah will suffice you against them. And He is the All-Hearer, the All-Knower.}

(Qur'an 2: 137)

{And put your trust in the Ever Living One Who dies not...}

(Qur'an 25: 58)

{Perhaps Allah may bring a victory or a decision according to His Will.}

(Qur'an 5: 52)

{None besides Allah can avert it [, advance it, or delay it].}

(Qur'an 53: 58)

Depression weakens the body and the soul

Dr. Alexis Carrel, a Nobel laureate in medicine, said, "Working people who do not know how to deal with anxiety and stress are more prone than others are to a premature death."

Indeed, everything that takes place occurs according to a divine decree. A person must nonetheless take the necessary steps to avoid difficulties, and so Carrel rightly points out that anxiety is one of the factors that lead to the body being damaged.

Depression: A cause of ulcers

"You will not be afflicted by an ulcer by virtue of what you eat, but instead by virtue of what eats you." This is a quote taken from Dr. Joseph F. Montague's book, Nervous Stomach Trouble. The renowned Arab poet, al-Mutanabbi, said:

> And stress transforms obesity into scrawniness,
>
> It whitens the hair of the young man and makes him a mess.

Some other effects of depression

I recently read the translation of Dr. Edward Podolsky's book, Stop Worrying and Get Well. Here are some of the chapter titles from his book:

- What Worry Does to the Heart
- High Blood Pressure is Fed by Worry
- Rheumatism Can be Caused by Worry
- Worry Less for Your Stomach's Sake
- How Worry Can Cause a Cold
- Worry and the Thyroid
- The Worrying Diabetic

Dr. Karl Menninger, a specialist in psychology, wrote a book called Man Against Himself. In it, he says:

Dr. Menninger will not give you the principles of how to avoid anxiety, but instead he will give you an astonishing report on how we destroy our own body and minds through anxiety and nervousness, malice and rancor, fear, and feelings of revenge.

﴿And those who pardon men: verily, Allah loves the good-doer.﴾

(Qur'an 3: 134)

Among the more salient lessons that we should learn from this verse is that we should have a sound heart, peace of mind, calm nerves, and a feeling of happiness. The French philosopher Montaigne once said, "I wish to help you in dealing with your problems with my hands, but not with my liver and lungs."

What depression and anger do

Dr. Russell Cecil of Cornell University mentioned four widespread causes of arthritis:

1. Marital strife.
2. Financial difficulties and depression.
3. Loneliness and anxiety.
4. Malice and rancor.

Dr. William Mark Gaungil, while addressing the American Dental Association, remarked, "Unhappy feelings like anxiety and fear possibly affect the distribution of calcium in the body, and in consequence, can lead to tooth decay."

Hold a good opinion of your Lord

William James said, "The Lord may forgive us our sins, but our nervous system never does."

Ibn al-Wazeer wrote in his book al-Awâşim wal-Qawâşim:

Verily, to be hopeful of Allah's mercy opens the doors of optimism for one of His slaves, making him more avid in worship, and inspiring him to be more enthusiastic in performing voluntary acts of worship and racing to perform good deeds.

This is true, especially because some people are not moved to do good deeds except when they recall Allah's mercy, forgiveness, and generosity. As a consequence of reflecting on these qualities, they seek closeness to Allah through diligently performing good deeds.

When your thoughts wander

Thomas Edison said, "Tre is no expedient to which a man will not go to avoid the labour of thinking."

One can confirm the accuracy of this statement from experience, for even when reading or writing, one is constantly diverted by inappropriate thoughts. One of the best means of controlling such thoughts is to work at something that is at once interesting and useful.

Embrace constructive criticism

Andre Moro said, "Everything that is in harmony with our personal inclinations, appears to us as a truth, and everything else only serves to provoke our anger."

A prime example of this is when we are given advice or criticism. For the most part, we adore praise, and our spirits are lifted when we are the objects of such attentions, even if we are praised for the wrong reasons. On the other hand, we hate criticism and disparagement, even if what is said about us happens to be true.

{And when they are called to Allah [that is, His words, the Qur'an] and His Messenger, to judge between them, lo! A party of them refuse [to come] and turn away. But if the right is with them, they come to Him willingly with submission.}

(Qur'an 24: 48-49)

William James said, "When once a decision is reached and execution is the order of the day, dismiss absolutely all responsibility and care about the outcome."

What he means is that when you make a judicious decision based on logic and a sound premise, then you should carry out that decision. Furthermore, you must not give way to doubts, for doubts beget nothing but more doubts. Then do not look back. An Arab poet said:

If you are of sound judgment, show resolution,

For ill judgment is in hesitation.

Showing courage in making decisions can save you from anxiety and confusion.

{And when the matter is resolved on, then if they had been true to Allah, it would have been better for them.}

(Qur'an 47: 21)

Dr. Richard Cabot of Harvard University wrote in his book What Men Live by: Work, Play, Love, Worship:

As a physician, I have had the happiness of seeing work cure many persons who have suffered from that trembling palsy of the soul which results from overmastering doubts, hesitation, vacillation, and fear.

{Then when the [Friday congregational] prayer is finished, you may disperse through the land, and seek the bounty of Allah [by working, et cetera.]...}

(Qur'an 62: 10)

George Bernard Shaw wrote:

The secret of being miserable is to have leisure to bother about whether you are happy or not. The cure for it is occupation, because occupation means pre-occupation, and the pre-occupied person is neither happy nor unhappy, but simply alive and active, which is pleasanter than any happiness until you are tired of it.

{And say [O Muhammad]: Do deeds! Allah will see your deeds, and [so will] His Messenger and the believers.}

(Qur'an 9: 105)

And a wise saying of the Arabs goes, "Life is too short to make it even shorter through disputes."

{He [Allah] will say: What number of years did you stay on earth? They will say: We stayed a day or part of a day. Ask of those who keep account. He [Allah] will say: You stayed not but a little – if you had only known!}

(Qur'an 23: 112-114)

Most rumors are baseless

{They think that every cry is against them.}

(Qur'an 63: 4)

{Had they marched out with you, they would have added to you nothing except disorder, and they would have hurried about in your midst [spreading corruption] and sowing sedition among you...}

(Qur'an 9: 47)

Dean Hawkes of Columbia University told Dale Carnegie that he had taken as his motto this Mother Goose rhyme:

For every ailment under the sun

There is a remedy, or there is none;

If there be one, try to find it;

If there be none, never mind it.

In an authentic hadith, the Prophet (bpuh) said:

«Allah has not sent down a sickness except that He has also sent down for it a cure. He knows it who knows it, and he is ignorant of it who is ignorant of it (so even if the most famous doctor is ignorant of it, it still exists).»

Gentleness averts confrontations

A Japanese teacher said to his pupils, "To bow is to be like the willow, and to not return force is to be like the oak tree."

In a hadith, the Prophet (bpuh) said:

«The believer is like the green plant; the wind blows it to the left and to the right.»

The wise person is like water, for water does not crash into a rock, trying to pass through it. Instead, it comes to it from the left and from the right, from above and from below.

In another hadith, the Prophet (bpuh) said:

«The believer is like a camel whose reins are on its nose. If it were made to kneel on a rock, it would do so.»

Yesterday is gone forever

{In order that you may not be sad over matters that you fail to get...}

(Qur'an 57: 23)

Adam said to Moses (peace be upon them), "Do you blame me for that which Allah had decreed upon me forty years before He created me?"

Concerning this last saying, the Prophet (bpuh) said:

«Adam overcame Moses in his arguments; Adam overcame Moses in his arguments; Adam overcame Moses in his arguments.»

Search for happiness inside of you, not around you or outside of you. The prolific English poet, Milton, said:

The mind is its own place, and in itself can make

A heaven of hell, or a hell of heaven.

Al-Mutanabbi wrote:

The one who is talented suffers because of

(His unbalanced genius) while he is rich,

Meanwhile the ignorant one is poor,

And yet he is smiling.

This life does not deserve our grief

Napoleon exclaimed in Saint Helena, "I have not known (even) six happy days in my whole life."

The Caliph, Hishâm ibn 'Abdul-Malik, said, "I have attempted to recall and enumerate the number of happy days in my life, and I have found them to be thirteen in total."

His father would often state sadly, "Would that I had never become the Caliph."

The eminent preacher Ibn Sammack once visited Haroon ar-Rasheed, who felt thirsty and asked for water to drink. Ibn Sammack said, "Commander of the Faithful, if you were refused this drink, would you bargain for it with half of your empire?" He replied, "Yes." When he finished drinking it, Ibn Sammack followed up with another question, "If, due to some sickness, you were unable to discharge this drink (through urine), would you pay half of your empire's wealth to be able to remove it from your body?" He answered, "Yes." Ibn Sammack then said, "Therefore, there is no good in a kingdom that is not even equal to a drink of water."

The whole world and whatever is in it has no value, weight, or meaning if it is devoid of faith. Iqbal said:

When faith is lost then so is peace,

And there is no life for the one who is not enlivened by religion,

Whoever is pleased with a life bereft of faith

Has made total ruin to be life's substance.

Emerson concluded his essay on self-reliance with the following:

A political victory, a rise in rents, the recovery of your sick, or return of your absent friend, or some other quite external event, raises your spirits, and you think good days are preparing for you. Do not believe it. Nothing can bring you peace but yourself. Nothing can bring you peace but the triumph of principles.

{Come back to your Lord, well-pleased [yourself] and well-pleasing unto Him! Enter you, then, among My honored slaves.}

(Qur'an 89: 28-29)

A renowned philosopher and novelist said:

> The indispensability of removing wicked notions from our thoughts is more critical than that of removing tumors and diseases from our bodies.

There are more warnings in the Qur'an about diseases of ideas and beliefs than there are concerning bodily ailments. The French philosopher Montaigne said, "A person is not influenced by what happens as much as he is by his opinion regarding what happens."

In the following hadith, the Prophet (bpuh) supplicated:

> «O Allah, make me pleased with Your decree, so that I may know that whatever has befallen me was not meant to miss me, and what has passed me by was not meant to be my lot.»

Ponder these points

Don't be sad, because sadness causes you to regret the past, to have misgivings concerning the future, and to make you waste away your present.

Don't be sad, because it causes the heart to contract, the face to frown, the spirit to weaken, and hope to vanish.

Don't be sad, because your sadness pleases your enemy, angers your friend, and makes the jealous rejoice.

Don't be sad, because by being sad, you are complaining against the divine decree and showing displeasure at what is written for you.

Don't be sad, because grief cannot bring back the one who is lost or has gone away. It cannot resurrect the dead, change fate, or bring any benefit whatsoever.

Don't be sad, because sadness is often from the devil and is a kind of hopelessness.

{Have We not opened your breast for you [O Muhammad]? And removed from you your burden, which weighed down on your back? And raised high your fame? So verily, with hardship, there is relief; verily, with hardship, there is relief. So when you have finished [from your occupation], then stand up for Allah's worship [that is, stand up for prayer]. And to your Lord [alone] turn [all your intentions and hopes and] your invocations.}

(Qur'an 94: 1-8)

As long as you have faith in Allah, don't be sad

Faith in Allah (the Exalted) leads to happiness and peace, while disbelief leads to confusion and misery. I have read about many intelligent people of a certain kind, some who might even be called geniuses, geniuses though whose hearts are bereft of the light of guidance. As such, they spoke wicked words about the Sharia (Islamic law). These are two examples that come to mind: The first is what Abu al-'Ulâ al-Ma'arri said about the Sharia, "Contradiction, concerning which we can do nothing but stay quiet.'" The second is the saying of Ibn Seena, "The element that influences nature is the active intellect."

I thus came to know that to the degree that one has faith in his or her heart, one will be happy. More recent sayings, similar in meaning to the two above, are the offspring of the evil words of old that were spoken by Pharaoh:

{Pharaoh said: O chiefs! I know not that you have a god other than me.}

(Qur'an 28: 38)

{Pharaoh said: I am your lord, most high.}

(Qur'an 79: 24)

James Allen wrote in As a Man Thinketh:

Man has but to right himself to find that the universe is right; and during the process of putting himself right, he will find that as he alters his thoughts toward things and other people, things and other people will alter toward him. The proof of this truth is in every person, and it therefore admits of easy investigation by systematic introspection and self-analysis. Let a man radically alter his thoughts, and he will be astonished at the rapid transformation it will effect in the material conditions of his life.

Regarding incorrect thinking and its effects, Allah (the Exalted) says:

{Nay, but you thought that the Messenger [Muhammad] and the believers would never return to their families; and that seemed fair in your hearts, and you did think an evil thought and you became a useless people going for destruction.}

(Qur'an 48: 12)

{And they thought wrongly of Allah – the thought of ignorance. They said: Have we any part in the affair? Say you [O Muhammad]: Indeed the affair belongs wholly to Allah.}

(Qur'an 3: 154)

James Allen also wrote:

All that a man achieves and all that he fails to achieve is the direct result of his own thoughts... A man can only rise, conquer, and achieve by lifting up his thoughts. He can only remain weak, and abject, and miserable by refusing to lift up his thoughts. Allah, the Almighty, All-Merciful, said of true determination and correct thought:

﴾And if they had intended to march out, certainly, they would have made some preparation for it, but Allah was averse to their being sent forth, so He made them lag behind...﴿

(Qur'an 9: 46)

﴾Had Allah known of any good in them, He would indeed have made them listen...﴿

(Qur'an 8: 23)

﴾He knew what was in their hearts, and He sent down tranquility upon them, and He rewarded them with a near victory...﴿ (Qur'an 48: 18)

Don't grieve over trivialities, for the entire world is trivial

Rumi was once thrown into the cage of a lion, and Allah then saved him from its claws. He was later asked, "What were you thinking about at the time?" He replied, "I was considering the saliva of a lion – whether it is considered by scholars to be pure or impure (whether, when I die, I will be in a state of purity or not)."

Allah (the Exalted) described those who were with the Prophet (bpuh) according to their intentions:

﴾Among you are some that desire this world and some that desire the hereafter.﴿

(Qur'an 3: 152)

Ibn al-Qayyim mentioned that a person's value is measured according to the person's determination and goals. A wise person once said words to the same effect, "Inform me of a man's determination, and I will tell you what kind of man he is."

A vessel capsized at sea, and a worshipper was hurled into the water. He began to make ablution, one limb at a time. He managed to get to shore and was saved. When asked about the ablution and why he made it, he replied, "I wanted to make ablution so that I would die in a state of purity."

Imam Ahmad, during the pangs of death, was pointing to his beard while others were making his ablution for him, reminding them not to miss a spot.

{So Allah gave them the reward of this world, and the excellent reward of the hereafter.}

(Qur'an 3: 148)

Do not grieve when you are shown overt enmity, for if you forgive and forget, you will have achieved nobility in this world and honor in the next.

{But whoever forgives and makes reconciliation, his reward is due from Allah.}

(Qur'an 42: 40)

Someone said to Sâlim ibn 'Abdullâh ibn 'Umar, a scholar from the early generations of Islam, "You are an evil man." He quickly replied, "None knows me except you."

A man said in a verbal attack on Abu Bakr (may Allah be pleased with him): "By Allah, I will curse you with such curses that will enter with you into your grave." He calmly answered, "No, but they shall enter with you into yours."

Someone said to 'Amr ibn al-'Âs, "I will dedicate myself to waging war against you." 'Amr replied, "Now have you fallen into what supersedes all else, and it will be your preoccupation (your misery)."

General Eisenhower once exclaimed, "Never waste a minute thinking about people you don't like."

The mosquito said to the tree, "Remain firm, for I wish to fly away and leave you." The tree answered, "By Allah, I did not feel your landing on me! Then why would I feel you when you fly away?"

Hâtim said, "I forgive the generous one when he saves some of his wealth, and I turn away from the curses of the accursed one generously."

{And if they pass by some evil play or evil talk, they pass by it with dignity.}

(Qur'an 25: 72)

{And when the foolish address them [with bad words] they reply with mild words of gentleness.}

(Qur'an 25: 63)

Confucius said, "An angry man is always full of poison."

One man asked the Prophet (bpuh) three times to give him advice. He answered each time:

«Don't be angry.»

The Prophet (bpuh) said of anger in the following hadith:

«Anger is an ember from the fire.»

The devil overcomes people on three occasions: when they are angry, when they feel lust, and when they are in a state of forgetfulness.

This is the way of the world

Marcus Aurelius, one of the wiser Roman Emperors, stated one day:

I am going to meet people today who talk too much – people who are selfish, egotistical, ungrateful. But I won't be surprised or disturbed, for I couldn't imagine a world without such people.

Strive to help others

Aristotle said:

The ideal person is he who takes pleasure in serving others, and who is ashamed when others do things for him, since showing compassion is a sign of superiority, while receiving it is a sign of failure.

More concise and to the point is the following hadith:

«The upper hand is better than the lower hand.»

The upper hand refers to the giving hand, and the lower one refers to the receiving hand.

You're not deprived as long as you have a loaf of bread, a glass of water, and clothes on your back

Jonathan Swift said that the best doctors in the world are 'the proper diet doctor,' 'the rest doctor' and 'the doctor of happiness...'

The reasoning behind Swift's comment is that overeating and obesity often have negative effects on one's physical and psychological wellbeing. Meanwhile, rest, moderation and happiness are satisfying forms of nourishment for the mind, heart, and soul.

Blessings in disguise

Dr. Samuel Johnson said that the habit of looking on the bright side in every circumstance is more valuable than having a large income.

{See they not that they are tried once or twice every year [with different kinds of calamities, disease, famine, et cetera.]? Yet, they turn not in repentance, nor do they learn a lesson [from it].}

(Qur'an 9: 126)

One of our pious predecessors said to someone, "Verily, I see upon you the signs of blessings, and my advice to you is to lock your blessings up and keep them safe by being thankful."

{And [remember] when your Lord proclaimed: If you give thanks [by accepting faith and worshipping none but Allah], I will give you more [of My blessings], but if you deny, verily! My punishment is indeed severe.}

(Qur'an 14: 7)

{And Allah puts forward the example of a township [Makkah], that dwelt secure and well content, its provision coming to it in abundance from every place, but it [its people] denied the favors of Allah [with ungratefulness]. So Allah made it taste the extreme of hunger [famine] and fear, because of that [evil, that is, denying Prophet Muhammad] which they [its people] used to do.}

(Qur'an 16: 112)

You are unique, so be yourself

James Gordon Gilkey said:

> The dilemma of wanting your own identity is as ancient as the beginning of history, and it is common to all human life. Similar is the problem of not wanting to be your own self, which is the source of much personal imbalance and disturbance.

Someone else said:

> You are a unique entity among creation: nothing is exactly similar to you, nor are you exactly similar to anything, because the Creator has brought diversity to the creation.

{Certainly, your efforts and deeds are diverse [different in aims and purposes].}
(Qur'an 92: 4)

{He sends down water [rain] from the sky, and the valleys flow according to their measure...}
(Qur'an 13: 17)

Every person has unique idiosyncrasies, talents, and abilities, so no one should fuse his or her personality into that of another. Undoubtedly, you have been created with restricted means and abilities that will help you to accomplish very specific and limited goals. It has been wisely said, "Read yourself and know yourself; you will then know your mission in life."

Emerson said in his essay, Self-Reliance:

There is a time in every man's education when he arrives at the conviction that envy is ignorance; that imitation is suicide; that he must take himself for better, for worse, as his portion; that though the wide universe is full of good, no kernel of nourishing corn can come to him but through his toil bestowed on that plot of ground which is given to him to till. The power which resides in him is new in nature, and none but he knows what that is which he can do, nor does he know until he has tried.

{And say [O Muhammad]: Do deeds! Allah will see your deeds, and [so will] His Messenger and the believers.}
(Qur'an 9: 105)

Contemplate these verses:

{Say: O My slaves, who have transgressed against themselves [by committing evil deeds and sins]! Despair not of the mercy of Allah, verily Allah forgives all sins. Truly, He is Oft-Forgiving, Most Merciful.}

(Qur'an 39: 53)

{And those who when they have committed Faḥshâ [illegal sexual intercourse et cetera.] or wronged themselves with evil, remember Allah and ask forgiveness for their sins – and none can forgive sins but Allah – and do not persist in what [wrong] they have done, while they know.}

(Qur'an 3: 135)

{And whoever does evil or wrongs himself but afterwards seeks Allah's forgiveness, he will find Allah Oft-Forgiving, Most Merciful.}

(Qur'an 4: 110)

{And when My slaves ask you [O Muhammad] concerning Me, then [answer them], I am indeed near [to them by My knowledge]. I respond to the invocations of the supplicant when he calls on Me [without any mediator or intercessor]. So let them obey Me and believe in Me, so that they may be led aright.}

(Qur'an 2: 186)

{Is not He [better than your gods] Who responds to the distressed one, when he calls Him, and Who removes the evil, and makes you inheritors of the earth, generations after generations. Is there any god with Allah? Little is that you remember!}

(Qur'an 27: 62)

{Those [that is, believers] unto whom the people [hypocrites] said: Verily, the people [pagans] have gathered against you [a great army], therefore, fear them. But it [only] increased them in faith, and they said: Allah [alone] is Sufficient for us, and He is the Best Disposer of affairs [for us]. So they returned with grace and bounty from Allah. No harm touched them; and they followed the good pleasure of Allah. And Allah is the Owner of great bounty.}

(Qur'an 3: 173-174)

{And my affair, I leave it to Allah. Verily, Allah is the All-Seer of [His] slaves. So Allah saved him from the evils that they plotted [against him]...}

(Qur'an 40: 44-45)

Much that seems harmful is in fact a blessing

William James said:

> Our handicaps help us to an extent that we never expected. If Dostoevsky and Tolstoy had not lived painful lives, they would not have been capable of writing their ageless journals. So being an orphan, blind, poor, or away from home and comfort are all conditions that may lead you to accomplishment and distinction, to advancement and contribution.

A poet said:

> Allah can bestow His blessings through trials
>
> That are small or large,
>
> And He puts some to trial
>
> By giving them of His blessings.

Even children and wealth can be the cause of misery:

{So let not their wealth or their children amaze you [O Muhammad]; in reality Allah's plan is to punish them with these things in the life of this world...}

(Qur'an 9: 55)

Upon becoming crippled, Ibn Atheer was afforded the opportunity to complete his two famous books, Jamay' al-Uṣool and an-Nihâyah. As-Sarakhsi wrote his acclaimed book, al-Mabṣoot, all fifteen volumes of it, while being imprisoned at the bottom of a well. Ibn al-Qayyim wrote Zâd al-Ma'âd while journeying on a riding animal. Al-Qurṭubi wrote a commentary on Ṣaḥeeḥ Muslim while traveling on a boat. Most of Ibn Taymiyah's Fatâwâ was written while he was in jail. The scholars of Hadith gathered hundreds and thousands of hadiths; these were people who were poor and who were strangers to the word 'home'. A righteous person informed me that he was imprisoned for a while, and during the period of his incarceration, he memorized the entire Qur'an and studied forty large volumes on Islamic jurisprudence. Abu al-'Ulâ dictated his books to others because he was blind. Ṭâhâ Ḥussain lost his sight, and forthwith he began writing his renowned journals and books. Many bright people, upon being removed from their positions or jobs, contributed to the world in knowledge and thought much more than they ever had previously. Francis Bacon said that, "A little philosophy inclineth man's mind to atheism, but depth in philosophy bringeth men's minds about to religion."

{And these similitudes We put forward for mankind, but none will understand them except those who have knowledge [of Allah and His signs, et cetera].}

(Qur'an 29: 43)

{It is only those who have knowledge among His slaves that fear Allah.}

(Qur'an 35: 28)

{And those who have been bestowed with knowledge and faith will say: Indeed you have stayed according to the decree of Allah, until the Day of Resurrection...}

(Qur'an 30: 56)

{Say: I only advise you of one [thing] – that you stand for Allah, [seeking truth] in pairs and individually, and then give thought. There is not in your companion any madness. He is only a warner to you before a severe punishment.}

(Qur'an 34: 46)

Dr. A. A. Brill said, "Anyone who is truly religious does not develop a neurosis."

{Verily, those who believe [in the Oneness of Allah and in His Messenger (Muhammad)] and work deeds of righteousness, the Most Beneficent [Allah] will bestow love for them [in the hearts of the believers].}

(Qur'an 19: 96)

{Whoever works righteousness, whether male or female, while he [or she] is a true believer [of Islamic monotheism] verily, to him We will give a good life [in this world with respect, contentment and lawful provision], and We shall pay them certainly a reward in proportion to the best of what they used to do [that is, paradise in the hereafter].}

(Qur'an 16: 97)

{And verily, Allah is the Guide of those who believe, to the straight path.}

(Qur'an 22: 54)

Faith is the greatest remedy!

One of the foremost experts in psychology of our time, Dr. Carl Jung, mentioned on page 264 of his book Modern Man In Search of a Soul:

Over the last thirty years, people from all over the world have come to me seeking advice. I treated hundreds of patients and most of them were middle-aged, or more than thirty-five years old. The problem with every one of them returned to one issue -seeking refuge in religion, and by doing so, being able to have a perspective or outlook on life. I can reasonably say that every one of them became sick because they missed out on what religion has to offer to the believer. And the one who does not develop a true faith cannot be healed.

{But whosoever turns away from My reminder [that is, neither believes in this Qur'an nor acts on its orders, et cetera,] verily, for him is a life of hardship...} (Qur'an 20: 124)

{We shall cast terror into the hearts of those who disbelieve, because they joined others in worship with Allah...} (Qur'an 3: 151)

{Darkness, one above another, if a man stretches out his hand, he can hardly see it! And he for whom Allah has not appointed light, for him there is no light.} (Qur'an 24: 40)

Don't lose hope

Allah answers the prayer of the disbeliever who is in distress; so how much more can the Muslim, who doesn't associate partners with Him, expect? Mahatma Gandhi, perhaps second in popularity in India only to the Buddha, was on the verge of slipping were it not for his dependence on the strength of prayer. How do I know this? Because he himself said, "If I didn't pray, I would have gone mad a long time ago." This was the effect of prayer, and Gandhi was not even a Muslim. Although he was not following the right path, what kept him going was that he was on a path.

{And when they embark on a ship, they invoke Allah, making their faith pure for Him only, but when He brings them safely to land, behold, they give a share of their worship to others.}

(Qur'an 29: 65)

{Is not He [better than your gods] Who responds to the distressed one, when he calls Him...}

(Qur'an 27: 62)

{And they think that they are encircled therein, they invoke Allah, making their faith pure for Him alone, saying: If You [Allah] deliver us from this, we shall truly be of the grateful.}

(Qur'an 10: 22)

Despite a thorough search through the biographies of Muslim scholars, Muslim historians, and Muslim writers as a group, I have failed to find a single one of them who fell prey to anxiety, confusion, or mental illness. The reason is that they lived in peace and serenity, and that they lived uncomplicated lives that were free from all forms of affectation.

{But those who believe and do righteous good deeds, and believe in that which is sent down to Muhammad, for it is the truth from their Lord, He will expiate from them their sins, and will make good their state.}

(Qur'an 47: 2)

Contemplate the following statement of Ibn Hâzim:

There is only one day separating kings and me. As for yesterday, their taste of it has vanished, and both they and I equally fear what tomorrow will bring. Thus there is only today. And what will today bring?

The Prophet (bpuh) said:

«O Allah, I ask you for goodness today: in its blessings, success, light, and guidance.»

{O you who believe! Take your precautions...}

(Qur'an 4: 71)

{And let him be careful and let no man know of you.}

(Qur'an 18: 19)

{And they said nothing but: Our Lord! Forgive us our sins and our transgressions [in keeping our duties to You], establish our feet firmly, and give us victory over the disbelieving folk.}

(Qur'an 3: 147)

Don't be sad – Life is shorter than you think

Dale Carnegie related the story of a man who had an ulcer that became aggravated to a dangerous level. Doctors informed him that he had very little time left to live. They insinuated that it would be wise for him to make funeral arrangements. Suddenly, Hani – the patient –made a spontaneous decision: He thought to himself that if he had such little time left to live, why not enjoy it to the utmost? He thought, "How often have I wished to travel around the world before I die? This is certainly the chance to realize my dreams." He bought his ticket, and when the doctors became aware of his plans, they were shocked. They said to him, "We most strongly remonstrate with you and warn you: If you go forward on this journey, you will be buried at the bottom of the ocean." Their arguments were in vain; he only answered, "No, nothing of the sort will happen. I have promised my relatives that I will come back to be buried in the family plot."

He thus began his trip of mirth and joy. He wrote to his wife saying, "I eat the most delectable of dishes on the cruise ship. I read poetry, and I eat tasty fatty foods that I have hitherto refrained from. I have enjoyed life during this period more than I have in my entire life previously."

Dale Carnegie claimed that the man became cured of his sickness and that the energizing path he took is one that is successful in defeating disease and pain.

The moral: happiness, cheerfulness, and calmness are often more efficacious than doctors' pills.

As long as you have life's basic necessities – Don't be sad

{And it is not your wealth, nor your children that bring you nearer to Us [that is, please Allah], but only he [will please Us] who believes [in the Islamic monotheism] and does righteous deeds: as for such, there will be twofold reward for what they did, and they will reside in the high dwellings [paradise] in peace and security.}

(Qur'an 34: 37)

Dale Carnegie said:

Statistics have proven that stress and anxiety are the number one killers in America. As a result of the last world war, one third of a million of our soldiers were killed. In the same period, heart disease was the cause of two million deaths. And from this latter group, stress, anxiety, and nervous tension were the source of sickness for one million people.

Yes, heart disease is one of the main reasons that prompted Dr. Alexis Carrel to say, "Those who do not know how to fight worry die young." Though the reasoning and logic that prompted Carrel to say this are sound, we must still remember:

{And no person can ever die except by Allah's leave and at an appointed term.}

(Qur'an 3: 145)

Those who live life with tranquility and calmness are less likely to suffer from heart disease. On the other hand, you will find that the number of doctors who die of heart attacks is high because they live a tough and stress-filled life, for which they pay a heavy price.

Contentment repels sadness

The Messenger of Allah (bpuh) said:

«We do not say other than what pleases our Lord.»

Upon you is a sacred duty to surrender yourself to what is preordained for you. If you fulfill this duty, you will be successful in the long run.

Your only escape is to believe in preordainment, since whatever has been decreed must inevitably take place. No subterfuge or artifice can protect you from it. Emerson said:

> From where has the idea come to us which says that a luxurious stable life, free from obstacles and hardships, creates prosperous and great men? The case is quite the opposite. Those who have made a habit of living the easy life will continue to further develop lazy habits as they go on in life. History witnesses that greatness has surrendered its reins to men of different backgrounds. From these backgrounds are environments that have both good and bad, or environments where good and bad cannot be distinguished. And from such environments have sprouted up men who have carried great responsibilities on their shoulders without ever negligently casting them off.

Who were those that carried the flag of divine guidance in the early days of Islam? They were the freed slaves, the poor, and the destitute. Most of the people who stood defiantly against them were the nobles, the chiefs, and the rich:

{And when Our clear verses are recited to them, those who disbelieve [the rich and strong among the pagans of Quraysh who lived a life of luxury] say to those who believe [the weak, poor Companions of Prophet Muhammad]: Which of the two groups [that is, believers and disbelievers] is best in position and station [place in council for consultation]?}

(Qur'an 19: 73)

{And they say: We are more in wealth and in children, and we are not going to be punished.}

(Qur'an 34: 35)

{Thus We have tried some of them with others, that they might say: Is it these [poor believers] that Allah has favored from amongst us? Does not Allah know best those who are grateful?}

(Qur'an 6: 53)

{And those who disbelieve [strong and wealthy] say of those who believe [weak and poor]: Had it [Islamic monotheism to which Muhammad is inviting humankind] been a good thing, they would not have preceded us thereto!}

(Qur'an 46: 11)

{Those who were arrogant said: Verily, we disbelieve in that which you believe in.}

(Qur'an 7: 76)

{And they say: Why is not this Qur'an sent down to some great man of the two towns [Makkah and Taif]? Is it they who would portion out the mercy of your Lord?}

(Qur'an 43: 31-32)

I often recall the verses of Antara, in which he establishes that his worth is in his character and deeds, and not in his lineage or connections. He said:

Despite being a slave, I am a noble chief;

And despite being black in color, I have a white character.

If you lose a limb, you still have others to compensate for it

Ibn 'Abbâs (may Allah be pleased with him) said:

If Allah removes the light from my eyes,

My tongue and ears still have in them light.

My heart is intelligent and my mind is not crooked,

And my tongue is sharp like a warrior's sword.

When harm befalls you, perhaps there is a benefit that comes with it, a benefit that you cannot perceive.

{And it may be that you dislike a thing which is good for you...} (Qur'an 2: 216)

Bashhar ibn Burd said:

My enemies disparage me, and the defect is in them,

It is not a disgrace to be called defective.

If a person can see gallantry and truth,

Blindness in the eyes will not be a hindrance.

In blindness I see rewards, savings, and protection,

And for these three, I am most needy.

Observe the difference between what Ibn 'Abbâs or Bashhar said and what Ṣâleḥ ibn 'Abdul-Quddoos said when he became blind:

Farewell to the world; the old man who is blind

Has no share whatsoever of this life.

He dies and people consider him to be of the living,

False hopes have betrayed him from the beginning.

All divine decrees will come to pass, both upon the one who accepts them and upon the one who rejects them. The difference is that the former will find reward and happiness, while the latter will find only sin and misery. 'Umar ibn 'Abdul-'Azeez wrote to Maymoon ibn Mehran:

You have written to console me for losing 'Abdul-Malik. For this matter I had been in waiting, and when it finally came to pass, I had no misgivings about it.

The days rotate in bringing good and bad

It has been related that Imam Aḥmad visited Baqi ibn Mukhalid while he was sick and said to him, "O Baqi, rejoice in Allah's reward. The days of health are devoid of sickness, and the days of sickness are devoid of health."

This means that during days of health, one never contemplates sickness, for plans and ambitions then increase, as do hopes and desires. During days of severe sickness, however, one forgets matters that pertain to times of health; weak despair encamps itself within the sick soul, and thus hopelessness prevails. Allah (the Exalted) said:

{And if We give man a taste of mercy from Us, and then withdraw it from him, verily! He is despairing, ungrateful. But if We let him taste good [favor] after evil [poverty and harm] has touched him, he is sure to say: Ills have departed from me. Surely, he is exultant, and boastful [ungrateful to Allah]. Except those who show patience and do righteous good deeds: theirs will be forgiveness and a great reward [paradise].}

(Qur'an 11: 9-11)

Commenting on this verse, Ibn Katheer wrote:

Allah is describing man and the base characteristic that he is the possessor of (with the exception of those believers upon whom Allah has bestowed His mercy). In general, if man is afflicted with hardship after ease, he becomes hopeless of ever seeing good in the future; he shows disdain for the past – as if he never experienced good days – and despair for the future as if he never expected succor and relief.

Analogous is his attitude when he experiences ease after hardship:

{Ills have departed from me.} (Qur'an 11: 10)
Or in other words, "Nothing evil or bad will befall me after this."

{Surely, he is exultant, and boastful.} (Qur'an 11: 10)
{Except those who show patience and do righteous good deeds: theirs will be forgiveness and a great reward [paradise].} (Qur'an 11: 11)

Travel throughout Allah's wide earth

It has rightly been said that traveling drives away worries. Ramhumuzi enumerated in his book, The Noble Scholar of Hadeeth, the various benefits of traveling for the purpose of seeking knowledge. He was refuting those who think that no tangible benefit can be derived by traveling through the lands. He said:

There is much profit to be derived from seeing new lands and new houses, in seeing beautiful gardens and fields, in seeing different faces and coming across different languages and colors, and in witnessing the wonders of different countries. The peace that one finds under the shades of large trees is unparalleled. Eating in the mosques, drinking from streams, and sleeping wherever one finds a place when night comes -these all instill affability and humbleness in a person. The traveler befriends all those whom he loves for Allah's sake and he has no reason to flatter or to be artificial. Add to these benefits all of the happiness that the traveler's heart feels when he reaches his destination, and the thrill he experiences after having overcome all of the obstacles that were in his way. If those who are averse to leaving their homelands knew all of this, they would learn that all of the individual pleasures of the world are combined in the noble pursuit of traveling. There is nothing more enjoyable to a traveler than the beautiful sights and the wonderful activities that are part of traveling through Allah's wide earth. And the non-traveler is deprived of all of this.

Contemplate these sayings of the Prophet (bpuh)

«If Allah loves a people, He tests them. Whoever is pleased, for him there is pleasure, and whoever is angry, upon him there is wrath.»

«The most harshly tested people are the Prophets, followed in succession by those who are best after them. A man is tested according to his religion. If his religion is strong with him, his test will be more intense. If his religion is weak with him, he will be tested according to the level of his religion. (Allah's) slave will continually be tested until he is left to walk on the earth without a mistake (to have to account for).»

«Wonderful is the situation of the believer. All of his affairs are good (for him)! And this is only for the believer. If good befalls him, he is thankful, and that is good for him. If harm afflicts him, he is patient, and that is good for him.»

«And know that if the entire nation were to gather upon benefiting you with something, they would only benefit you with something that Allah has (already) written for you. And if they were to gather upon harming you with something, they would only harm you with something that Allah has (already) written for you.»

«The righteous ones are tested: first, the best of them, then the next, and so on.»

«The believer is like a tiny branch; the wind blows it to the right and to the left.»

In the last moments of life...

Abu ar-Reyhân al-Bayrooni was a prolific thinker and writer whose pen rarely left his hand. He lived to the ripe age of seventy-eight, and throughout his life, he never unnecessarily took a break from reading, writing, or teaching. Abul-Ḥasan 'Ali ibn 'Eesâ said:

> ...I visited Abu ar-Reyhân when he was on his deathbed. Upon entering, I immediately recognized that he was on the verge of leaving this life. While in that state, he said to me that there was an issue in (Islamic) inheritance law that we had discussed the last time we met and that I had said something then that he now realized was a mistake. I felt compassion for him, and asked him if it was proper for him to discuss something like that, with him being so ill. He answered: I know that I am leaving this world, but don't you think it is better for me to understand the issue in question than to be ignorant of it? I then repeated to him the issue, and he started to explain it to me. After we finished our conversation, I left, and upon exiting, I heard a scream and I knew that he had died. It is only lofty souls like his that remain strong right until the end.

When 'Umar (may Allah be pleased with him) was bleeding to death after being stabbed, he asked his companions whether he had completed the prayer or not.

Ibrâheem ibn al-Jarraḥ said:

> Abu Yusuf became sick and was vacillating between wakefulness and unconsciousness. When he regained consciousness, he asked me about a religious issue. When he saw the wonder with which I received his question, he said to me: O matter, we will study this issue in the hope that the knowledge of it perpetuates until it becomes the cause of saving someone.

This is how our pious predecessors were. Every time they revived, while yet being on their deathbeds, they would talk about Islamic knowledge, either as a teacher or as a student. How precious was knowledge to their hearts! In the last moments of their lives, they remembered neither family nor wealth; they only remembered the knowledge that was the toil of their lives. May Allah have mercy upon them.

Don't let calamity shake you

Aḥmad ibn Yusuf wrote that human beings positively know that ease comes after difficulty, just as the light of day comes after the dark of night. In spite of this knowledge, the weaker part of their nature takes over when calamity strikes. Persons who go through trials should take steps to remedy their situation, or else hopelessness will take control of them. Contemplating the patience of those who were tested in the past is a means of strengthening one's determination.

He mentioned later that hardship before comfort is analogous to hunger before food: food comes at a time when it has its greatest effect on the taste buds. Plato said, "Hardship is as beneficial to the soul as it is unwelcome in one's life. Comfort is as harmful to the soul as it is welcome in life."

When we begin to understand our purpose in life, we will know that we are being tested either to gain reward from Allah or to gain atonement for our sins.

After reading a book written by at-Tanookhi, I derived three conclusions:

1. Relief comes after hardship. This is a consistent pattern in the life of humankind, as consistent as the coming of morning after darkness.

2. Hardship is more beneficial to the soul than are comfort and ease.

3. The One Who brings good and drives away evil is Allah. Know that whatever happens to you was decreed for you, and whatever you have missed out on was never meant for you.

Don't grieve – This world isn't worth it

The Prophet (bpuh) said:

> «If this world were worth the wing of a mosquito to Allah, He would not have given the disbeliever (even) a drink of water.»

This world is not even worth the wing of a mosquito! If this is the worth of this world, why do we grieve over it?

Don't be sad: Remember that you believe in Allah

{Nay but Allah has conferred a favor upon you, that He has guided you to the faith...}

(Qur'an 49: 17)

One particular blessing overlooked by most people is the vantage point afforded to the believers when they are observing the disbelievers. The believers remember Allah's favor of guiding them to Islam. They are thankful that Allah has not decreed for them to be like the disbelievers, who rebel, deny His signs, and disbelieve in His perfect attributes, in His messengers, and in the hereafter.

Furthermore, the believers perform all obligatory acts of worship. Perhaps their execution of those acts is not perfect, yet simply performing them is in itself a great blessing. It is a blessing for which few are grateful.

{Is then he who is a believer like him who is Fâsiq [disbeliever and disobedient to Allah]? Not equal are they.}

(Qur'an 32: 18)

Some commentators of the Qur'an have said that among the pleasures of paradise for the believers is to be able to look upon the people of the fire and then thank their Lord for what He has given them.

Pause to reflect

There is none worthy of worship except Allah. This means that none truly deserves, or has the right, to be worshipped except Allah, the Almighty, since He alone possesses those perfect qualities that are associated with omnipotence, divinity, and godhood.

The spirit and secret of this monotheistic phrase is to single out Allah for love, fear, hope, veneration, and glorification. It also includes our depending upon Allah and our repenting to Him. So our love is pure for none except Him, and everyone other than Him is only loved as a by-product of our love for Him, or as a means of increasing our love for Him.

Therefore we must fear Allah alone, and we must depend upon Him alone; in Him alone do we place our hopes, and of Him alone are we in awe. We take an oath by His name only; we repent to Him alone; and all obedience is for Him. In times of hardship, we invoke none but Him and we seek refuge in none save in Him. Also, we prostrate to Him only, and when we slaughter an animal, we mention His name only.

All of the above can be summarized in one phrase: None has the right to be worshipped except Allah. This phrase is comprehensive of all forms of worship.

Despair not - Disabilities don't prevent success

An interview was published in the Arabic daily 'Ukkâdh, with a blind man named Maḥmood ibn Muhammad al-Madani. He studied books of Arabic literature through the eyes of others, listening as others read to him books of history and commentaries on the classics. He used to have one of his friends read to him until three o'clock in the morning. Today, he is considered to be a reference book in literature and history. Muṣṭafa Ameen, a columnist for ash-Sharq al-Awsaṭ, wrote:

Be patient with oppressors and wrongdoers for only five minutes. After a short time, the whip will fall, the shackles will break, the prisoner will be released, and the clouds will dissipate; upon you, then, is only to be patient and to wait.

An Arab poet wrote:

How many calamities cause one to lose patience?

But from them, the exit is with Allah.

I once met in Riyadh with the Mufti of Albania. He told me of how the ruling Communists imprisoned him with hard labor for twenty years. While serving his sentence in prison, he was constantly subjected to torture, darkness, and hunger. He would perform the five daily prayers secretly in a corner of the washroom, for fear of being caught. Through all of this he was patient and anticipating his reward with Allah, until finally relief came.

{So they returned with grace and bounty from Allah.}

(Qur'an 3: 174)

Consider Nelson Mandela, the one-time President of South Africa, who for twenty-seven years endured imprisonment. He sought freedom for his people to break off the shackles of tyranny and oppression. He was steadfast and firm, and he almost appeared to be seeking out death. As a result, he reached his goal and achieved his worldly glory. Allah (the Exalted) said:

{To them We shall pay in full [the wages of] their deeds therein.}

(Qur'an 11: 15)

{If you are suffering [hardships] then surely, they [too] are suffering [hardships] as you are suffering, but you have a hope from Allah [for the reward, that is, paradise] that for which they hope not...}

(Qur'an 4: 104)

{If a wound [and killing] has touched you, be sure a similar wound [and killing] has touched the others.} (Qur'an 3: 140)

If you embrace Islam, there is no reason for you to be sad

Miserable are those souls who are ignorant of Islam or who know Islam but have not been guided to it. Today, Muslims need a slogan or advertisement to be broadcast worldwide, for Islam is a great message that must be conveyed to the masses. The words of this slogan need to be clear, concise, and inviting, because the happiness of humanity as a whole lies in this true religion.

{And whoever seeks a religion other than Islam, it will never be accepted of him...}

(Qur'an 3: 85)

A famous caller to Islam settled in Munich, Germany some years ago. Upon reaching the entrance of the city, he noticed a large placard on which was written, "You don't know Yokohama Tires." He later put up a sign beside it, and it was just as large. He wrote on it, "You don't know Islam. If you wish to know about it, call us at this number." There was an inundation of calls from native Germans. In one year alone, thousands of people accepted Islam at this man's hands. He also established a mosque, an Islamic centre, and a school.

Most human beings are confused and are in dire need of this great religion. They need Islam so that a peaceful and serene life can take the place of the chaotic one that they are presently leading:

{Wherewith Allah guides all those who seek His good pleasure to ways of peace, and He brings them out of darkness by His will unto light and guides them to a straight way [Islamic monotheism].}

(Qur'an 5: 16)

A worshipper who was found living in a remote area, and who never had prior contact with other people, said, "I never thought that anyone in the world worshipped other than Allah."

{But few of My slaves are grateful.}

(Qur'an 34: 13)

{And if you obey most of those on earth, they will mislead you far away from Allah's path.}

(Qur'an 6: 116)

{And most of humankind will not believe even if you desire it eagerly.}

(Qur'an 12: 103)

One scholar informed me that during the time when Sudan was a colony under the British Empire, a desert nomad came to the capital city, Khartoum. When he saw a British policeman walking in the center of the city, he asked a passerby, "Who is that?" He was told that the man was a foreign policeman and that he was a disbeliever. The nomad asked, "A disbeliever in what?" A disbeliever in Allah," was the reply. Living in the desert for so long, this man's inborn nature – unspoiled by evil ideas – had remained intact, and so, when he heard something so absurd, it made him astonished and sick. He said, "And does anyone disbelieve in Allah?" He then grabbed hold of his stomach and vomited from sheer disgust at what he had heard.

{What is the matter with them, that they believe not?}

(Qur'an 84: 20)

{Then, by the Lord of the heaven and the earth, it is the truth [that is, what has been promised to you], just as it is the truth that you can speak.}

(Qur'an 51: 23)

We should think well of our Lord and seek His favor and mercy. In an authentic hadith, the Prophet (bpuh) said that our Lord laughs. After hearing this, a desert Bedouin said, "We are not bereft of a Lord who laughs well."

{And He it is Who sends down the rain after they have despaired...}

(Qur'an 42: 28)

{Surely, Allah's mercy is [ever] near unto the good-doers.}

(Qur'an 7: 56)

{Yes! Certainly, the help of Allah is near!}

(Qur'an 2: 214)

By reading the biographies of successful people, one finds that they have certain things in common, whether it is in their background, their qualities, or the circumstances that surrounded their success. Here are some of the conclusions I arrived at after having read some of their biographies.

1. A person's value is based on the good he or she does. This is a saying of 'Ali (may Allah be pleased with him), and it means that a person's knowledge, character, worship, and generosity are the yardsticks by which we measure his or her worth.

    {And verily, a believing slave is better than a polytheist, even though he pleases you.}
    (Qur'an 2: 221)

2. One's status in this life and in the hereafter depends on determination, striving, and sacrifice.

    {And if they had intended to march out, certainly, they would have made some preparation for it...}
    (Qur'an 9: 46)

    {And strive hard in Allah's cause as you ought to strive [with sincerity and with all your efforts that His name should be superior].}
    (Qur'an 22: 78)

3. Each of us – by the will of Allah – is the maker of our own history. We write our life's story with our good and bad deeds.

    {Indeed it is We Who bring the dead to life and record what they have put forth and what they have left behind, and all things We have enumerated in a clear register.}
    (Qur'an 36: 12)

4. Life is short and passes quickly. Do not make it shorter by sinning, by worrying, or by quarrelling.

    {The Day they see it, [it will be] as if they had not tarried [in this world] except an afternoon or a morning.}
    (Qur'an 79: 46)

What brings about happiness

1. Good deeds:

   {Whoever works righteousness, whether male or female, while he [or she] is a true believer [of Islamic monotheism] verily, to him We will give a good life [in this world with respect, contentment and lawful provision]...}

   (Qur'an 16: 97)

2. A pious wife:

   {Our Lord! Bestow on us from our wives and our offspring who will be the comfort of our eyes...}

   (Qur'an 25: 74)

3. A spacious house:

   The Prophet (bpuh) said:

   «O Allah, make my house spacious for me.»

4. Sustenance that is derived and earned through honest means:

   The Messenger of Allah (bpuh) said:

   «Verily, Allah is good and pure, and He does not accept other than what is good and pure.»

5. Good manners and a spirit of fellowship with people:

   {And He has made me blessed wheresoever I be...}

   (Qur'an 19: 31)

6. Being debt-free and not being a profligate spender:

   {Those, who, when they spend, do so not excessively or sparingly...}

   (Qur'an 25: 67)

   {And let not your hand be tied [like a miser] to your neck, nor stretch it forth to its utmost reach [like a spendthrift]...}

   (Qur'an 17: 29)

The ingredients of happiness

1. A thankful heart and a tongue that is moist with the remembrance of Allah (the Exalted). An Arab poet said:

   Thankfulness, remembrance, and patience,

   In them are blessings and rewards.

2. Another ingredient of happiness is the keeping of secrets, especially one's own secrets. Among the Arabs there is a famous story of a Bedouin who was entrusted with a secret for a fee of twenty dinars. At first he remained true to the deal and then suddenly, in a fit of impatience, he went and returned the money – he wanted to unburden himself from the load of the secret. This is basically because secrecy requires steadfastness, patience, and willpower.

{O my son! Relate not your vision to your brothers...} (Qur'an 12: 5)

A weakness of people – which is just one of their many weak traits – is that they constantly feel the urge to reveal the details of their personal affairs to others. This sickness is an old one in the annals of history. The soul loves to spread secrets and disseminate stories. The connection between this topic and that of this book is that those who spread their secrets will inevitably feel regret, sadness, and misery.

{And let him be careful and let no man know of you.} (Qur'an 18: 19)

You won't die before your appointed time

{When their term is reached, neither can they delay it nor can they advance it an hour [or a moment].} (Qur'an 7: 34)

This verse contains within it a consolation for cowards, those who die many deaths before their actual death. This verse tells us that for every person there is an appointed time to die: it cannot be brought forward, nor can it be held back, even if all of the creation were to join together in the attempt.

{And the stupor of death will come in truth...}

(Qur'an 50: 19)

And know that hoping in other than Allah is misery:

{Then he had no group or party to help him against Allah, nor was he one of those who could save themselves.}

(Qur'an 28: 81)

Adh-Dhahabi's Sayr A'lâm an-Nubalâ' is a twenty-volume work containing the biographies of scholars, kings, ministers, rulers, and poets. Their stories illustrate that when people place their hopes or trust in something or someone other than Allah, Allah abandons them and makes that thing or person the cause of their ruin.

{And verily, the devils hinder them from the path [of Allah], but they think that they are guided aright!}

(Qur'an 43: 37)

For Pharaoh it was status, for Qâroon it was wealth, for Umayyah it was business, and for Waleed it was his child:

{Leave Me alone [to deal] with whom I created lonely [without any means, that is, al-Waleed ibn al-Mugheerah al-Makhzoomi]!}

(Qur'an 74: 11)

For Abu Jahl it was status; for Abu Lahab it was lineage; for Abu Muslim it was the throne; for al-Mutanabbi it was fame, and for al-Hajjâj it was power and authority.

As for those who seek honor with Allah (the Exalted) and do righteous deeds, Allah will honor them and bestow upon them ranking even if they have no wealth, status, or noble lineage.

For Bilâl it was the call to prayer; for Salmân it was the hereafter; for Ṣuhayb it was his sacrifice; and for 'Aṭâ' it was knowledge (may Allah be pleased with them all):

{And made the word of those who disbelieved the lowermost, while it was the word of Allah that became the uppermost, and Allah is All-Mighty, All-Wise.}

(Qur'an 9: 40)

'O Allah, Who is full of majesty and honor...'

In an authentic hadith, the Prophet (bpuh) advised us to repeat this phrase often:

«O (Allah) Who is full of majesty and honor.»

He also advised us to say:

«O Ever Living, O one Who sustains and protects all that exists.»

Therefore, for one's own wellbeing, one should use these phrases to invoke Allah (the Exalted) and seek His help and the answer will surely then follow.

{[Remember] when you sought help of your Lord and He answered you.}

(Qur'an 8: 9)

In the life of Muslims, there are three truly joyful days:

1. The day that they renounce committing sins and they perform their obligatory prayers in congregation.

   {Answer Allah [by obeying Him] and [His] Messenger when he calls you...}

   (Qur'an 8: 24)

2. The day that they repent from a sin, forsake it, and return to their Lord.

   {Then, He accepted their repentance, that they might repent [unto Him].}

   (Qur'an 9: 118)

3. The day that they die, ready to meet their Lord, having performed a final deed that is both good and pure.

   «Whosoever loves to meet Allah, Allah loves to meet him.»

After having studied the life of the Prophet's Companions (may Allah be pleased with them all), I found in them five characteristics that distinguish them from others:

1. They led simple lives that were free from ostentation and extravagance.

   {And We shall make easy for you [O Muhammad] the easy way [that is, the doing of righteous deeds].}

   (Qur'an 87: 8)

2. Their knowledge of religious matters was as blessed as it was profound. More importantly, they accompanied that knowledge with practical application.

    {It is only those who have knowledge among His slaves who fear Allah.}

    (Qur'an 35: 28)

3. They gave precedence to deeds of the heart over deeds that others could see. Thus, they had sincerity; they depended upon Allah (the Exalted); they loved Him; they hoped from Him only; and they feared none except Him. Furthermore, they assiduously performed voluntary acts of worship, such as prayer and fasting.

    {He knew what was in their hearts…}

    (Qur'an 48: 18)

4. They did not seek the world and its pleasures. They turned their backs in disdain on material possessions, and they reaped the fruits of this noble stance: happiness, peace of mind, and sincerity.

    {But whoever desires the hereafter and exerts the effort due to it while he is a believer…}

    (Qur'an 17: 19)

5. Jihad was a priority for them over other good deeds until it became a banner by which they were recognized. Through jihad, they annihilated their worries and troubles, because all of the following are a part of jihad: remembrance, striving, effort, and activity.

{As for those who strive hard in Us [Our cause], We will surely guide them to Our paths [that is, Allah's religion – Islamic monotheism]. And verily, Allah is with the good doers.}

(Qur'an 29: 69)

The Qur'an mentions truths and realities concerning this life that are constant and do not change. Here are the ones that are related to the subject matter of this book. If you work for Allah (the Exalted), He will help you:

{If you help [in the cause of] Allah, He will help you, and make your foothold firm.}

(Qur'an 47: 7)

If you ask of Allah, He will answer you:

{And your Lord said: Invoke Me, I will respond to your [invocation].}

(Qur'an 40: 60)

If you ask Allah for forgiveness, He will forgive you:

{He said: My Lord! Verily, I have wronged myself, so forgive me. Then He forgave him.}

(Qur'an 28: 16)

{And He it is Who accepts repentance from His slaves...}

(Qur'an 42: 25)

If you place your trust in Allah, He will be sufficient for you:

{And whosoever puts his trust in Allah, then He will suffice him.}

(Qur'an 65: 3)

There are three kinds of people whose punishment is certain: those who are rebellious against Allah, those who break their pledges, and those who plot evil deeds:

{Your rebellion [disobedience to Allah] is only against your own selves.}

(Qur'an 10: 23)

{Then whosoever breaks his pledge, breaks only to his own harm...}

(Qur'an 48: 10)

{But the evil plot encompasses only him who makes it.}

(Qur'an 35: 43)

Oppressors will not escape from Allah's punishment:

{These are their houses in utter ruin, for they did wrong.}

(Qur'an 27: 52)

The fruits of righteousness are harvested both in the short and long term:

{So Allah gave them the reward of this world, and the excellent reward of the hereafter.}

(Qur'an 3: 148)

If you obey Allah, He will love you and provide sustenance for you:

{Verily, Allah is the All-Provider...} (Qur'an 51: 58)

Allah (the Exalted) will punish the enemies of his obedient slaves:

{Verily, We will exact retribution.} (Qur'an 44: 16)

Shaykh 'Abdur-Raḥmân ibn Sa'di wrote a valuable book called Practical Means to a Happy Life. In it he said:

> By enumerating Allah's blessings, one will realize that he is better off than a great number of people and that he should truly be thankful for Allah's favors upon him.

Even in matters of religion, we find that in spite of the negligence we are all guilty of, some of us are better than others in performing the obligatory congregational prayers regularly, in reading the Qur'an, in remembering Allah, and so on. These are all favors for which we should be thankful. Allah (the Exalted) said:

> {Do you not see that Allah has made subject to you whatever is in the heavens and whatever is in the earth and amply bestowed upon you His favors, [both] apparent and unapparent?}
>
> *(Qur'an 31: 20)*

Adh-Dhahabi mentioned that the great scholar of Hadith, Ibn 'Abdul-Ba'qi, observed the people as they were leaving the central mosque of Baghdad. He was looking for someone with whom he would wish to change places, in all aspects of his life, yet he reported that he found no one:

> {And We have preferred them above many of those whom We have created with a marked preference.}
>
> *(Qur'an 17: 70)*

Pause to reflect

Asmâ' bint 'Umays related that the Messenger of Allah (bpuh) said to her:

> «Shall I not teach you words that you should say when in distress? Say: Allah, Allah, My Lord; I do not associate any partners with Him.»

In another hadith, the Prophet (bpuh) informed us that when we are afflicted with sickness or hardship, we will find relief if we say:

> «Allah, My Lord; He has no partner.»

At times, we may become afflicted with a severe trial. If we turn to our Lord and surrender our will to Him, without associating any partners with Him, this hardship will go away.

Steps to take if you fear a jealous person

Recite the last two chapters of the Qur'an, remember Allah (the Exalted) and supplicate to Him:

{And from the evil of the envier when he envies.}

(Qur'an 113: 5)

Hide or keep secret your affairs from the jealous person:

{O my sons! Do not enter by one gate, but enter by different gates...}

(Qur'an 12: 67)

Be generous to those who attempt to harm you, for perhaps they will then desist:

{Repel evil with that which is better.}

(Qur'an 23: 96)

Good manners

Good manners lead to prosperity, while bad ones lead to misery. In a hadith, the Prophet (bpuh) said:

«Through good manners, one reaches the status of the person who not only fasts, but who also stands late in the night to pray.»

He also said:

«Shall I not inform you of the most beloved to me and the one seated closest to me on the Day of Resurrection: Those of you who are best in manners.»

{And verily, you [O Muhammad] are on an exalted standard of character.}

(Qur'an 68: 4)

{And by the mercy of Allah, you dealt with them gently. Had you been severe and harsh-hearted, they would have broken away from about you...}

(Qur'an 3: 159)

{...And speak good to people...}

(Qur'an 2: 83)

Â'ishah (may Allah be pleased with her) described the Prophet (bpuh) with the following words:

«His character was the Qur'an»

Sleepless nights

If you toss and turn during the night without being able to fall asleep, do the following:

1. Remember Allah with supplications from the Prophet (bpuh) or from the Qur'an:

    {Verily, in the remembrance of Allah do hearts find rest.}

    (Qur'an 13: 28)

2. Avoid sleeping during the day, except when you have no other choice:

    {And have made the day for livelihood.}

    (Qur'an 78: 11)

3. Read or write until sleep comes:

    {And say: 'My Lord! Increase me in knowledge.}

    (Qur'an 20: 114)

4. Work hard during the day:

    {And it is He Who has made the night for you as clothing and sleep [a means for] rest and has made the day a resurrection.} (Qur'an 25: 47)

5. Consume stimulants, such as coffee and tea, in moderation.

The evil consequences of sinning

Listed below are some of the evil consequences of sinning.

1. A barrier develops between Allah and the evildoer:

    {Nay! Surely, they [evildoers] will be veiled from seeing their Lord that day.}

    (Qur'an 83: 15)

2. When people perpetrate evil deeds on a continual basis, they become despondent, losing hope of being saved.

3. The evildoer often falls into a state of depression and anxiety:

   ⦃The building which they built will never cease to be a cause of hypocrisy and doubt in their hearts...⦄

   (Qur'an 9: 110)

4. Fear permeates the heart of the evildoer:

   ⦃We shall cast terror into the hearts of those who disbelieve, because they joined others in worship with Allah...⦄

   (Qur'an 3: 151)

5. Life becomes wretched for the evildoer:

   ⦃...Verily, for him is a life of hardship...⦄

   (Qur'an 20: 124)

6. The heart of the evildoer blackens and becomes hard:

   ⦃...And made their hearts grow hard.⦄

   (Qur'an 5: 13)

7. An evildoer's face loses its light and becomes morbid:

   ⦃As for those whose faces will become black [to them will be said]: Did you reject faith...⦄

   (Qur'an 3: 106)

8. People feel contempt for an evildoer.

9. The worldly circumstances of an evildoer become straitened:

   ⦃And if only they had acted according to the Torah, the Injeel [Gospel], and what has [now] been sent down to them from their Lord [the Qur'an], they would surely have gotten provision from above them and from underneath their feet.⦄

   (Qur'an 5: 66)

10. The wrath of Allah, a decrease in faith, and calamity – all of these are the lot of the evildoer:

{So they have drawn on themselves wrath upon wrath.}

(Qur'an 2: 90)

{Rather, the stain has covered their hearts of that which they were earning.}

(Qur'an 83: 14)

{And they say: Our hearts are wrapped [that is, we do not hear or understand Allah's Word].}

(Qur'an 2: 88)

Strive for your sustenance, but don't be covetous

The Lord of the worlds provides even for the worm in the ground:

{And there is no creature on [or within] the earth or a bird that flies with its wings except [that they are] communities like you.}

(Qur'an 6: 38)

Allah (the Exalted) provides for the birds in the sky and for the fish in the sea:

{And it is He Who feeds but is not fed.}

(Qur'an 6: 14)

You are worthier than a worm, bird, or fish, so don't worry about sustenance.

I have known people who were stricken by poverty simply because of their distance from Allah. Some of them were rich and healthy, but instead of being thankful they turned away from obedience to Allah, they abandoned prayer, and they perpetrated major sins. Allah took away their health and their wealth, replacing these with poverty, sickness, and anxiety. They were then afflicted with hardship upon hardship, calamity upon calamity.

{But whosoever turns away from My reminder, verily, for him is a life of hardship...}

(Qur'an 20: 124)

{That is because Allah would not change a favor which He had bestowed upon a people until they change what is within themselves.}

(Qur'an 8: 53)

{And whatever of misfortune befalls you, it is because of what your hands have earned. And He pardons much.}

(Qur'an 42: 30)

{And [Allah revealed] that if they had remained straight on the way, We would have given them abundant provision.}

(Qur'an 72: 16)

The secret of guidance

Contentment and happiness are blessings that are given only to those who follow the straight path. Muhammad (bpuh) left us upon one end of this path, and at the other end of it are the gardens of paradise.

{And indeed We should then have guided them to a straight way.}

(Qur'an 4: 68)

By happiness we mean this: when you adhere to the straight path, though you may be afflicted with hardships along the way, you are confident of a happy ending and a future abode in paradise. As a result, you will follow the Prophet (bpuh), who spoke not from his own desires, who was immune to the whisperings of the devil, and whose sayings are a proof for humankind.

{For each [person], there are angels in succession, before and behind him. They guard him by the command of Allah.}

(Qur'an 13: 11)

One can sense the joy of a righteous person by his mannerisms and by his treading the straight path. He knows that he has a Lord and that he has a role model in the Messenger (bpuh); he has the Book of Allah in his hand, illumination in his heart, and a conscience that prompts him to do well. He is advancing to a greater state of bliss and is always striving for betterment.

{This is the guidance of Allah with which He guides whomsoever He will of His slaves.}

(Qur'an 6: 88)

There are two paths: one that is figurative and the other that has a physical reality. The first path is that of faith, which one treads in this transient life – a life that is fraught with temptations and desires. The second path is in the hereafter. Every person will have to go across that second path in order to reach paradise. Anyone who fails will plunge into the fire. This path or bridge is teeming with spikes. Whoever is guided to the path of faith and belief in this life will safely cross the path of the hereafter – the speed at which the person crosses will be proportional to the level of his or her faith. Know that if you are blessed with being guided to the straight path, your worries and anxieties will quickly vanish.

Ten gems for a good and noble life

1. Wake up in the last third of the night to beg forgiveness from Allah (the Exalted).

   {And those who pray and beg Allah's pardon in the last hours of the night.}

   (Qur'an 3: 17)

2. At least once in a while, seclude yourself from people in order to contemplate.

   {And [those who] think deeply about the creation of the heavens and the earth...}

   (Qur'an 3: 191)

3. Stay in the company of the righteous.

   {And keep yourself patiently with those who call on their Lord...}

   (Qur'an 18: 28)

4. Remember Allah (the Exalted) often.

   {Remember Allah with much remembrance.}

   (Qur'an 33: 41)

5. Pray two units of prayer with sincerity and devotion.

   {Those who offer their prayer with all solemnity and full submissiveness.} (Qur'an 23: 2)

6. Recite the Qur'an with understanding and reflection.

   {Do they not then consider the Qur'an carefully?}

   (Qur'an 4: 82)

7. Fast on a hot, dry day.

   «He abandons his food, drink, and desire – all for Me.»

8. Give charity secretly.

   «Until the left hand doesn't know what the right hand has spent.»

9. Provide relief and aid to the afflicted Muslim.

   «Whoever gives relief to a Muslim from one of the vicissitudes of this life, Allah will relieve him from a calamity that is from the calamities of the Day of Judgment.»

10. Be as abstemious and abstinent as possible in this fleeting world.

    {The hereafter is better and more lasting.}

    (Qur'an 87: 17)

Among the delusions of Prophet Noah's son was his saying:

{I will betake myself to a mountain, and it will save me from the water.}

(Qur'an 11: 43)

Had he taken refuge with Allah, his outcome would have been very different. The cause of misery for An-Namrood (Nebuchadnezzar) was his saying, "I bring about life, and I cause death." He tried wearing a garb that wasn't his, and he claimed to have a quality that he didn't in fact have – and thus his downfall became complete.

The key to our happiness can be summed up in one simple yet profound phrase, the phrase of Tawḥeed (Islamic monotheism): "There is none worthy of worship except Allah, and Muhammad is His Messenger."

When you pronounce this phrase on earth, it will be said to you in the heavens, "You have spoken the truth."

{And he [Muhammad] who has brought the truth [this Qur'an and Islamic monotheism] and [those who] believed therein...}

(Qur'an 39: 33)

When you live your life in harmony with this phrase on a practical level, you will be saved from destruction, shame, and the hellfire.

{And Allah will deliver those who are the Muttaqoon [pious] to their places of success [paradise].}

(Qur'an 39: 61)

When you not only apply the phrase of Tawheed, but also call others to it, your name will be remembered and you will be made victorious:

{And that Our hosts, they verily would be the victors.}

(Qur'an 37: 173)

When you love the phrase of Tawheed, you will be elevated in ranking and endowed with honor.

{But honor, power and glory belong to Allah, His Messenger [Muhammad], and the believers...}

(Qur'an 63: 8)

Bilâl (may Allah be pleased with him) called out with the phrase of Tawheed, and his situation underwent a dramatic inward change that ran parallel to his outward change of being freed from slavery.

{He brings them out from darkness into light.}

(Qur'an 2: 257)

Abu Lahab balked at and desisted from saying the phrase of Tawheed. He died in a weak and pathetic state.

{And whosoever Allah disgraces, none can honor him.}

(Qur'an 22: 18)

The phrase of Tawheed is an elixir that transforms the base human being into a paragon of pureness and devotion.

{But We have made it [this Qur'an] a light wherewith We guide whosoever of Our slaves We will.}

(Qur'an 42: 52)

Whatever you do, do not exult in wealth acquired if you have turned your back on the hereafter. If you do turn your back on the hereafter, a harsh punishment and severe chastisement will lie in wait for you:

{My wealth has not availed me. My power and arguments [to defend myself] have gone from me!} *(Qur'an 69: 28-29)*
{Verily, your Lord is Ever Watchful [over them].}

(Qur'an 89: 14)

Also, don't exult excessively in your child if you have forgotten your Lord. Turning away from Him is the ultimate failure.

{And they were covered with humiliation and misery…}

(Qur'an 2: 61)

And finally, do not be complacent about your wealth if your deeds are evil, for such deeds will be your disgrace in the hereafter.

{But surely the torment of the hereafter will be more disgracing…}

(Qur'an 41: 16)

{And it is not your wealth, nor your children that bring you nearer to Us [that is, please Allah], but only he [will please Us] who believes [in the Islamic monotheism], and does righteous deeds…}

(Qur'an 34: 37)

Don't be sad – Learn to deal with your reality

In this life, if you inwardly disparage something you can't have, its value will diminish for you. On the other hand, if you are contented with not getting something that you really wanted, then your heart will find solace.

{Allah will give us of His bounty, and [also] His Messenger [from alms, et cetera]. We implore Allah [to enrich us].}

(Qur'an 9: 59)

I once read about a man who fell out of a window. The ring he was wearing became stuck around a nail on the ledge that wasn't nailed down completely; consequently, his ring finger was pulled from its root, leaving him with four fingers. The amazing thing is not the incident itself, but the contentment shown by the man long after the accident, contentment that is illustrated in the following words, "It hardly ever crosses my mind that I have four fingers on one hand or that I have lost a finger. It only comes back when I remember the accident; Otherwise, my work is going well, and I am content with what happened."

«Allah has made His decree, and as He pleases, He does.»

Be Happy

I know a man who lost his left arm as a result of a disease; He has lived for many years since; he got married and has children; He drives his car without difficulty and performs the various tasks of his work with ease; He is so at ease that it is as if Allah created him with only one arm to begin with.

«Be content with what Allah has apportioned for you and you will be the richest of people.»

How quickly we adapt to our circumstances! It is amazing how we adapt our thinking when a change in lifestyle is imposed upon us; Fifty years ago, a house consisted of a carpet made from palm tree leaves, a jug for water, a small amount of coal, and a few other paltry items. People managed as they do now, and a lack of resources or comfort did not make life any less important than it is now. An Arab poet said:

The soul desires more if you encourage it,

But it returns to contentment when it is disciplined.

A battle broke out in the central mosque of Kufa when members of one tribe began to hurl insults at the members of another tribe. A man who was in the mosque stealthily made his escape in order to seek out al-Aḥnaf ibn Qays, who was recognized by all as a consummate peacemaker. The man found him in his house milking a goat. Al-Aḥnaf was dressed in a garment that was not even worth ten dirhams (in other words, it was ragged and cheap). He looked emaciated and haggard, and one of his legs was longer than the other, which gave him a bad limp. When he was informed of the news, no change became manifest on his countenance and he remained calm. This display of fortitude stemmed from the fact that al-Aḥnaf had witnessed much strife and hardship during his life, so he had become used to such an occurrence. He told the man, "By the will of Allah, everything will be all right." He then began to take his breakfast as if nothing had happened. His breakfast consisted of a morsel of dry bread, oil, salt, and a glass of water. He mentioned Allah's name and ate. Then he praised Allah and said, "Wheat from Iraq, oil from Syria, water from the Tigris, and salt from Merv. Verily, these are great blessings." He put on his clothes, took his walking stick, and made his way to the people. When they saw him, their gazes became fixed on him, and they listened attentively to what he had to say. He spoke words of peace and of compromise, words that pleased both sides, and he requested them to depart and go their own ways. They all acquiesced. Each of them left without a trace of rancor remaining in his heart, and in this way the ordeal ended peacefully. An Arab poet said: One can reach nobility even if His clothes are tattered and his pocket is patched.

There are many lessons to be learned from this narrative. One of them is that greatness is not in appearance or clothes; other lessons are that having few material possessions is not an indication of misery and that happiness does not reside in comfort and wealth.

{As for man, when his Lord tries him by giving him honor and gifts, then he says [puffed up]: My Lord has honored me. But when He tries him, by straitening his means of life, he says: My Lord has humiliated me!}

(Qur'an 89: 15-16)

Another lesson we should take away from the narrative is that a person's character and qualities are the yardsticks of his worth, not his clothes, shoes, or house. His worth is weighed by his knowledge, generosity, manners, and deeds.

{Verily, the most honorable of you with Allah is that [believer] who is pious.}

(Qur'an 49: 13)

The connection between the narrative and the subject matter of this book is that happiness is not found in opulence, mansions, gold, or silver; instead, happiness is something that manifests itself in the heart through faith, contentment, and knowledge.

{So let not their wealth or their children amaze you.}

(Qur'an 9: 55)

{Say: In the bounty of Allah, and in His mercy [that is, Islam and the Qur'an] – therein let them rejoice. That is better than what [wealth] they amass.}

(Qur'an 10: 58)

Train yourself to surrender your will to whatever is decreed for you. What will you do if you do not believe in the decree of Allah? Whatever you plan other than complete submission to Allah's divine decree will provide no benefit for you. And so, you may ask, what is the solution to hardships?

The solution is to say sincerely, "We are contented and pleased, and we have surrendered our wills."

{Wheresoever you may be, death will overtake you even if you are in fortresses built up strong and high!}

(Qur'an 4: 78)

One of the most difficult days of my life, and a most painful day it was, was when the doctor told me that the arm of my brother Muhammad had to be amputated. The news fell upon my ears like thunder. I was overcome (with emotion) and my soul sought comfort in Allah's sayings:

{No disaster strikes except by permission of Allah. And whoever believes in Allah – He will guide his heart...}

(Qur'an 64: 11)

{But give glad tidings to the patient ones who, when afflicted with calamity, say: Truly! To Allah we belong and truly, to Him we shall return.}

(Qur'an 2: 155-156)

These verses instilled a sense of peace and comfort in my soul. There is no form of artifice that can prevent the occurrence of that which is decreed. Therefore we must keep faith and submit our wills.

{Or have they plotted some plan? Then We too are planning.}

(Qur'an 43: 79)

{And Allah has full power and control over His affairs.}

(Qur'an 12: 21)

{When He decrees a matter, He only says to it: Be! – and it is.}

(Qur'an 2: 117)

Al-Khansâ an-Nakhâ'iyah was told in one breath of the death of her four boys, who all died in the path of Allah at the battle of al-Qâdisiyah. Her only reaction was to praise Allah and thank Him for choosing what was best. Faith fortifies one's ability to persevere through hardship; through gratitude, one achieves happiness in this life and in the hereafter. If you are loath to follow this advice, then ask yourself this: is there a viable alternative? If that alternative is bitterness, complaining, and a refusal to accept what has happened, then you will only bring upon yourself pain in this life and in the hereafter.

«Whoever is contented, then for him is pleasure, and whoever (displays) anger, then for him is wrath.»

The best remedy and course of action after a calamity is to say with sincerity, "Verily, We belong to Allah and indeed, to Him is our return." This means that we are all from Allah's creation; that we belong to Him; that we are in His kingdom; and that we shall return to Him.

The beginning is with Him, and the return is to Him. The whole affair is in the hands of Allah. An Arab poet said:

> My own soul that possesses things is itself departing,
>
> So why should I cry over a possession when it leaves?

Allah (the Exalted) said:

{Everything will perish save His face.}

(Qur'an 28: 88)

{Whatsoever is on it [the earth] will perish.}

(Qur'an 55: 26)

{Verily, you [O Muhammad] will die and verily, they [too] will die.}

(Qur'an 39: 30)

If you suddenly learned that your house burned down, that your child died, or that your life's savings were lost, what would you do? From this moment, prepare yourself mentally. Trying to escape or elude what is decreed is a fruitless endeavor that brings no benefit. Be satisfied with what has been decreed, acknowledge your reality, and earn your reward. You have no other option. Sure, you might say that there is another option, but it is a base one, and I warn you to stay clear from it: it is to complain and grumble, and to lose your composure by flaring into rage and anger. What can this attitude and behavior possibly accomplish? You will earn anger from your Lord, and people will revile you. Furthermore, what you have lost will not return and your calamity will not be lightened for you:

{Let him extend a rope to the ceiling, then cut off [his breath], and let him see: will his effort remove that which enrages [him]?}

(Qur'an 22: 15)

Don't be sad – Sooner or later everything in this world perishes

Death is the end of us all: the oppressor and the oppressed, the mighty and the feeble, the rich and the poor. Your death is no novelty. Nations before have gone, and nations after will perish.

Ibn Baṭooṭa related that in the north, there is a graveyard with one thousand kings buried in it. At the entrance of this graveyard is a sign that reads:

The Kings: ask the dirt about them,

And about the great leaders; they are all bones now.

A cause for wonder is the forgetfulness of humankind and how we remain heedless of death, the menace of which hangs over us day and night. People delude themselves thinking that they are immortal on this earth.

{O humankind! Fear your Lord and be dutiful to Him! Verily, the earth-quake of the Hour [of Judgment] is a terrible thing.}

(Qur'an 22: 1)

{Draws near for humankind their reckoning, while they turn away in heedlessness.}

(Qur'an 21: 1)

When Allah (the Exalted) destroyed a nation and wiped out a transgressing people, He said:

{Can you find a single one of them or hear even a whisper of them?}

(Qur'an 19: 98)

Depression leads to misery

The newspaper al-Muslimoon reported that in 1990 two million people around the world suffered from depression. Depression is a sickness that has quietly wreaked havoc on humankind. It does not distinguish between people from the West or East, or between the rich and poor. It is a malady that attacks all kinds of people... and may in certain cases lead to suicide.

Depression does not recognize or stand in awe of wealth, nobility, or power. However, it does stay aloof from the believer. Some statistics indicate that 200 million people are now suffering from depression.

The findings of a recent study showed that at least one out of every ten people has at one time or another suffered from this dangerous sickness. The danger is not restricted to adults; even the young are now susceptible to depression. Even the fetus in the womb is at risk, for a depressed mother can turn to abortion as a means of escaping from her problems.

Depression may lead to suicide

{And do not kill yourselves.}

(Qur'an 4: 29)

{And do not throw yourselves into destruction...}

(Qur'an 2: 195)

Reports were leaked that former President Ronald Reagan fell victim to a state of severe depression. His situation was attributed to his being over seventy years of age while still having to face tremendously stressful problems and to his having undergone periodic operations.

{Wheresoever you may be, death will overtake you even if you are in fortresses built up strong and high!}

(Qur'an 4: 78)

Many famous people, and in particular those in the arts, suffer from depression. The main reason, if not the only reason, for poet Ṣâleḥ Jâheen's death was indeed depression. It has also been said that Napoleon Bonaparte, while still in exile, died in a state of depression.

{And that their souls shall depart [die] while they are disbelievers.}

(Qur'an 9: 55)

Not too long ago, a German woman killed three of her children. It later became clear that her reason for doing this horrible act stemmed from her state of depression. Since she loved her children a great deal, she feared that they would have to go through the pain and hardship that she had undergone in her life. Thus, she decided to 'give them comfort' and 'to save each one of them' from the difficulties and vicissitudes of life. After murdering them, she took her own life.

The numbers issued by the World Health Organization indicate the severity of the situation. In 1973, it reported that three percent of the world's population was afflicted with depression. The figures increased dramatically, and in 1978 the figure was up to five percent. What might come as a surprise to some is that some studies have shown that one out of every four Americans suffers from depression. During the conference of Mental Disorders that was held in Chicago in 1981, the chairman of the conference announced that one hundred million people in the world suffer from depression.

Contrary to what some might expect, most of them were from developed countries. Other studies have even proclaimed a number of two hundred million.

{See they not that they are tried once or twice every year [with different kinds of calamities, disease, famine, et cetera]?}

(Qur'an 9: 126)

It is said that, "The intelligent person is not he who is able to increase his profits, but he who transforms his losses into profits)."

{There did Allah give you one distress after another by way of requital to teach you not to grieve for that which had escaped you.}

(Qur'an 3: 153)

The meaning of this verse is that things that are over and finished with should not be dwelt upon, since doing so leads only to anxiety, worry, and wastage of time.

If you have no work to do, you can fill your time with many useful activities, such as doing good deeds, helping others, visiting the sick, visiting the graveyard (to remember and reflect on your final destination), volunteering in the mosque, participating in charitable work, doing physical exercise, visiting loved ones, organizing one's affairs, and lending aid to the old, the poor, and the weak.

{Verily, you are returning towards your Lord – with your deeds and actions [good or bad], a sure returning.}

(Qur'an 84: 6)

An Arab poet said:

A generous deed is singular in its sweet taste

And in its beautiful appearance.

Look through any history book and you will find among its pages stories of pain, privation, and misery. An Arab poet said:

Read History, as it is filled with morals.

A nation will sink if it knows nothing of its annals.

{And all that We relate to you of the news of the Messengers is in order that We may make strong and firm your heart thereby.}

(Qur'an 11: 120)

{Indeed in their stories, there is a lesson for men of understanding.}

(Qur'an 12: 111)

{So relate the stories, perhaps that they may reflect.}

(Qur'an 7: 176)

'Umar (may Allah be pleased with him) said, "My goal now remains to find enjoyment in the different things that have been decreed for me," a statement that indicates his contentment with Allah's decree for him.

In the span of one year, eight of Abi Thuayb al-Hathali's sons died during a plague. What do you suppose he said? He kept faith, was resigned, and submitted to Allah's decree, saying:

Patience will I show to those who rejoiced in my pain,

I will not shake or tremble with the vicissitudes of time,

When death looms and bares its claws,

No charm or trinket can ward it off.

{No disaster strikes except by permission of Allah.}

(Qur'an 64: 11)

Ibn 'Abbâs (may Allah be pleased with him) lost his eyesight, and he said to himself these words of solace:

If Allah takes from me the light of my eyes,

My heart remains illuminated,

My heart understands and my mind is not perverse,

And my tongue is like a blade of an unsheathed sword.

He comforted himself by remembering the many favors of Allah that remained for him after having lost only one of them.

In a single day, 'Urwah ibn Zubayr (may Allah be pleased with him) lost one of his legs and was informed that his son had died. This was his reaction:

O Allah, to You belongs all praise. If You have taken away, then You have also given. And if You have tested (me) with hardship, You have also saved me and cared (for me). You have bestowed upon me four limbs and have taken only one away. You have blessed me with four sons and have taken only one away.

{And their recompense shall be paradise, and silken garments, because they were patient.}

(Qur'an 76: 12)

{Peace be upon you for that you persevered in patience!}

(Qur'an 13: 24)

The following words of consolation have been attributed to Imam Shâfi'i:

Let the days bring what they may,

And be contented when a decree has come to pass.

When the execution of it comes in a land of some nation,

Neither earth nor sky can prevent it.

How many times have we feared death and then nothing came of it? How many times have we felt the end near, yet we then returned stronger than before? How many times have we found ourselves in difficulties, yet after a short time been allowed to taste the sweetness of ease and relief?

{Say [O Muhammad]: Allah rescues you from it and from all [other] distresses...}

(Qur'an 6: 64)

Or how many times have we been sick only to be restored to health?

{And if Allah touches you with harm, none can remove it but He...}

(Qur'an 6: 17)

When we know with certainty that Allah controls everything, how then can we feel any fear of anyone other than Him? And when we fear Allah, how can we fear others alongside Him, especially considering that Allah (the Exalted) said:

{...so fear them not, but fear Me...} (Qur'an 3: 175)

He is All Powerful:

{And that Our hosts, they verily would be the victors.}

(Qur'an 37: 173)

{Verily, We will indeed make victorious Our Messengers and those who believe in this world's life and on the day when the witnesses will stand forth [that is, Day of Resurrection].}

(Qur'an 40: 51)

Ibn Taymiyah said that with the phrase, "There is neither might nor power except with Allah," heavy things are carried, obstacles are overcome, and honor is achieved. So remember this phrase constantly, since it is a treasure from the treasures of paradise and a pillar of happiness and contentment.

Asking Allah for forgiveness opens locked doors

Ibn Taymiyah said:

> When I am confused in my understanding of an issue in religion, I forthwith beseech Allah to forgive me one thousand times – maybe a little more or maybe a little less. Then Allah opens what was closed for me and I come to understand.

{I said [to them]: Ask forgiveness from your Lord. Verily, He is Oft-Forgiving; he will send rain to you in abundance.}

(Qur'an 71: 10-11)

One way of finding inner peace is to constantly seek forgiveness from Allah. Even a sin can be a blessing if it causes the believer to turn to his Lord in repentance. In al-Musnad, it is related that the Prophet (bpuh) said:

> «Allah does not make a decree for his slave except that it is better for him.»

In regard to this hadith, Ibn Taymiyah was asked, "Even the sin?" He replied, "Yes, if it is followed by repentance, regret, asking for forgiveness, and a sincere feeling of remorse for having transgressed."

{If they [hypocrites], when they had been unjust to themselves, had come to you [Muhammad] and begged Allah's forgiveness, and the Messenger had begged forgiveness for them, indeed, they would have found Allah All--Forgiving, Most Merciful.}

(Qur'an 4: 64)

{And so are the days [good and not so good], We give to men by turns...}

(Qur'an 3: 140)

{The day they see it, [it will be] as if they had not tarried [in this world] except an afternoon or a morning.}

(Qur'an 79: 46)

I always feel wonder when reflecting on some famous historical figures. Even though they faced hardships, it seems as if to them their hardships were as gentle as drops of water. In the forefront of this elite group is the leader of the creation, Muhammad (bpuh). He was in the cave with Abu Bakr (may Allah be pleased with him), with his enemies near them, and he said to his Companion:

{Be not sad [or afraid], surely Allah is with us.}

(Qur'an 9: 40)

Glad tidings from the unseen at the mouth of the cave: Revelation that led to happiness for the world. Just before the battle of Badr, the Prophet (bpuh) eagerly put on his armor while saying:

{Their multitude will be put to flight, and they will show their backs.}

(Qur'an 54: 45)

In the battle of Uḥud, after some of his Companions were martyred and others were injured, the Prophet (bpuh) said to his Companions:

«Line up behind me so that I can praise my Lord.»

It was the determination and willpower of a Prophet that could even, by the will of Allah, shake mountains.

Qays ibn 'Âṣim al-Manqari, famous among the Arabs for his patience, was once narrating a story to some of his companions when a man came and told Qays, "Your son has been murdered. The son of So-and-so was the culprit." Qays didn't cut his story short, but instead continued relating it in a calm demeanor until he finished. Then he said, "Wash my son, shroud him, and allow me to pray over him!"

{And those who are patient in extreme poverty and ailment [disease] and at the time of fighting [during the battles].} (Qur'an 2: 177)

Ikrimah ibn Abi Jahl (may Allah be pleased with him) was offered water on his deathbed, and he said, "Offer it to So-and-so." There were a number of them, all on the verge of dying, and each preferred the person beside him to his own self; with this wonderful display of brotherhood, they all died.

Let others depend on you, not you on them

The noble hearted one works for people and does not allow them to serve him. Therefore he doesn't embark on a project that will require him to rely upon others.

In helping others, people have a limit, or point, up to which they are willing to strive and sacrifice for others. This limit is seldom exceeded.

Consider Ḥusayn ibn 'Ali, the grandson of the Prophet (bpuh). He was murdered, and the nation did not stir. Instead, his murderers danced in the streets, chanting praises to Allah for their victory – may Allah be pleased with Ḥusayn. An Arab poet wrote:

They came with your head, O grandson of Muhammad (bpuh),

Rejoicing at its dripping blood with joy and mirth,

Praising Allah for having killed you, but

They only killed their praises and their religion.

Imam Aḥmad was tortured by being severely beaten with a whip. He was on the verge of dying, and nobody moved a finger to help him.

{So invoke not with Allah another god...}

(Qur'an 26: 213)

Ibn Taymiyah was captured and was made to mount a mule, to be paraded on it and humiliated. Throngs of people who later attended his funeral did nothing while that happened, simply because people, with the rare exception, have a certain limit they will not go beyond in helping others.

{And they possess neither hurt nor benefit for themselves, and possess no power [of causing] death, nor [of giving] life, nor of raising the dead.}

(Qur'an 25: 3)

{O Prophet [Muhammad]! Allah is Sufficient for you and for the believers who follow you.}

(Qur'an 8: 64)

{And put your trust [O Muhammad] in the Ever Living One Who dies not...}

(Qur'an 25: 58)

{Verily, they can avail you nothing against Allah [if He wants to punish you].} (Qur'an 45: 19)

Prudence

Those who spend prudently are saved from having to depend on others. A poet said:

Save your money, for with wealth comes respect,

And you can do without asking uncle or cousin.

The philosophy that promotes extravagance in spending is false and is detrimental to one's wellbeing. The roots of such ideas are found in India, or originate from the ignorant among the Sufis. Indeed, Islam promotes earning money honestly and spending it in a proper way. Applying these two principles is what makes us honorable through our wealth. The following saying of the Prophet (bpuh) is proof of this:

«Blessed is good wealth (that which is earned honestly) in the hands of a righteous man.»

In contrast are those who are inundated in debt or indigent. The former are always troubled and worried that all of their possessions will be taken away from them, and the latter are continuously struggling just to find the means of staying alive.

The Prophet (bpuh) said:

«O Allah, I seek refuge in You from disbelief and from poverty.»

He also said:

«Poverty is almost disbelief.»

There is no contradiction between the previous hadith and the hadith in Ibn Mâjah:

«Seek to have little in this world, and Allah will love you; do not seek what others have, and people will love you.»

This hadith has a defect in terms of its authenticity. Yet suppose it to be other than weak, and the meaning is that you should be content with having the bare necessities, and you should be satisfied with that amount of provision which saves you from having to beg or ask for people's help. At the same time, you should be noble and self-dependent and have sufficient means to prevent you from asking others for help.

«Whoever wishes to be free from dependence on others, Allah will make him so.»

Be Happy

An Arab poet said:

I never had my hands outstretched except to the Creator,

And I never sought a dollar from one who reminds others of his favors.

In an authentic hadith, the Prophet (bpuh) said:

«For you to leave rich those who inherit from you is better than leaving them poor, (in which case) they will have to ask of people.»

In another authentic hadith, the Prophet (bpuh) said:

«The upper hand is better than the lower one.»

The meaning of this hadith is that the giver is better than the receiver.

{The one who knows them not, thinks that they are rich because of their modesty.}

(Qur'an 2: 273)

The following verse indicates that one should not be fulsome in praising people in order to receive financial assistance from them, since Allah has guaranteed our sustenance:

{Do they seek honor, power and glory with them? Verily, then to Allah belongs all honor, power and glory.}

(Qur'an 4: 139)

An Arab poet said:

I have no intention of kissing someone's hand,

For me, cutting it off is better than that kiss,

When one gives me a favor he enslaves me,

Or if not, at least I feel ashamed.

Don't cling to other than Allah

If Allah (the Exalted) is the One Who brings life and causes death, and if He alone provides for all creation, why fear people or be distressed by their actions? I think that in our society, much grief and anxiety is caused by our attachment to people – in seeking to please them, trying to gain their favor, striving to praise the important ones among them, and feeling wounded by their disparaging treatment. All of this indicates a weakness in one's belief in Allah. An Arab poet said:

> Would that you were pleased when life is bitter,
>
> And would that you were contented when people are angry,
>
> If your love for Allah is true, then all else is insignificant,
>
> And all above the dirt is dirt.

Do those things that bring you peace

Ibn al-Qayyim enumerated some of the factors that bring about tranquility:

1. Islamic monotheism, or worshipping Allah exclusively without associating any partners with Him (in worship), and without associating any partners with Him in all qualities that belong to Him alone. The disbeliever and the one who associates partners with Allah the Almighty are, for all practical purposes, dead and not alive.

    {But whosoever turns away from My reminder [that is, neither believes in this Qur'an nor acts on its orders, et cetera] verily, for him is a life of hardship, and We shall raise him up blind on the Day of Resurrection.}

    (Qur'an 20: 124)

    {And whosoever Allah wills to guide, He opens his breast to Islam...}

    (Qur'an 6: 125)

    {Is he whose breast Allah has opened to Islam, so that he is in light from His Lord [as he who is non-Muslim]?}

    (Qur'an 39: 22)

Allah (the Exalted) warned His enemies with the following verse:

{We shall cast terror into the hearts of those who disbelieve, because they joined others in worship with Allah, for which He had sent no authority...}

(Qur'an 3: 151)

{So, woe to those whose hearts are hardened against remembrance of Allah!}

(Qur'an 39: 22)

{And whosoever He wills to send astray, He makes his breast closed and constricted, as if he is climbing up to the sky.}

(Qur'an 6: 125)

2. Useful knowledge, because the most happy, easygoing, and contented kind of person is the scholar. Why should scholars not be so, for they are the inheritors of Muhammad (bpuh)?

{And [Allah] taught you that which you knew not.}

(Qur'an 4: 113)

{So know [O Muhammad] that none has the right to be worshipped but Allah...}

(Qur'an 47: 19)

3. Good deeds. A good deed brings light both to the heart and to the face. Doing good deeds results in being blessed in one's sustenance, and the hearts of people are naturally attracted to the doer of good.

{We should surely have bestowed on them water [rain], in abundance.}

(Qur'an 72: 16)

4. Bravery, for the courageous person is firm and strong and fears Allah alone. Difficulties and hardship neither shake nor disturb him.

5. Avoiding sins. Sinning ruins one's peace of mind and makes one feel lonely and in the dark:

I saw that sins cause the heart to die

And addiction brings disgrace to the addicted.

6. Not being extravagant in that which is lawful. In other words, one should be moderate in speaking, sleeping, and mixing with people, and likewise one should be abstemious in one's eating habits.

{And they who turn away from ill speech.}

(Qur'an 23: 3)

{Not a word does he [or she] utter, but there is a watcher by him ready [to record it].}

(Qur'an 50: 18)

{And eat and drink but waste not by extravagance...}

(Qur'an 7: 31)

An Arab poet said:

O companion of the bed, you have slept excessively,

Don't you know that after death is a long sleep?

Preordainment

A man who had a mental disorder and an extreme anxiety problem sought advice from a Muslim doctor, who advised him, "Know that no matter what the plans are that someone has for the future, there is no movement, not so much as a whisper, in this world but that it occurs by the permission of Allah."

The following is related in a hadith:

«Verily, Allah wrote the Maqâdeer (everything that will happen) of the creation fifty thousand years before He created them.»

Al-Mutanabbi wrote:

Small things are greatly magnified in the eyes of the small one,

And great things are diminished in size in the eyes of the great one.

The sweet taste of freedom

Ar-Râshid wrote in al-Masâr:

Whoever possesses three hundred sixty loaves, a canister of oil, and one thousand six hundred dates (that is, enough provision for one year), then none can enslave him.

One of our pious predecessors once said, "The one who is satisfied with dry bread and water will be free from slavery except for slavery to Allah."

{And have in his mind no favor from anyone for which a reward is expected in return.}

(Qur'an 92: 19)

My aspirations and desires enslaved me since I obeyed them. If I had only been contented, I would have been free.

Those who seek to make wealth or status a means to happiness will come to know in the end how futile and fruitless their efforts were.

{And truly you have come unto Us alone [without wealth, companions or anything else] as We created you the first time. You have left behind all that which We had bestowed on you.}

(Qur'an 6: 94)

{Nay, you prefer the life of this world although the hereafter is better and more lasting.}

(Qur'an 87: 16-17)

Dirt was the pillow of Sufyân ath-Thawri

The lives of eminent scholars of the past are filled with lessons in humility. During the pilgrimage season, Sufyân ath-Thawri wanted to rest for the night, so he placed his cheek on a tiny mound of dirt. The people said to him, "You rest your head on dirt, yet you are the greatest scholar of Hadith in the world." He answered, "This pillow of mine is indeed better than that of the Caliph."

{Say: Nothing shall ever happen to us except what Allah has ordained for us.}

(Qur'an 9: 51)

Don't pay attention to the telltale

Predictions of calamity (which rarely come to pass) and evil premonitions (which are most often false) instill fear into the hearts of many:

{[Satan] threatens you with poverty and orders you to commit Faḥshâ [evil deeds, illegal sexual intercourse, sins et cetera]; whereas Allah promises you forgiveness from Himself and bounty, and Allah is All-Sufficient for his creatures' needs, All-Knower.}

(Qur'an 2: 268)

Anxiety, sleeplessness, and ulcers are the ill consequences of hopelessness and worry. An Arab poet said:

Don't punish us, for we have already been tortured

By anxiety that keeps us awake long through the night.

The curses of the foolish are of no consequence to you

Abraham Lincoln, America's sixteenth President, said:

I never read malicious, hostile letters that are sent to me. I never open the envelopes and never bother responding to them. If I were to become busy in dealing with such matters, I would have no time left to do things for my people.

{So turn aside from them [do not punish them]...}

(Qur'an 4: 63)

{So overlook their faults with gracious forgiveness.}

(Qur'an 15: 85)

{So turn away from them [O Muhammad], and say: Salâm [peace]!}

(Qur'an 43: 89)

The commander of the American Navy during World War II was a brilliant leader and tactician, and he earned a considerable amount of fame as a result. However, he had to deal with those under his command – inferiors who harbored jealousy towards him and subordinates who constantly attacked him behind his back with curses and criticism.

As is usually the case in such instances, he was well aware of what they said about him. He commented on this, saying:

> I now have an immunity from criticism. I have become old and am now cognizant of the fact that words cannot destroy greatness, nor can they bring down a sturdy fence.

An Arab poet said:

> What do the poets want from me (through attacking me verbally),
>
> And I have passed in age the limit of forty.

It has been claimed that Jesus (pbuh) said, "Love your enemy."

The meaning of this saying is that you should give a general pardon to your enemies. This way, you will be free from feelings of revenge, and free from hatred and rancor.

{And those who pardon men; verily, Allah loves the good doers.}

(Qur'an 3: 134)

After gaining control of Makkah, the Messenger of Allah (bpuh) said to those who had previously inflicted much harm on him:

«Go forth, for you are the freed ones.»

{No reproach on you this day...}

(Qur'an 12: 92)

{Allah has forgiven what is past...}

(Qur'an 5: 95)

Appreciate the beauty of the universe

By studying and appreciating the wonders of Allah's creation, you will find peace. Allah (the Exalted) says:

{We cause to grow wonderful gardens full of beauty and delight.}

(Qur'an 27: 60)

{Say: Behold all that is in the heavens and the earth.} (Qur'an 10: 101)

{Our Lord is He Who gave to each thing its form and nature, then guided it aright.}

(Qur'an 20: 50)

Learn from the bright sun, shining stars, rivers, streams, mountains, trees, fruits, air, and water.

{So blessed be Allah, the best of creators.}

(Qur'an 23: 14)

A poet said:

In everything there is a sign,

Indicating that He is One.

Ilyâ Abu Mâdi said:

O complainer who has no cause to grumble,

Imagine how you would be if you became ill,

Do you see the thorn and the roses, yet remain blind?

Or the dewdrops: did you miss them?

He who himself is void of beauty,

Sees nothing beautiful in nature.

{Do they not look at the camels, how they are created?}

(Qur'an 88: 17)

Einstein said that whoever looks reflectively at the universe knows that the One who created it perfectly is All-Wise and is not playing with dice.

{The One Who made everything, He has created good.}

(Qur'an 32: 7)

{We created them not except with truth [that is, to examine and test those who are obedient and those who are disobedient and then reward the obedient ones and punish the disobedient ones]...}

(Qur'an 44: 39)

{Did you think that We had created you in play [without any purpose]?}

(Qur'an 23: 115)

The meaning of these verses is that everything is planned and measured according to divine wisdom. Whoever studies the creation knows that there is One All-Powerful God Who sustains and manages everything, and that the notion that everything happens by coincidence is false.

{The sun and the moon run on their fixed courses [exactly] calculated with measured out stages for each [for reckoning, et cetera].}

(Qur'an 55: 5)

{It is not for the sun to overtake the moon, nor does the night outstrip the day. They all float, each in an orbit.}

(Qur'an 36: 40)

Avarice is of no avail

The Prophet (bpuh) said:

> «No soul dies until it takes its full portion of provision and until it reaches its appointed time of death.»

So why the ambition and why the covetousness?

{Everything with Him is in [due] proportion.}

(Qur'an 13: 8)

{And the command of Allah is a decree determined.}

(Qur'an 33: 38)

Bearing hardship atones for sins

The Messenger of Allah (bpuh) said:

«Worry, anxiety, pain, fatigue, sickness or even a thorn that pricks him – when a believer is afflicted with any of these, Allah grants him pardon for some of his sins (through or because of those afflictions).»

This reward is for those who are patient, who seek their reward with Allah, who repent to Him, and who know that all their dealings are solely with Allah, the Most Gracious. Al-Mutanabbi wrote:

Don't receive what time brings except with indifference,

As long as your soul is a companion for your body,

Whatever you are happy with is fleeting,

And sadness revives not lost loved ones.

{In order that you may not be sad over matters that you fail to get, nor rejoice because of that which has been given to you.}

(Qur'an 57: 23)

Allah is sufficient for us, and He is the best Disposer of our affairs

Prophet Abraham (pbuh) said this phrase when he was thrown into the fire, and it became cool and peaceful for him. The Prophet (bpuh) said it at the battle of Uḥud, and Allah made him victorious.

When Abraham was placed where the fire was to be set, the angel Gabriel came to him and asked, "Do you need anything from me?" Abraham confidently responded, "From you, no. But from Allah, yes!"

Prophet Moses (pbuh) saw the sea in front of him and the enemy behind him, and he said:

{Nay, verily! With me is my Lord, He will guide me.}

(Qur'an 26: 62)

It is mentioned in some narrations that when the Prophet (bpuh) was hiding in the cave, a pigeon came by the will of Allah and made its nest at the entrance, and a spider built its house at the mouth of the cave. The disbelievers said, "This is a sign that the cave had not been disturbed," and they said, "Muhammad has not entered here." Protection from the Lord of all that exists reaches those who have faith in Him and faith in His being All-Powerful and Most Merciful. Shawqi said:

> If this protection is directed at you,
>
> Sleep, since everything that happens is peace.

{For verily, you are under Our eyes...}

(Qur'an 52: 48)

{Allah is the best to guard, and He is the Most Merciful of those who show mercy.}

(Qur'an 12: 64)

The ingredients of happiness

In a hadith related by Tirmidhi, the Prophet (bpuh) said:

> «Whoever spends the night safely in his place of sleep, while he is physically healthy and has sufficient sustenance for his day, it is as if he achieved the world in its entirety.»

The meaning of this is that if one has enough food and a safe place to sleep, then he has achieved the best of the good things in this world. And many are those who are at this level in life but are thankless nonetheless. Allah (the Exalted) said to His Messenger (bpuh):

{...I have completed my favor upon you...}

(Qur'an 5: 3)

After reading this verse, you should ask yourself this question: what blessing was complete for the Prophet (bpuh)? Was it material wealth? Was it the possession of castles, mansions, gold, or silver? It is none of these blessings that Allah is referring to, since the Prophet (bpuh) was not wealthy.

The Prophet (bpuh) used to sleep in a room made of mud. His roof was made of branches from palm trees. Extreme hunger often forced him to tie two stones around his stomach - something he did in order to alleviate the pangs of hunger. His mattress was the branch of a date-palm tree, which would give him pains in his sides. He had to leave his armor with a Jew as collateral for thirty measures of wheat, until he would be able to pay him back. He would go three days straight without finding so much as a rotten date to eat.

{And indeed the hereafter is better for you than the present [life of this world]. And verily, your Lord will give you [all that is good] so that you shall be well-pleased.}

(Qur'an 93: 4-5)

The fatigue and stress that come with an important position

People who have important positions are taxed heavily. Their responsibilities take away from their health and peace. Very few people remain unaffected and unharmed by the stresses that are related to having strenuous and demanding jobs.

«Don't seek to be the Ameer (leader or governor).»

{My power and arguments [to defend myself] have gone from me!}

(Qur'an 69: 29)

Imagine that the world came to you with everything. Where will it all go in the end? Without a doubt, all of it will perish.

{And the face of your Lord full of Majesty and Honour will abide forever.}

(Qur'an 55: 27)

A wise man warned his son, "Do not seek to be the head, for the head is constantly aching."

In other words, do not always aspire to be the leader or the one in charge. Bitter criticisms, curses, and tough problems are the lot of the leader. A poet justly said:

Half of the people are enemies of

The governor, so very few, only if he is just.

Come to the prayer

{And seek help in patience and the prayer.}

(Qur'an 2: 45)

Whenever the Prophet (bpuh) was in a difficult situation, he would hasten to prayer. He would say to Bilâl (may Allah be pleased with him), whose responsibility it was to say the call to prayer:

«O Bilâl, give us comfort with it.»

When you feel stressed or in difficulty, or when you find yourself to be the victim of deception, hurry to the mosque and pray.

Especially on important occasions, the Prophet (bpuh) would find peace in prayer, such as in the battle of Badr and the Battle of the Trench. Ibn Ḥajar, who wrote the most important commentary on Ṣaḥeeḥ al-Bukhâri, was once trapped in a castle that was surrounded by robbers. When he stood up for prayer, Allah saved him.

Ibn 'Asâkir and Ibn al-Qayyim both related the story of a thief who accosted a righteous man on his way to Shâm (the present-day area of Syria and Palestine). The thief intended to kill him, but before he came close, the righteous man asked for a respite of a few minutes so that he could say a prayer. He stood, began his prayer, and remembered Allah's saying:

{Is not He [better than your gods] Who responds to the distressed one, when he calls Him?}

(Qur'an 27: 62)

He repeated this verse three times. An angel descended from the sky with a spear and killed the transgressor. The angel said, "I am the angel of the One Who answers the distressed ones when they supplicate."

{And enjoin the prayer on your family, and be patient in offering them [the prayers].}

(Qur'an 20: 132)

{...Indeed, prayer prohibits immorality and wrongdoing.}

(Qur'an 29: 45)

{Verily, the prayer is enjoined on the believers at fixed hours.}

(Qur'an 4: 103)

Sending prayers upon the Prophet (bpuh) also helps to remove hardship:

{O you who have believed, ask [Allah to confer] blessing upon him and ask [Allah to grant him] peace.}

(Qur'an 33: 56)

«Ubay ibn Ka'b asked the Messenger of Allah (bpuh): How much of my prayer should I dedicate to sending Ṣalât upon you? He replied: As much as you please. Ubay inquired: One-fourth? He responded: As much as you please, and if you increase, it is better. He questioned: Two-thirds? The Prophet answered: As much as you please, and if you increase, it is better. He then said: I will make it all for you. The Prophet responded: Then you will be forgiven, and your worries will be taken care of.»

The last line of the previous hadith proves that sending prayers and greetings on the Prophet (bpuh) removes worries.

«O Allah, send prayers (that is, praise and exalt him in the highest of gatherings, that of the closest angels to Allah) upon Muhammad and the followers of Muhammad, just as You sent prayers upon Abraham and upon the followers of Abraham. Verily, You are full of praise and majesty. O Allah, send blessings upon Muhammad and upon the family of Muhammad, just as You sent blessings upon Abraham and upon the family of Abraham. Verily, You are full of praise and majesty.»

Charity brings peace to the giver

Among the factors that contribute to one's happiness are performing acts of kindness to others and giving charity.

{Spend of that with which We have provided for you...}

(Qur'an 2: 254)

{The men and the women who give Ṣadaqah [that is, zakâh, and alms, et cetera].}

(Qur'an 33: 35)

{And the likeness of those who spend their wealth seeking Allah's pleasure while they in their ownselves are sure and certain that Allah will reward them [for their spending in His cause], is the likeness of a garden on a height: heavy rain falls on it and it doubles its yield of harvest. And if it does not receive heavy rain, light rain suffices it.}

(Qur'an 2: 265)

{And let not your hand be tied [like a miser] to your neck...}

(Qur'an 17: 29)

Miserly people are deplorable in their manners and are always ill at ease. They are stingy in sharing the favors of Allah. If the miser only knew that he would achieve happiness by spending money on those who are poor, then he would surely race to give charity.

{If you lend to Allah a goodly loan [that is, spend in Allah's cause] he will double it for you, and will forgive you.}

(Qur'an 64: 17)

{And whosoever is saved from his own covetousness, such are they who will be the successful.}

(Qur'an 59: 9)

{And those who spend out of what we have provided for them [that is, give zakâh, spend on themselves, their parents, their children, their wives, et cetera and also give charity to the poor and also in Allah's cause – jihad, et cetera].}

(Qur'an 2: 3)

A man said to his wife:

If you have prepared a meal, invite

A voracious eater, for I cannot bear to eat by myself.

Then he said to her, proclaiming his philosophy:

Name a generous person who died from being generous,

Or a miserly one who lived forever, and I will desist.

Don't be angry

{And if an evil whisper comes to you from Satan then seek refuge with Allah. Verily, He is All-Hearer, All-Knower.}

(Qur'an 7: 200)

The Prophet (bpuh) advised one of his Companions:

«Don't be angry...»

He repeated this three times. Once when a man became angry in his presence, the Prophet (bpuh) ordered him to seek refuge in Allah from the accursed Satan.

{And I seek refuge with You, My Lord! Lest they may attend [or come near] me.}

(Qur'an 23: 98)

{Indeed, those who fear Allah -when an impulse touches them from Satan, they remember [Him], and at once they have insight.}

(Qur'an 7: 201)

Anger is one of the factors that cause depression and sadness. The following are some of the ways of controlling your anger:

1. Combat feelings of anger as if anger itself is your enemy.

   {And those who repress anger, and who pardon men; verily, Allah loves the good-doers.}

   (Qur'an 3: 134)

   {And when they are angry, they forgive.}

   (Qur'an 42: 37)

   {And when the anger of Moses was appeased, he took up the Tablets...}

   (Qur'an 7:154)

2. Make ablution. Since anger is an ember of the fire, it can be extinguished by water.

3. If you are standing, sit; if you are sitting, lie down.

4. When you are angry, remain silent.

5. Remind yourself of the rewards of those who repress their anger and of those who forgive.

Supplications of the morning

If you say the supplications listed in this section on a daily basis, they will help to bring you happiness, protect you from the devils of humankind and jinn, and protect you for the remainder of your day, until the evening.

> «We have reached the evening, and at this very time unto Allah belongs all sovereignty, and all praise is for Allah. None has the right to be worshipped but Allah alone, without partner. To Him belongs all sovereignty and praise, and He is over all things omnipotent. My Lord, I ask You for the good of this night and the good of what follows it, and I take refuge in You from the evil of this night and the evil of what follows it. My Lord, I take refuge in You from laziness and senility. My Lord, I take refuge in you from the torment of the fire and punishment in the grave.»

> «O Allah, by Your leave we have reached the morning, and by Your leave we have reached the evening; by Your leave we live and die, and unto You is our resurrection.»

> «O Allah, verily I have reached the morning and call on You, the bearers of Your throne, Your angels, and all of Your creation to witness that You are Allah – none has the right to be worshipped except You alone, without partner – and that Muhammad is Your servant and Messenger.»

> «I take refuge in Allah's perfect words from the evil He has created.» (Three times)

> «O Allah, Knower of the unseen and the seen, Creator of the heavens and the Earth, Lord and Sovereign of all things, I bear witness that none has the right to be worshipped except You. I take refuge in You from the evil of my soul and from the evil and shirk (associating partners with Allah in worship) of the devil, and from committing wrong against my soul or bringing the same upon another Muslim.»

> «How perfect is Allah, and I praise Him by the number of His creation and His pleasure, and by the weight of His throne and the ink of His words.»

> «None has the right to be worshipped except Allah alone, without partner. To Him belongs all sovereignty and praise, and He is over all things omnipotent.»

> «We rise upon the fiṭrah (the religion of Islam, the way of Prophet Abraham), and the word of pure faith, and upon the religion of our Prophet Muhammad and the religion of our forefather Abraham, who was a Muslim of true faith and was not of those who associate partners with Allah.»

Pause to reflect

Those who have knowledge about Allah agree that when you get to the point of losing all hope, it means that Allah has entrusted to you your own affairs. When you have trust and hope in Allah, it means that Allah has guided you to goodness.

Allah's slaves are always swaying between the first state and the second. During the period of a single hour, we can have our share of both. So we obey Allah and please Him, remember Him and thank Him – and we are only able to do these through His help. Shortly afterwards, though, we disobey Allah, go against His commands, earn His anger, and are generally in a state of forgetfulness – all because Allah has left us to ourselves. Therefore Allah's slave is always oscillating between His divine care and being forsaken.

As Allah's slaves, whenever we witness this phenomenon -that of changing from one state to the other – we should appreciate the dubious nature of our situation and our extreme need to be guided by Allah (the Exalted) in every breath we take and in every moment we live. Our faith and belief are in Allah's hand. If Allah were to leave us alone for even the blinking of an eye, our faith would plunge to the ground. We should therefore realize that the One Who is protecting our faith is the One Who is preventing the sky from falling to the earth.

The Qur'an: The Blessed Book

When you recite the Qur'an and contemplate its meanings, you take a positive step toward achieving happiness. Allah described the Qur'an as being guidance, light, and a cure for what is in the breasts of people. He also described it as being a mercy.

{There has come to you a good advice from your Lord [that is, the Qur'an, ordering all that is good and forbidding all that is evil], and a healing for that [disease of ignorance, doubt, hypocrisy and differences, et cetera] which is in your breasts...}

(Qur'an 10: 57)

{Then do they not reflect upon the Qur'an, or are there locks upon [their] hearts?}

(Qur'an 47: 24)

{Do they not then consider the Qur'an carefully? Had it been from other than Allah, they would surely have found therein much contradiction.}

(Qur'an 4: 82)

{[This is] a Book [the Qur'an] which We have sent down to you, full of blessings that they may ponder over its verses.}

(Qur'an 38: 29)

Reciting the Qur'an is blessed, as are acting upon it and turning to it for judgment and guidance. A righteous person (and many have had a similar experience) once said:

> I felt that a cloud of depression and anxiety was hanging over me. I picked up the Qur'an, and I read it for a period of time. Then, by Allah, the depression and anxiety disappeared, and happiness along with tranquility took their place.

{Verily, this Qur'an guides to that which is most just and right…}

(Qur'an 17: 9)

{And thus We have revealed to you an inspiration of Our command.}

(Qur'an 42: 52)

Don't aspire to fame, or else you will be taxed with stress and worries

By seeking to be the center of attention and by trying to please others, you lose both peace and stability in your life.

{That home of the hereafter [that is, paradise], We shall assign to those who rebel not against the truth with pride and oppression in the land nor do mischief by committing crimes.}

(Qur'an 28: 83)

A poet said:

> Whoever is satisfied in following and not leading, brings serenity to himself and spends his nights peacefully.
>
> Verily, when the wind blows strong and violently,
>
> It only tosses about the high part of the tree.

{They stand with laziness and to be seen of men.}

(Qur'an 4: 142)

{And those who love to be praised for what they have not done…}

(Qur'an 3: 188)

{And be not like those who come out of their homes boastfully and to be seen of men…}

(Qur'an 8: 47)

A poet said:

Transparent is the gown of the one who does deeds for show,

Even if he wraps it around himself, he remains naked.

The good life

Everything that we discussed in previous chapters concerning happiness can be summed up in the following: Have faith in Allah, Lord of all that exists. All else that we mentioned hitherto is useless and is of no benefit unless you have faith in Allah. Believing in Allah (the Exalted) as your Lord, in Muhammad as His Messenger and in Islam as your religion – these must be your foundations.

{Whoever works righteousness, whether male or female, while he [or she] is a true believer [of Islamic monotheism] verily, to him We will give a good life [in this world with respect, contentment and lawful provision], and We shall pay them certainly a reward in proportion to the best of what they used to do [that is, paradise in the hereafter].}

(Qur'an 16: 97)

There are two conditions for gaining a good life: faith in Allah and performing good deeds.

{Verily, those who believe and work deeds of righteousness, the Most Beneficent [Allah] will bestow love for them [in the hearts of the believers].}

(Qur'an 19: 96)

The one who believes in Allah (the Exalted) and does good deeds derives two benefits:

1. A good and prosperous life in this world and in the hereafter.

2. A tremendous reward from Allah (the Exalted).

{For them are glad tidings in the life of the present world and in the hereafter.} (Qur'an 10: 64)

Bear trials patiently

Don't let hardships bother you excessively. The Prophet (bpuh) said:

> «Verily, if Allah loves a people, He makes them go through trials. Whoever is satisfied, for him is contentment, and whoever is angry, upon him is wrath.»

Worship Allah by surrendering your will to Him

Among the necessities or elements of faith is to be contented with all that is decreed: both what is good and what is bad.

> {And certainly, We shall test you with something of fear, hunger, loss of wealth, lives and fruits, but give glad tidings to the patient ones.}
>
> *(Qur'an 2: 155)*

What is decreed for us is not always in harmony with our desires, but then we are not in a position to give suggestions. On the contrary, the appropriate station and position for us is that of worshippers who surrender their wills.

We are all tested according to the level of our faith. The Prophet (bpuh) said:

> «The pangs of death I feel are equal to what two of your men feel.»

> «The most severely tested of people are the Prophets and then the righteous ones.»

> {Therefore be patient [O Muhammad] as were the Messengers of strong will...}
>
> *(Qur'an 46: 35)*

If Allah (the Exalted) wants good for a person, He afflicts him.

> {And surely, We shall try you until We test those who strive hard [for the cause of Allah] and the patient ones, and We shall test your facts [that is, the one who is a liar, and the one who is truthful].}
>
> *(Qur'an 47: 31)*

> {And We indeed tested those who were before them.}
>
> *(Qur'an 29: 3)*

From governor to carpenter

'Ali ibn al-Maymoon al-'Abbassi was a governor and the son of the caliph. He lived a life of opulence in a large castle. Anything he wanted in this world was easy for him.

One day, looking down from a balcony in the castle, he saw a man toiling in the fields. On succeeding days, 'Ali paid more and more attention to the man and witnessed that he always worked straight through the morning, after which he would take a break, make ablution from a stream, and pray two units of prayer. Only when the evening came would he quit his work and go home to his family. To learn more about him, 'Ali invited him one day and asked him many questions. He soon learned that the worker had a wife, two sisters, and a mother that were all under his care, and it was for their sake that he toiled so assiduously. He fasted every day, and when nightfall came, he would break his fast from what he had reaped during the day. 'Ali asked, "And do you have any cause to complain?" He answered, "No. All praise is due to Allah, Lord of all that exists."

'Ali was so impressed by the simple laborer that he left the castle, resigned from his position, and traveled abroad. He was found dead years later in the vicinity of Khorasan. After leaving the castle, he had worked as a carpenter, and he found happiness in his new life – happiness that had eluded him in his former life.

{While as for those who accept guidance, He increases their guidance, and bestows on them their piety.}

(Qur'an 47: 17)

This narrative reminds me of the story of the People of the Cave. They were in a castle with the king, yet they felt constricted, confused, and troubled. The life of opulence, for the most part, is one wherein disbelief and extravagance reign. So they departed, and one of them said:

{Then seek refuge in the cave; your Lord will open a way for you from His mercy and will make easy for you your affair [that is, will give you what you will need of provision, dwelling, et cetera].}

(Qur'an 18: 16)

Mixing with people of low character ruins a person's peace

Books written by eminent Islamic scholars are replete with sayings that indicate an aversion to people who are referred to as being thaqeel, which means burdensome. They are people whose company is unbearable. Imam Aḥmad said that they are the people of innovation. Some have said that they are the foolish ones in society, and others have stated that they are people with coarse personalities, or that they are people of cold and colorless character.

{They are as blocks of wood propped up.}

(Qur'an 63: 4)

{So what is wrong with these people that they fail to understand any word?}

(Qur'an 4: 78)

Imam Shâfi'i said: When a dull person comes to sit with me, I begin to feel that the earth beneath him is sinking from the heaviness of his company.

Al-A'mash, upon seeing this kind of person, would recite:

{Our Lord! Remove the torment from us, really we shall become believers!}

(Qur'an 44: 12)

Allah (the Exalted) said:

{And when you see those who engage in a false conversation about Our verses [of the Qur'an] by mocking them, stay away from them...}

(Qur'an 6: 68)

{...Then sit not with them...}

(Qur'an 4: 140)

People who are devoid of virtues, who have low aims, and who easily succumb to their desires are among the most unbearable of people to share company with:

{Then sit not with them, until they engage in a talk other than that; [but if you stayed with them] certainly in that case you would be like them.}

(Qur'an 4: 140)

A poet said:

Your company upon me is heavy, heavy, heavy,

You are in appearance a man yet an elephant in the scale of bad company.

Ibn al-Qayyim said:

If you are forced to converse with someone who is unbearable, lend him your body and deny him your spirit, and travel away with your soul. Lend him a deaf ear and a blind eye until Allah makes a way for you to part from his company.

{And obey not him whose heart We have made heedless of Our remembrance, one who follows his own lusts and whose affair [deeds] has been lost.}

(Qur'an 18: 28)

For the calamity-stricken

In an authentic hadith, the Prophet (bpuh) related that Allah (the Exalted) said:

«When I have taken away from someone a most beloved one [to him], and then he [patiently] expects a reward [from Me], I will compensate him with paradise.»

In another authentic hadith, the Prophet (bpuh) related that Allah (the Exalted) said:

«Whoever I have tested in his two beloved ones -meaning his eyes [by taking away his sight] – I will compensate him for them with paradise.»

{Verily, it is not the eyes that grow blind, but it is the hearts which are in the breasts that grow blind.}

(Qur'an 22: 46)

In an authentic hadith related by Tirmidhi, the Prophet (bpuh) said:

«Verily, when Allah takes away the son of one of His believing slaves, He says to the angels: Have you taken the son of my believing slave? They answer: Yes. He then says: You took (away) the fruit of his heart? They answer: Yes. Allah (the Exalted) says: What did My slave say? They answer: He praised you and said: Verily, to Allah do we all belong, and to Him is our return. Allah orders them: Build for My slave a house in paradise, and call it the house of praise.»

{Only those who are patient shall receive their rewards in full, without reckoning.}

(Qur'an 39: 10)

{Salâmun 'Alaykum [peace be upon you] for that you persevered in patience!}

(Qur'an 13: 24)

{Our Lord! Pour forth on us patience.}

(Qur'an 2: 250)

{And endure you patiently [O Muhammad]; your patience is not but from Allah.}

(Qur'an 16: 127)

{So be patient [O Muhammad]. Verily, the promise of Allah is true.}

(Qur'an 30: 60)

The Prophet (bpuh) said:

«Verily, the greatness of reward is proportionate to the greatness of the test. Indeed, if Allah loves a people, He tests them. Whoever is contented, for him is pleasure, and whoever is angry, upon him is wrath.»

Patience, preordainment, and reward from Allah are important issues to be considered when calamity strikes, and we should know that the One Who took away is the One Who gave in the first place.

{Verily! Allah commands that you should render back the trusts to those to whom they are due.}

(Qur'an 4: 58)

A poet said:

Wealth and family are only loans for a period.

And the day must come when a loan is returned.

The positive effects of having true faith in Allah alone

Only when you are the victim of some wrongdoing do certain positive effects of Islamic monotheism become manifest in your life. When others hurt you, remember that having faith in Allah (the Exalted) will help you in many ways:

1. By having a strong faith in Allah, you will forgive those who transgress against you. Better yet is to have good wishes for those same people, and the highest and best level – higher than simply forgiving them or wishing them well – is to benefit or help them in some way. The first stage of forgiveness is to repress your anger, which means that you don't reciprocate injury with injury. Then comes actual forgiveness, which means to pardon and to discard any feelings of ill will. The final stage is to do good, in other words, to recompense the harm done to you by doing a good deed or showing kindness to them.

   {Those who repress anger, and who pardon men; verily, Allah loves the good-doers.}

   (Qur'an 3: 134)

   {But whoever forgives and makes reconciliation, his reward is due from Allah.}

   (Qur'an 42: 40)

   {Let them pardon and forgive.}

   (Qur'an 24: 22)

   It is reported that the Prophet (bpuh) said:

   «Verily, Allah has ordered me to join (seek to make relations amicable) with the one who has cut me off, to forgive the one who wronged me, and to give to the one who refused me.»

2. You will develop a stronger faith in preordainment. In other words, you will realize that the person who injured you only did so based on Allah's preordainment and decree.

   People are only means, but the One Who decrees and decides is Allah, so surrender your will to Him.

3. You will realize that the harm that was perpetrated against you was atonement for your sins and can result in an increase in ranking with Allah.

   {So those who emigrated and were driven out from their homes, and suffered harm in My cause, and who fought, and were killed [In My cause], verily, I will remit from them their evil deeds...}

   (Qur'an 3: 195)

Be Happy

The believers are able to perceive that putting out the fire of enmity is a wise course to follow in life:

{Repel [evil] by that [deed] which is better, and thereupon the one whom between you and him is enmity [will become] as though he was a devoted friend.}

(Qur'an 41: 34)

«The Muslim is he from whose tongue and hand other Muslims are safe.»

The meaning of the previous verse is that you should repay the ones who harm you, by means of a pleasant face and gentle words. Thus you will be able to extinguish the fire of hatred from their hearts.

{And say to My slaves [that is, the true believers of Islamic monotheism] that they should [only] say those words that are the best. [Because] Satan indeed sows disagreements among them.}

(Qur'an 17: 53)

4. You will come to know your shortcomings. In other words, you will be aware of the fact that a person was afforded the opportunity to harm you because of your own sins.

{[What is the matter with you?] When a single disaster smites you, although you smote [your enemies] with one twice as great, you say: From where does this come to us? Say [to them]: It is from yourselves [because of your evil deeds].}

(Qur'an 3: 165)

{And whatever of misfortune befalls you, it is because of what your hands have earned.}

(Qur'an 42: 30)

5. When you are wronged, praise and thank Allah for making you the oppressed one and not the oppressor. Some of our pious predecessors used to say, "O Allah, cause me to be the oppressed one and not the oppressor."

This tone is similar to that of the worthier of Adam's two sons when he said to the other:

{If you do stretch your hand against me to kill me, I shall never stretch my hand against you to kill you, for I fear Allah; the Lord of the 'Ālameen [humankind, jinns, and all that exists].}

(Qur'an 5: 28)

6. You should show mercy to the ones who hurt you. They are deserving of your pity and mercy. Their persistence in doing evil and in openly challenging Allah's commandment of not hurting a Muslim makes them worthy recipients of your gentleness and mercy. Perhaps you can save them from their downfall. The Prophet (bpuh) said:

«Help your brother, whether he is an oppressor or he is oppressed.»

When Misṭaḥ harmed Abu Bakr (may Allah be pleased with him) by tainting the honor of him and his daughter 'Â'ishah, Abu Bakr vowed to cut off any further support for him. Prior to that, Abu Bakr used to spend on Misṭaḥ and support him because he was poor. Forthwith, Allah (the Exalted) sent down this verse:

{And let not those among you who are blessed with graces and wealth swear not to give [any sort of help] to their kinsmen, al-Masâkeen [the poor], and those who left their homes for Allah's cause. Let them pardon and forgive. Do you not love that Allah should forgive you?}

(Qur'an 24: 22)

Abu Bakr said, "Yes, I do love that Allah should forgive me." He then resumed spending on Misṭaḥ, and he also forgave him.

'Uyaynah ibn Ḥasan said to 'Umar (may Allah be pleased with him), "O 'Umar, what is this? By Allah, you don't give us generously, and you don't judge justly between us." 'Umar moved towards him, but al-Ḥurr ibn Qays said:

O Commander of the Faithful, Allah (the Exalted) says:

{Show forgiveness, enjoin what is good, and turn away from the foolish [that is, don't punish them].}

(Qur'an 7: 199)

Al-Ḥurr later said:

By Allah, 'Umar did not go beyond the bounds of this verse. And he always stopped (without transgressing the limits set by Allah) and followed what is in the Book of Allah.

Prophet Joseph (pbuh) said to his brothers:

{No reproach on you this day, may Allah forgive you, and He is the Most Merciful of those who show mercy!}

(Qur'an 12: 92)

When the Messenger of Allah (bpuh) returned to Makkah victorious, he saw the faces of those who had hurt him, expelled him, and then waged war on him from among the disbelievers of Quraysh. He announced to them:

«Go forth, for you are the freed ones.»

He said in another hadith:

«The strong one is not he who is strong in combat. Verily, the strong one is he who controls himself when he is angry.»

A poet said:

If you are in the company of a loving people,

Treat them with the softness of a loving relative,

And don't take people to account for all of their mistakes,

So as not to stay companionless throughout your life.

Some have said that in the Gospel, it is written, "Forgive seven times the one who wronged you once."

This means that when someone wrongs you one time, repeat your forgiveness of this person seven times, in order to keep your religion safe and your heart clean. Desiring revenge will only subtract from your nerves, sleep, stability, and peace, while taking nothing away from others.

{But whoever forgives and makes reconciliation, his reward is due from Allah.}

(Qur'an 42: 40)

The Indians say in one of their proverbs, "The one who overcomes his own self is more brave than the one who conquers a city."

{Verily, the [human] self is inclined to evil...}

(Qur'an 12: 53)

Take care of your outside as well as your inside

A person who has a pure soul cares about wearing clean clothes. Some wise people have even said, "When one's garment becomes soiled, his soul will follow suit."

The root of vexation for many people is in being neither neat nor organized nor punctual; for others, it is in having bad hygiene, dirty clothes, or a sloppy appearance.

The universe is based on order. In fact, to truly understand the depth and wisdom of our religion, one should appreciate that it came to organize our lives in both small and large matters. Everything with Allah (the Exalted) is according to a measure. Tirmidhi related the following hadith:

«Verily, Allah is beautiful and He loves beauty.»

Imam Bukhari related the following hadith in his Ṣaḥeeḥ: «It is a right (incumbent) upon a Muslim to take a shower at least one day out of every seven. In it, he washes his head and his body.»

This is the least that can be expected. Some of our pious predecessors would take a shower once a day, as has been transmitted to us about 'Uthmân ibn 'Affân (may Allah be pleased with him).

{This is a spring of water to wash in, cool and a [refreshing] drink.}

(Qur'an 38: 42)

Growing a beard, trimming one's moustache, cutting one's nails, brushing one's teeth, using perfume, washing one's clothes, and generally taking care of one's outward appearance – these are all acts that are intrinsic to people. Performing these acts of hygiene makes one feel comfortable and good. It is also recommended to wear white, for the Prophet (bpuh) said:

«Wear white, and use it as a shroud for your dead.»

You should organize your appointments in a small journal or notebook, allocating time to read, to worship, to exercise, and so on.

{[For] each and every matter there is a decree [from Allah].}

(Qur'an 13: 38)

{And there is not a thing, but with Us are the stores thereof. And We send it not down except in a known measure.} (Qur'an 15: 21)

In the Library of Congress hangs a large placard on which is written, "The Universe is Based on Order"'. This is true, for the divinely revealed religion calls for order, organization, and harmony in action.

Allah informed us that the affairs of the universe are not based on play and frivolity, but are by preordainment, decree, measurement, and organization.

{The sun and the moon run on their fixed courses [exactly] calculated with measured out stages for each [for reckoning, et cetera].}

(Qur'an 55: 5)

{It is not for the sun to overtake the moon, nor does the night outstrip the day. They all float, each in an orbit.}

(Qur'an 36: 40)

{And the moon, We have measured for it mansions [to traverse] until it returns like the old dried curved date stalk.}

(Qur'an 36: 39)

{And We have made the night and day two signs, and We erased the sign of the night and made the sign of the day visible that you may seek bounty from your Lord and may know the number of years and the account [of time]. And everything We have set out in detail.}

(Qur'an 17: 12)

{Our Lord! You have not created [all] this without purpose, glory be to You!}

(Qur'an 3: 191)

{And We did not create the heaven and earth and that between them in play. Had We intended to take a diversion, We could have taken it from [what is] with Us -if [indeed] We were to do so.}

(Qur'an 21: 16-17)

{And say: Do [as you will], for Allah will see your deeds.}

(Qur'an 9: 105)

When mentally ill patients were brought to the sages of Greece for treatment, they would be forced to work in farming and in gardens. Only a short time would pass before they would return to good health.

Tradesmen who work with their hands are, as a class, more happy, easygoing, and calm than others. If you observe laborers, you will notice strength of body and peace of mind. Both of these are consequences of a satisfaction that comes with movement, exercise, and work.

«And I seek refuge in You (Allah) from incapability and laziness.»

Seek refuge with Allah

Allah: the great and glorious name. Going back to the root of the word, we learn a special meaning. Some say that the name Allah comes from the root A-La-Ha. This means the one whom the hearts of people love, find peace in, are happy with, turn to, and accept as their God. Also, it is impossible for the heart to find peace or comfort with other than Him. For this reason, Fâṭimah (may Allah be pleased with her) taught her daughter the supplication of the one who is in distress:

«Allah, Allah, My Lord, I do not associate any partners with Him.»

{Say: Allah [sent it down]. Then leave them to play in their vain discussions.}

(Qur'an 6: 91)

{And He is the Irresistible, above His slaves...}

(Qur'an 6: 18)

{Allah is very Gracious and Kind to His slaves.}

(Qur'an 42: 19)

{They made not a just estimate of Allah such as is due to Him. And on the Day of Resurrection the whole of the earth will be grasped by His hand and the heavens will be rolled up in His right hand. Glorified be He, and High is He above all that they associate as partners with Him!}

(Qur'an 39: 67)

{And [remember] the day when We shall roll up the heavens like a scroll rolled up for books...}

(Qur'an 21: 104)

{Verily! Allah grasps the heavens and the earth lest they should move away from their places.}

(Qur'an 35: 41)

Trust Him completely

Always turning to Allah (the Exalted), placing one's trust in Him, and being satisfied with His care and protection – these are among the most important of factors that bring happiness to the believer.

{Do you know of any similarity to Him?}

(Qur'an 19: 65)

{Indeed, my protector is Allah, Who has sent down the Book, and He is an ally to the righteous.}

(Qur'an 7: 196)

{Unquestionably, [for] the allies of Allah there will be no fear concerning them, nor will they grieve.}

(Qur'an 10: 62)

They agree on three points

After steeping myself in books that deal with anxiety and mental ailments, I found that Muslim scholars agree upon three fundamentals for those who seek a cure:

1. They should have a close relationship with Allah, by worshipping Him, being obedient to Him, and turning to Him when in hardship or in ease. This is the paramount issue in faith:

   {So worship Him and have patience for His worship. Do you know of any similarity to Him?}

   (Qur'an 19: 65)

2. They must close the files of the past. Episodes of the past, which when recalled only induce pain, should be forgotten and eradicated from their memory. Thus, a new life for a new day!

3. They should leave the future alone. Whatever has yet to occur is from the world of the unseen; it should be left alone until it comes.

More particularly, they should avoid being preoccupied with predictions, expectations, and apprehensions. Life should be lived within the boundaries of today. 'Ali (may Allah be pleased with him) said, "Beware of having long-term expectations (for this world), for verily it makes one forget (his true purpose)."

{And they thought that they would never return to Us.}

(Qur'an 28: 39)

Beware of believing in superstitions and rumors:

{They think that every cry is against them.}

(Qur'an 63: 4)

I know people who for years now have been waiting for predictions of disaster and calamity to come true, predictions that, at least until now, have not materialized. They are putting fear into their own hearts and the hearts of others. (How perfect is Allah!) Leading such a life is pathetic and deplorable. The example of these people is that of the tortured prisoner in China, whose captors place him under a tap, releasing from it a drop of water every minute. The prisoner desperately waits for each drop until he loses his mind. Allah (the Exalted) described the people of the fire in the following verses:

{Neither it will have a complete killing effect on them so that they die, nor shall its torment be lightened for them.}

(Qur'an 35: 36)

{Wherein he will neither die [to be in rest] nor live [a good living].}

(Qur'an 87: 13)

{As often as their skins are roasted through, We shall change them for other skins that they may taste the punishment.}

(Qur'an 4: 56)

The wrongdoing of the transgressor

To judgment is our destination on the Day of Gathering,

And in front of Allah will be gathered all adversaries.

Sufficient justice and retribution for the believer is that he waits for the day wherein Allah will gather the first and the last (of creation). The judge on that day will be Allah (the Exalted), and the witnesses will be the angels:

{And We shall set up balances of justice on the Day of Resurrection, then none will be dealt with unjustly in anything. And if there be the weight of a mustard seed, We will bring it. And sufficient are We as reckoners.} (Qur'an 21: 47)

Khosrau and the old woman

Buzrjamhar, the wise man of Persia, related the story of Khosrau the king and the old woman. The woman possessed a chicken and a small hut, which was situated on a small plot of land that bordered the palace of Khosrau. One day, she had to travel to another village, and before departing she prayed, "O my Lord, I entrust my chicken to You." During her absence, Khosrau usurped her property in order to expand the gardens of his palace. His army slaughtered the chicken and destroyed the cottage. When she returned and discovered the deplorable act, she turned her gaze to the sky and said, "O my Lord, I was absent and where were You?" Then Allah the Exalted, the All-Powerful granted revenge for her. It came to pass that the son of Khosrau attacked his father with a knife and killed him.

{Is not Allah sufficient for His slave? Yet they try to frighten you with those [whom they worship] besides Him! And whom Allah sends astray, for him there will be no guide.}

(Qur'an 39: 36)

Would that we were all like the worthier of Adam's sons, who said to the other:

{If you do stretch your hand against me to kill me, I shall never stretch my hand against you to kill you...}

(Qur'an 5: 28)

The Prophet (bpuh) said:

«Be the slave of Allah, the murdered, and not the slave of Allah, the murderer.»

The Muslim has a mission and a message that are more important than revenge, malice, and hate.

A handicap in one area can be compensated for by excellence in another

{Consider it not a bad thing for you. Nay, it is good for you.}

(Qur'an 24: 11)

Most people who are remembered today for their greatness had to overcome many obstacles on their path: their perseverance was akin to obstinacy. They felt a weakness in one faculty or area that required compensation in another. Many great scholars of Islam were actually freed slaves. Many Islamic scholars, who in the vastness of their knowledge were like oceans, were afflicted with blindness – Ibn 'Abbâs (may Allah be pleased with him), Qatâdah, Ibn Umm Maktoom (may Allah be pleased with him), al-A'mash and Yazeed ibn Hâroon, to mention only a few.

Among contemporary scholars, Shaykh Muhammad ibn Ibrâheem Âl-Shaykh, Shaykh 'Abdullâh ibn Humayd, and Shaykh Ibn Bâz are all blind.

Many great scholars had physical disabilities of some sort; some were blind, others were deaf, and yet others were missing limbs. Despite this, they influenced generations to come, and they were able to contribute a great deal to humankind.

{... He will give you a light by which you shall walk [straight]...}

(Qur'an 57: 28)

A diploma from a prestigious university is not everything. Do not be down or despondent because you weren't able to earn a university degree. Even without a diploma in your hand, you can still shine and contribute greatly to humankind. There are many famous and eminent people who do not have degrees. They made their way in life and overcame insurmountable obstacles with an iron will and a strong determination. Speaking of present day Islamic scholars, there are many prominent ones without degrees. Shaykh Ibn Bâz, Malik ibn Nabi, al-'Aqqâd, at-Tantawi, Abi-Zahrah, al-Mawdoodi, and an-Nadawi all come to mind as examples, yet there are many more.

On the other hand, there are thousands of holders of Ph.D. degrees in the Islamic world who remain obscure and who have had no impact on society.

{Can you [O Muhammad] find a single one of them or hear even a whisper of them?}

(Qur'an 19: 98)

You have a great treasure with you if you are of the type who is contented with any situation. The Prophet (bpuh) said in an authentic hadith:

«Be contented with what Allah has apportioned for you, and you will be the richest of people.»

Be contented with your family, your income, your car, and your job. If you are contented with all of these, then you will have found happiness and peace. In another authentic hadith, the Prophet (bpuh) said:

«Richness is the richness of the soul.»

He also said:

«O Allah, make his wealth be in his heart.»

A man related that he once got into a taxi at the airport and ordered the driver to take him to the city. He said:

I noticed that the driver was happy and good-humored. He would constantly praise Allah, thank Him, and remember Him. I asked him about his family, and he said that he was the breadwinner for two families. Meanwhile, his monthly salary was a paltry sum of 800 Riyals, and he and his family had to live in a run-down building. Yet his mind was at peace because he was thankful for what Allah had allotted for him.

The narrator went on to say,

I felt amazed when I compared this man to others who lead a life of affluence – with money, luxury cars, and large mansions. In spite of such opulence, they live such miserable lives, and upon reflection, I realized that happiness is not in wealth.

I knew a tycoon who had hundreds of millions and a number of mansions. He was miserable in his relationships, always seething with anger and always brooding in a state of depression. He died estranged from his family, and he went through all of this misery because he was not satisfied with what Allah gave him.

{After all that he desires -that I should give more: Nay! Verily, he has been stubborn and opposing Our Âyât [proofs, evidences, verses, lessons, signs, revelations, et cetera].}

(Qur'an 74: 15-16)

Centuries ago in Arabia, one would find peace by isolating oneself in the desert. In the desert and far away from human activity, a poet said:

The whine of the fox, I've developed a liking for it,

Then I heard the voice of a man and I almost flew away (out of contempt for it).

Sufyân ath-Thawri said, "I long to be in an obscure valley without anyone knowing me."

The Prophet (bpuh) said in a hadith:

«The time is near when the best wealth of a Muslim will be sheep, with which he follows the places of rain and the paths of mountains; he will be fleeing with his religion from trials.»

In times of tribulation (meaning the struggles of Muslims among themselves), the safest option for a Muslim is to run away from them. When 'Uthmân was wrongfully murdered, Ibn 'Umar, Usâmah ibn Zayd, and Muhammad ibn Muslimah all stayed away from the ensuing discord, may Allah be pleased with them all.

I know people who have been afflicted with poverty, misery, and depression. In every case, the cause of their downfall was that they were far away from Allah. You will find that one of them was rich, comfortable, and in a state of good health from his Lord. But then he turned away from the obedience of Allah. He was negligent in performing his prayers and he began to commit major sins. So Allah, the Almighty, took away his health and wealth and replaced them with the hardships of poverty, worry, and anxiety. He went from misery to misery, from a low point to a point that was even lower.

{But whosoever turns away from My reminder [that is, neither believes in this Qur'an nor acts on its orders, et cetera] verily, for him is a life of hardship...}

(Qur'an 20: 124)

{That is so because Allah will never change a grace which He has bestowed on a people until they change what is in their ownselves.}

(Qur'an 8: 53)

{And whatever of misfortune befalls you, it is because of what your hands have earned. And He pardons much.}

(Qur'an 42: 30)

{If they [non-Muslims] had believed in Allah, and went on the right way [that is, Islam] We should surely have bestowed on them water [rain] in abundance.}

(Qur'an 72: 16)

If I were able to perform a miracle, I would remove from you your troubles and grief; however, being unable to do to, I will suffice by prescribing for you a prescription that is given by the scholars of Islam. It is to worship the Creator (without associating any partner with Him in worship), to be contented with your provision, to live moderately, and to decrease the level of your expectations for this life.

The famous American psychologist, William James, spoke these words that caught my attention:

We, humankind, brood over what we don't own, and we don't thank God for what we do own. We always dwell on the tragic and dark side of our lives, and we don't look at the brighter side of our existence. We rue over what is missing in our lives and we are not happy with what is there.

{If you give thanks [by accepting faith and worshipping none but Allah], I will give you more [of My blessings]...}

(Qur'an 14: 7)

The Messenger of Allah (bpuh) supplicated:

«And I seek refuge in Allah from a soul that is insatiable.»

When your main concern becomes the hereafter, Allah will make things go well for you and will cause richness to dwell in your heart. The world will come to you despite its unwillingness. When this world becomes your main concern, Allah will scatter your affairs and place poverty between your eyes; also, the world will not come to you, except what was decreed for you.

{If you were to ask them: Who has created the heavens and the earth and subjected the sun and the moon? They would surely reply: Allah. How then are they deviating [as polytheists and disbelievers]?}

(Qur'an 29: 61)

A few words about the foolish

In the magazine ar-Risâlah, I found an interesting article on Communism, written by Zayyât. The Soviet Union sent a spacecraft to outer space, and after it returned, one of their astronauts was quoted in Pravda as saying, "We ascended to the sky, and we found no god there, no paradise, no hell, and no angels."

In response, Zayyât wrote:

> Truly amazing you are, O red fools. Do you think that you will see Allah on His throne in the open? Do you have the temerity to think that you will see the maidens of paradise walking around in silk? Or that you will hear the flowing of al-Kawthar (a river in paradise)? Or that you will smell the stench of those being punished in the fire? If you truly thought this, then your loss and failure is open for all to see. All that I can think of to explain your misguidance, wandering, and foolishness is the communism and atheism in your heads. Communism is a day without a tomorrow, a ground without a sky, work without an end, and a constant toiling without results...

{Or do you think that most of them hear or reason? They are not except like livestock. Rather, they are [even] more astray in [their] way.}

(Qur'an 25: 44)

{They have hearts wherewith they understand not, they have eyes wherewith they see not, and they have ears wherewith they hear not [the truth].}

(Qur'an 7: 179)

{And whomsoever Allah disgraces, none can honor him.}

(Qur'an 22: 18)

{Their deeds are like a mirage in a desert.}

(Qur'an 24: 39)

{...Their works are as ashes, on which the wind blows furiously on a stormy day...}

(Qur'an 14: 18)

In A Religion of Defects, al-'Aqqâd inveighed against communism and its false premise of atheism:

> The soul that is intrinsically sound accepts this true religion of Islam. As for those whose minds are crippled, or who have base and shortsighted ideas, it is plausible for them to be atheists.

﴾Their hearts are sealed up [from all kinds of goodness and right guidance], so they understand not.﴿

(Qur'an 9: 87)

Atheism is a death blow to one's thinking. It is an idea that is as farfetched as any imaginary world that a child is able to conjure up, and it is an error unsurpassed in the annals of errors. That is why Allah (the Exalted) says:

﴾What! Can there be a doubt about Allah, the Creator of the heavens and the earth?﴿

(Qur'an 14: 10)

Ibn Taymiyah said, "The Creator's existence has not been openly denied by anyone except Pharaoh, and even he recognized Him on the inside." That is why Prophet Moses said:

﴾Moses said: Verily, you know that these signs have been sent down by none but the Lord of the heavens and the earth as clear [evidences that is, proofs of Allah's Oneness and His Omnipotence, et cetera]. And I think you are, indeed, O Pharaoh, doomed to destruction [away from all good]!﴿

(Qur'an 17: 102)

Pharaoh proclaimed the following at the very end (when it was too late), revealing what was in his heart:

﴾He said: I believe that none has the right to be worshipped but He, in Whom the children of Israel believe, and I am one of the Muslims [those who submit to Allah's will].﴿

(Qur'an 10: 90)

Faith in Allah is the way to salvation

{And my affair I leave it to Allah.}

(Qur'an 40: 44)

{No calamity befalls, but with the leave [that is, decision and divine preordainments] of Allah, and whosoever believes in Allah, He guides his heart [to the true faith with certainty]...}

(Qur'an 64: 11)

Allah guides the heart of one who recognizes that a calamity is by preordainment and decree.

{He releases them from their heavy burdens [of Allah's Covenant], and from the fetters [bindings] that were upon them.}

(Qur'an 7: 157)

Some eminent Western writers – such as Alexis Carrel and Dale Carnegie – readily admit that the savior of the material-minded, declining West is a belief in Allah. They propound the view that the reason behind the increasingly alarming phenomenon of suicide in the West is atheism and a lack of faith in Allah, Lord of all that exists.

{Those who wander astray from the path of Allah [shall] have a severe torment, because they forgot the Day of Reckoning.}

(Qur'an 38: 26)

{And whoever assigns partners to Allah, it is as if he had fallen from the sky, and the birds had snatched him, or the wind had thrown him to a far off place.}

(Qur'an 22: 31)

Quzmân was at the battle of Uḥud, fighting on the side of the Muslims. He fought intrepidly and fiercely. The people exclaimed, "For him is the bliss of paradise." The Prophet (bpuh) said:

«Verily, He is from the dwellers of the fire!»

Why? Because when his wounds were serious, instead of being patient, he took his own life with his sword.

{Those whose efforts have been wasted in this life while they thought that they were acquiring good by their deeds!}

(Qur'an 18: 104)

﴾But whosoever turns away from My reminder [that is, neither believes in this Qur'an nor acts on its orders, et cetera] verily, for him is a life of hardship, and We shall raise him up blind on the Day of Resurrection.﴿

(Qur'an 20: 124)

A Muslim does not take the path of suicide, no matter how severe the hardship. Two units of prayer that are performed with humility and presence of mind after making ablution will guarantee the banishment of anxiety and worry from your life.

﴾So bear patiently what they say, and glorify the praises of your Lord before the rising of the sun, and before its setting, and during some of the hours of the night, and at the sides of the day [an indication for the five compulsory congregational prayers], that you may become pleased with the reward which Allah shall give you.﴿

(Qur'an 20: 130)

In the Qur'an there is a cogent and powerful question for the misguided ones:

﴾What is the matter with them, that they believe not?﴿

(Qur'an 84: 20)

What is it that makes them swerve away from belief, while the proofs and signs are clear?

﴾We will show them Our signs in the universe, and in their own selves, until it becomes manifest to them that this [the Qur'an] is the truth.﴿

(Qur'an 41: 53)

﴾And whosoever submits his face [himself] to Allah, while he is a good-doer, then he has grasped the most trustworthy handhold [none has the right to be worshipped except Allah].﴿

(Qur'an 31: 22)

Even the disbelievers are at different levels

George H. W. Bush wrote in his memoirs that he had attended the funeral of Brezhnev, who had been the President of the Soviet Union. Bush said, "I found the funeral to be dark and morbid; it was devoid of faith and spirit." He said this because he is Christian and they were atheists.

﴾And you will find the nearest in love to the believers [Muslims] those who say: We are Christians.﴿ (Qur'an 5: 82)

Observe that although he is misguided, he was able to discern their falsehood. Thus, the matter becomes relative. How matters would have been different had he known Islam, the true religion of Allah!

{And whoever seeks a religion other than Islam, it will never be accepted of him, and in the hereafter he will be one of the losers.}

(Qur'an 3: 85)

This incident brought to my mind a saying of Ibn Taymiyah. A member of a deviant Sufi sect asked him:

Why is it that when we come to you (the people of the Sunnah), our miracles lose their effect and become useless, but when we go to the Mongolian disbelieving Tartars, our miracles work?

Ibn Taymiyah replied:

Do you know what the example of you, the Tartars, and us is? As for us, we are white horses. You are spotted horses, and the Tartars are black ones. When the spotted one enters upon a throng of black, he appears to be white. And when he enters upon a crowd of white, he appears to be black. Now, you have some remnants of light, and when you mix with the people of disbelief, that light becomes visible. But when you come to us, the people of the Sunnah who have the greater light, your blackness and darkness is all that is left for you. And this is the example of you, the Tartars, and us.

{And for those whose faces will become white, they will be in Allah's mercy [paradise], therein they shall dwell forever.} (Qur'an 3: 107)

An iron will

A student from a Muslim country went to London to study. He boarded with a British family in order to enhance his language skills. He was true to his religious principles and would wake up early for the morning prayer. He would make his ablution, go to his place of prayer, prostrate to his Lord, glorify Him, and praise Him. An elderly woman in the house was always keen to observe his foreign habits. She asked him after a few days, "What are you doing?" "My religion orders me to do this," was his reply.

"Couldn't you delay saying this prayer until after you get your complete rest?" He answered, "But my Lord does not accept from me my prayer if I delay it until after its fixed time period." She shook her head and exclaimed, "A will that shatters steel!"

{Men whom neither trade nor sale diverts them from the remembrance of Allah [with heart and tongue], nor from performing the prayers.}

(Qur'an 24: 37)

Such action springs from the determination of faith, which was inspired to the sorcerers of Pharaoh. They were inspired to believe in Allah, the Lord of all that exists, at the moment when Prophet Moses (pbuh) and Pharaoh faced off against one another. They said to Pharaoh:

{We prefer you not over the clear signs that have come to us, and to Him [Allah] Who created us. So decree whatever you desire to decree.}

(Qur'an 20: 72)

It was a challenge to Pharaoh that was unheard of up until that moment. Their mission suddenly became to convey the true and powerful message of Islam to the haughty atheist.

Ḥabeeb ibn Zayd (may Allah be pleased with him) went to Musaylamah in order to call him to Islam. In response, Musaylamah began to chop off limb after limb from Ḥabeeb's body. During this process, which was drawn out in order to make Ḥabeeb suffer, he did not cry, scream, or shake – all the way until the very end, when he met his Lord as a martyr.

{And the martyrs with their Lord, they shall have their reward and their light.}

(Qur'an 57: 19)

The inborn disposition upon which we were created

When the wind blows violently, and the thunder roars, and darkness permeates the sky, man's inherent need to turn to Allah for help awakes from its slumber.

{Then comes a stormy wind and the waves come to them from all sides, and they think that they are encircled therein; they invoke Allah, making their faith pure for Him alone...}

(Qur'an 10: 22)

Except that the Muslim invokes his Lord in times of ease and prosperity as well as in times of hardship and difficulty.

{Had he not been of them who glorify Allah, He would have indeed remained inside of its belly [the fish] until the Day of Resurrection.}

(Qur'an 37: 143-144)

Most people ask Allah in times of need, and when their hopes are fulfilled, they turn away proudly. Do they think that Allah is to be deceived?

{Verily, the hypocrites seek to deceive Allah, but it is He Who deceives them.}

(Qur'an 4: 142)

Those who turn to Allah only during times of calamity are in that regard students of the deviant Pharaoh. It was said to him when it was too late:

{Now [you believe], while you refused to believe before and you were one of the evil-doers.}

(Qur'an 10: 91)

I heard on BBC radio that when Iraq occupied Kuwait, British Prime Minister Margaret Thatcher, who was in Colorado at the time, quickly rushed to church and knelt in prayer!

If so, the only explanation that I can think of is that her inborn nature awoke, and she turned to her Creator in spite of her misguidance. People have something inherent in them, which makes them believe in Allah.

> «Every baby is born on the fiṭrah (the natural and inborn disposition to believe in Allah and accept Islam), then his parents make him into a Jew, a Christian, or a Magian.»

Whatever is written for you will unerringly come to you

A person who is impatient about his sustenance, worried about why he has so little, and unsatisfied at being lower than others in worldly status is like one who precedes the imam when going from one stage of prayer to the next. At the end, he cannot make Salâms (the final action that makes the prayer complete) until after the imam has done so. Similarly, one does not die before receiving all of the provision that was decreed for him or her. Sustenance and provision were preordained and decided upon fifty thousand years before the creation was created.

{The event ordained by Allah will come to pass, so seek not to hasten it.}

(Qur'an 16: 1)

{And if He intends any good for you, there is none who can repel His favor...}

(Qur'an 10: 107)

'Umar (may Allah be pleased with him) said, "O Allah, I seek refuge in you from the stamina of the wicked person and from the feebleness that accompanies (a false) confidence."

This phrase has a very significant meaning. As I contemplated key events in history, I found that many of Allah's enemies had extraordinary levels of fortitude, hardiness, and perseverance. In contrast, I found that many Muslims were timid, lethargic, and feeble, all the while thinking – and falsely so – that they were putting their trust in Allah. A true trust in Allah (the Exalted) requires striving and working, and only then leaving the results to Allah.

Work hard for the fruitful end

Al-Waleed ibn al-Mugheerah, Umayyah ibn Khalaf, and al-'Âṣ ibn Wâ'il spent liberally from their wealth in the fight against Islam and its adherents:

{And so will they continue to spend it; but in the end it will become an anguish for them. Then they will be overcome.}

(Qur'an 8: 36)

Yet many Muslims are miserly, hoarding their wealth and keeping themselves aloof from good causes.

{And whoever is niggardly, it is only at the expense of his ownself.}

(Qur'an 47: 38)

In Golda Meir's memoirs, the former Prime Minister said that at one stage in her life, she would work sixteen hours continuously without breaks. But for what end did she strive? It was to serve her false principles and deviant ideas. She toiled until she and Ben Gurion established a country.

I then reflected on the many Muslims who will not work even for a single hour a day. Instead it is playing, eating, drinking, sleeping, and wasting time.

{What is the matter with you, that when you are asked to march forth in the cause of Allah [that is, jihad] you cling heavily to the earth?}

(Qur'an 9: 38)

'Umar (may Allah be pleased with him) was steadfast in working day and night, and he would sleep but a little. His family asked, "Do you not sleep?" He replied:

If I sleep at night, my soul will be lost (meaning that he spent his nights in worship) and if I sleep during the day, my people (citizens) will be lost (as Caliph, he spent his days taking care of the people's affairs).

The memoir of the assassin Moshe Dayan is replete with accounts of how he flew from one country to another, day and night, attending meetings and conferences, always making deals and pacts. I thought what a shame it was that such extraordinary fortitude was possessed by a man who used his God-given strengths not for good, but to occupy a peaceful land and its people, and to establish dominance over it through terrorist tactics and sheer force. To complete this somber thought, I reflected on the feebleness and incapability of so many Muslims. Here again I remembered 'Umar's words about the stamina of the evildoer and the feebleness of self-assurance.

Under 'Umar's rule, indolence and inactivity were not tolerated. He once evicted some youths who lived in the mosque, chastising them with blows and saying, "Go out and seek sustenance, for the sky does not send down rain of gold or silver." Laziness begets worry, depression, and manifold illnesses, while activity and work beget satisfaction and happiness. If we all do what we are supposed to do, all of the above-mentioned maladies can be eradicated, and our society will benefit from an increase in productivity and development.

{And say: Do deeds!}

(Qur'an 9: 105)

{... You may disperse through the land...}

(Qur'an 62: 10)

{Race one with another in hastening towards forgiveness from your Lord [Allah], and towards paradise...}

(Qur'an 57: 21)

{And march forth in the way [which leads to] forgiveness from your Lord, and for paradise...}

(Qur'an 3: 133)

The Prophet (bpuh) said:

«Verily, the Prophet David would eat from the labor of his hands.»

Though it might seem to be a paradox, many people are dead despite the fact that they are alive. They have no clue as to the purpose of life, and they do nothing for themselves or for others.

{They are content to be with those [the women] who sit behind [at home].}

(Qur'an 9: 87)

{Not equal are those of the believers who sit [at home], except those who are disabled [by injury or are blind or lame, et cetera], and those who strive hard and fight in the cause of Allah...}

(Qur'an 4: 95)

The dark-skinned woman who cleaned the Prophet's Mosque played out her role in life with enthusiasm and a sense of purpose. As a result, she entered paradise:

{And indeed a slave woman who believes is better than a polytheist, even though she pleases you.}

(Qur'an 2: 221)

Similarly, the boy who made the pulpit for the Prophet (bpuh) contributed according to his abilities, and for that he earned his reward. His talents were in carpentry, and he took advantage of those talents.

{... And those who could not find to give charity [in Allah's cause] except what is available to them...}

(Qur'an 9: 79)

In a move that expanded the opportunities for the call to Islam, the American government opened the doors for Muslim preachers to visit prisons in order to teach prisoners about Islam. The apparent reason or motive was that those criminals, drug dealers, and murderers who accept Islam during their stay in prison re-enter society as productive and good members.

{Is he who was dead [without faith by ignorance and disbelief] and We gave him life [by knowledge and faith] and set for him a light [of belief] whereby he can walk amongst men, like him who is in the darkness [of disbelief, polytheism and hypocrisy]...}

(Qur'an 6: 122)

An extreme attachment to this life, the yearning to live a long time, and an abhorrence of death that goes beyond normal limits -these all result in anxiety, worry, and sleeplessness.

Allah blamed the Jews for their strong attachment to the life of this world.

{And verily, you will find them [the Jews] the greediest of humankind for life and [even greedier] than those who ascribe partners to Allah. Every one of them wishes that he could be given a life of a thousand years. But the grant of such life will not save him even a little from [due] punishment. And Allah is All-Seer of what they do.}

(Qur'an 2: 96)

Regarding this verse, there are some important issues that we need to discuss. First, Allah mentioned that every one of them wishes for a long life. In other words, no matter what the quality of the life they lead, regardless of whether they lead a life that is worthless and trivial or not, they have strong aspirations to stay in this world for a long time.

Second, there is the choice of the words 'one thousand years'. Perhaps the reason for this stems from the tradition of Jews that when they would meet each other, their greeting was, "Live for a thousand years." Allah reproached them for desiring such a long life. And yet, suppose that they did live for one thousand years, what would be their end? It would still be the scorching fire of hell!

{But surely the torment of the hereafter will be more disgracing, and they will never be helped.}

(Qur'an 41: 16)

The following is a common Arab saying, "No worries, and supplication is to Allah."

In other words, since Allah above is the One Whom we ask for good, why should we worry? If you put your trust in Allah concerning your worries, He will remove them from you.

{Is not He [better than your gods] Who responds to the distressed one when he calls Him, and Who removes the evil...}

(Qur'an 27: 62)

{And when My slaves ask you [O Muhammad] concerning Me, then [answer them], I am indeed near [to them by My knowledge]. I respond to the invocations of the supplicant when he calls on Me [without any mediator or intercessor].}

(Qur'an 2: 186)

An Arab poet said:

The patient one is worthy of achieving his goal,

And the one addicted to knocking on doors is worthy of entering.

Your life is full of priceless moments

'Ali aṭ-Ṭanṭawi related two poignant experiences in his journals. The first was when he almost drowned on the shores of Beirut. Time was running out for him when he was finally rescued and carried unconscious to land. In the brief moments of struggle before losing consciousness, he recalls his utter submission to his Lord and his wish to return to life, even if it was for only an hour, to renew his faith, to do good deeds, and to try to reach the pinnacle of belief.

The second instance was when he accompanied a caravan traveling from Syria to Makkah. While in the desert of Tabuk, they lost their way and wandered aimlessly for three days. Their situation worsened when their supply of food and drink began to run out. Everyone felt that death might very well be imminent. At this point, he stood up and gave a speech to the people; it was tantamount to a farewell speech to life. It was a heartfelt sermon that moved both himself and his audience to tears. He felt his faith increase, and he truly felt that none could save or help them except Allah (the Exalted).

{Whoever is in the heavens and on earth begs of Him [its needs from Him]. Everyday He has a matter to bring forth [such as giving honor to some, disgrace to some, life to some, death to some, et cetera]!}

(Qur'an 55: 29)

{And many a Prophet fought [in Allah's cause] and along with him [fought] large bands of religious learned men. But they never lost heart for that which did befall them in Allah's way, nor did they weaken nor degrade themselves. And Allah loves the patient ones.}

(Qur'an 3: 146)

Verily, Allah loves those strong believers who challenge their enemies with patience and stamina. They don't give up, feel hopeless, or allow themselves to be humiliated at the hands of others. Instead, they struggle, strive, and toil. These are the taxes that a believer must pay for the ultimate property in this world: faith in Allah, His Messenger (bpuh), and His religion.

«The strong believer is better and more beloved to Allah than the weak believer. And in each of them there is good.»

Abu Bakr (may Allah be pleased with him) inserted one of his fingers into a crevice of the cave in order to protect the Prophet (bpuh) from a scorpion, and he himself was bitten in the process. The Prophet (bpuh) read upon him some Qur'anic verses, and he became cured by the permission of Allah (the Exalted).

A man asked 'Antara, "What is the secret to your bravery? You are known for your ability to overpower men." He replied, "Put your finger in my mouth, and let me put mine in yours." Each put his finger into the mouth of the other, and each one of them began to bite the finger of the other, slowly increasing in intensity. Within a very short span of time, the man could hold out no longer; he let out a shrill scream, so 'Antara loosened the hold his jaws had on the man's finger. 'Antara said, "This is how I overpower champions" – in other words, with patience and forbearance.

The spirits of the believers are raised when they appreciate that they are in close proximity to Allah's mercy, kindness, and forgiveness. They feel Allah's protection and care with an intensity of feeling that is proportionate to their belief.

{And there is not a thing but glorifies His praise. But you understand not their glorification.}

(Qur'an 17: 44)

Farmers in Arabia sometimes pass the time while sowing the earth by chanting:

A dry seed, in a dry country in Your Hands,

O Creator of the heavens and the earth.

{Tell Me! The seed that you sow in the ground. Is it you that make it grow, or are We the grower?}

(Qur'an 56: 63-64)

The eloquent orator 'Abdul-Ḥameed Kishk, who was blind, once ascended the podium to give a sermon. He took a date-palm tree leaf out of his pocket, and on it was written 'Allah' in beautiful writing. He then proclaimed to the congregation:

Look at that tree,

With its fresh branches,

Who made it grow?

And decorated it with green?

He is Allah, Who is All-Powerful, All-Capable.

Those who attended the sermon broke out into tears.

He is the Creator of the heavens and the earth. His signs are imprinted throughout the universe, and all of creation pronounces Him to be the Creator, the One with perfect qualities, and the only One Who deserves to be worshipped.

{Our Lord! You have not created [all] this without purpose, glory to You!}

(Qur'an 3: 191)

Among the pillars of happiness is to know that our Lord is merciful and forgives the faults of the one who repents. So rejoice in your Lord's mercy, a mercy that encompasses the heavens and the earth. Allah (the Exalted) says:

{My mercy embraces all things.}

(Qur'an 7: 156)

How tremendous is Allah's kindness! In an authentic hadith, it is related that a desert Arab prayed with the Prophet (bpuh), and when they reached the end of the prayer, the man said: "O Allah, be merciful to me and to Muhammad, and don't be merciful to anyone other than us." The Prophet (bpuh) said to him:

«Indeed, you have constricted what is vast.»

{And He is Ever Most Merciful to the believers.}

(Qur'an 33: 43)

After a battle, a woman prisoner rushed between the Prophet's Companions to grab and protect her child. Upon witnessing this scene, the Messenger of Allah (bpuh) said:

«Allah is more merciful to His slaves than this woman is to her child.»

In an authentic hadith, it has been related that before dying, a man ordered that his corpse be burned and his remains scattered throughout the land. Allah then put him together again and said to him, "O My slave, what was your motive for doing what you did?" He replied, "O my Lord, I feared You and dreaded my sins." Allah then made him enter paradise.

{But as for him who feared standing before his Lord, and restrained himself from impure evil desires and lusts. Verily, paradise will be his abode.}

(Qur'an 79: 40-41)

Allah took to account a man who spent extravagantly on himself and was wasteful. Nonetheless, he was someone who worshipped Allah and did not associate any partners with Him. Allah did not find the man to have any good deeds except one: he was a businessman and would pardon the debts of those who were insolvent. Allah said, "We are more worthy of generosity than you are." Allah pardoned him and let him enter paradise.

{And Who, I hope will forgive me my faults on the Day of Recompense, [the Day of Resurrection].}

(Qur'an 26: 82)

A hadith in Ṣaḥeeḥ Muslim mentions:

«The Prophet (bpuh) prayed with the people, and upon completing the prayer, a man suddenly stood and said: I have perpetrated a sin that is punishable by law, so implement the punishment on me. The Prophet asked: Did you pray with us? The man answered: Yes. The Prophet said: Go, for you have been forgiven.»

{And whoever does evil or wrongs himself but afterwards seeks Allah's forgiveness, he will find Allah Oft-Forgiving, Most Merciful.}

(Qur'an 4: 110)

There is an invisible mercy that surrounds the believer from every direction. The source of this invisible mercy is Allah, Lord of all that exists. He kept Muhammad (bpuh) safe in the cave, and He showed mercy to those known as the People of the Cave. He protected Abraham from the effects of the fire. He saved Moses from drowning, Noah from the flood, Joseph from the well, and Job from sickness (may peace be upon them all).

Pause to reflect

Umm Salamah (may Allah be pleased with her) related that she heard the Prophet (bpuh) say:

«When a Muslim is afflicted with a calamity, and then says what Allah orders him to say: Truly! To Allah we belong and truly, to Him we shall return, and to say: O Allah, reward me in my calamity, and compensate me with that which is better than it, then Allah will compensate him with that which is better than it.»

An Arab poet said:

My friend, by Allah, no calamity

Lasts, no matter how large it is,

If it descends today, do not succumb to it,

And don't complain too much when your foot slips.

How many noble people have been tried through disaster!

They were patient and vanished and went away.

My soul was attached to this world and was stubborn,

But when it witnessed my patience, it yielded.

Performing noble deeds is the way to happiness

If you love for good to befall others, then you have a blessed gift from Allah (the Exalted). Ibn 'Abbâs (may Allah be pleased with him) said:

> I have in me three qualities. The first is that whenever it rains, I praise and thank Allah. I feel happy for this blessing, even if I myself don't own camels or sheep to benefit from the rain. The second is that whenever I hear of a just judge, I supplicate to Allah for him, even if I don't have a case pending with him. The third is that whenever I gain knowledge of (the meaning of) a verse from the Qur'an, I long for others to learn what I know from it.

All of these qualities indicate a true longing for the wellbeing of others. Allah described those of an opposite nature:

{Those who are miserly and enjoin miserliness on other men and hide what Allah has bestowed upon them of His bounties.}

(Qur'an 4: 37)

Beneficial versus fruitless knowledge

{And those who have been bestowed with knowledge and faith will say: Indeed you have stayed according to the decree of Allah, until the Day of Resurrection, but you knew not.}

(Qur'an 30: 56)

There is knowledge that is useful, and there is knowledge that is harmful. As for the knowledge that is useful, the believer's faith is strengthened as a result of it. The disbeliever, on the other hand, does not reap any benefit whatsoever from gaining this kind of knowledge; though the information acquired is the same, the results are very different. Allah (the Exalted) says of His enemies:

{They know only the outside appearance of the life of the world [that is, the matters of their livelihood, like irrigation or sowing or reaping, et cetera], and they are heedless of the hereafter.}

(Qur'an 30: 7)

{Nay, they have no knowledge of the hereafter. Nay, they are in doubt about it. Nay, they are blind about it.}

(Qur'an 27: 66)

{That is what they could reach of knowledge.}

(Qur'an 53: 30)

{And recite [O Muhammad] to them the story of him to whom We gave Our Âyât [proofs, evidences, verses, lessons, signs, revelations, et cetera], but he threw them away, so Satan followed him up, and he became of those who went astray. And had We willed, We would surely have elevated him therewith but he clung to the earth and followed his own vain desire. So his description is the description of a dog: if you drive him away, he lolls his tongue out, or if you leave him alone, he [still] lolls his tongue out. Such is the description of the people who reject Our Âyât [proofs, evidences, verses, lessons, signs, revelations, et cetera]. So relate the stories, perhaps they may reflect.}

(Qur'an 7: 175-176)

Allah (the Exalted) said about the Jews and their knowledge of the truth:

{The likeness of those who were entrusted with the Torah, but who subsequently failed in those [obligations], is as the likeness of a donkey who carries huge burdens of books [but understands nothing from them]. How bad is the example of people who deny the Âyât [proofs, evidences, signs, verses, et cetera] of Allah.}

(Qur'an 62: 5)

They knew the truth from the Torah, yet they were not guided by it. They distorted its words, and if that failed to work, they distorted the meanings of the words. How could people who treated knowledge in this despicable manner ever have found happiness? It was certainly not possible in their case, for they always tried to eradicate the truth using any means at their disposal.

{...But they preferred blindness to guidance...}

(Qur'an 41: 17)

{And of their saying: Our hearts are wrapped [with coverings, that is, we do not understand what the Messengers say] – nay, Allah has set a seal upon their hearts because of their disbelief, so they believe not but a little.}

(Qur'an 4: 155)

There are millions of books in the Library of Congress in Washington. There are books that deal with every century, every people, every nation, and every culture. Yet who owns this venerable library? A nation where the majority of people are misguided concerning their Lord, a nation whose knowledge passes not the bounds of the tangible, material world. As for what is beyond the material world, they hear not, see not, feel not, nor do they understand.

{And We had assigned them the [faculties of] hearing, seeing, and hearts, but their hearing, seeing and their hearts availed them nothing.}

(Qur'an 46: 26)

The likeness between the truth and the disbeliever's aversion to it is as follows: The water is pure and sweet, but the person drinking it feels a bitter taste:

{How many clear Āyāt [proofs, evidences, verses, lessons, signs, revelations, et cetera] We gave them.}

(Qur'an 2: 211)

{And never an Āyāh [sign] comes to them from the Āyāt [proofs, evidences, verses, lessons, signs, revelations, et cetera] of their Lord, but that they have been turning away from it.}

(Qur'an 6: 4)

Read more, but with understanding and contemplation

To be blessed with a large store of knowledge, a mind that contemplates, a good understanding, and an intellect that delves beneath the surface for reasons and motives – these are all factors that contribute to giving a person peace of mind.

{It is only those who have knowledge among His slaves that fear Allah.}

(Qur'an 35: 28)

{Rather, they have denied that which they encompass not in knowledge...}

(Qur'an 10: 39)

A scholar usually has an open mind and is at peace. A thinker from the West said:

> I keep a large file in the drawer of my desk, and on it is written, 'Foolish things I have done.' I write in it all of the follies and errors that I perpetrate during the course of a day; I do this to know my faults in order to rid myself of them.

The earlier Muslim scholars preceded him in this endeavor. They would meticulously take account of their deeds.

{And I swear by the self-reproaching person [a believer].}

(Qur'an 75: 2)

Ḥasan al-Baṣri said, "The Muslim takes account of himself with more rigor than does a businessman with his partner." Ar-Rabeeʿ ibn Khuthaym would write everything that he said from one Friday to the next. If he found that he had spoken well and truthfully, he praised Allah (the Exalted); if he found an error in his speech, he repented to Allah. A righteous man from the early centuries of Islam said, "I committed a particular sin forty years ago, a sin that still bothers me today. I continue to ask Allah to forgive me for it."

{And they who give what they give while their hearts are fearful because they will be returning to their Lord...} (Qur'an 23: 60)

Take account of yourself

Keep a journal with you, and use it to take account of your actions. Write down the negative aspects of your personality and actions, and then think of solutions to rid yourself of them. ʿUmar (may Allah be pleased with him) said:

> Take account of yourselves before it is taken of you. Weigh your deeds before they are weighed for you (that is, on the Day of Judgment), and beautify yourselves (with good deeds) for the great display (on the Day of Judgment).

Three mistakes that are common in our everyday lives

1. Wasting time.

2. Talking about matters that don't concern us, matters that are none of our business.

   «From the goodness of one's Islam is leaving alone what does not concern him.»

3. Being preoccupied with trivial issues. Listening to rumors, predictions, and gossip are three common examples. Having this characteristic results in paranoia, anxiety, and a lack of purpose in life.

   {So Allah gave them the reward of this world, and the excellent reward of the hereafter.}
   (Qur'an 3: 148)

   {My guidance shall neither go astray, nor fall into distress and misery.}
   (Qur'an 20: 123)

Make plans and take proper precautions

When Muslims set out to do something, they must plan with caution and put their trust in Allah. The Prophet (bpuh), who was protected by Allah and who had a stronger trust in Allah than anyone else had, wore armor in battle.

«A man asked the Prophet (bpuh): Should I tie my camel to the post or should I put my trust in Allah? The Prophet (bpuh) said: Tie it up and put your trust in Allah.»

When you take appropriate steps to reach your goal, and at the same time you put your trust in Allah, you have implemented two important principles of Islamic monotheism. To trust in Allah without taking appropriate measures – without making an effort to achieve one's goals – is a contemptible misunderstanding of the religion, and to take appropriate measures without trusting in Allah means that there is a defect in one's faith in Allah. An Arab poet said:

The slow cautious person will achieve part of his goals,

While the impetuous hasty one will often fail.

By being circumspect in your affairs, you are not acting contrary to your belief in preordainment; you are actually implementing a fundamental part of it.

{And let him be careful...}

(Qur'an 18: 19)

{To protect you from the heat [and cold], and coats of mail to protect you from your [mutual] violence.}

(Qur'an 16: 81)

Winning people over

In indication of one's prosperity is the ability to gain people's love, respect and sympathy. Prophet Abraham (pbuh) said:

{And grant me an honorable mention in later generations.}

(Qur'an 26: 84)

Allah (the Exalted) said of Moses (pbuh):

{And I bestowed upon you love from Me...}

(Qur'an 20: 39)

The following two hadiths are both authentic:

«You are Allah's witnesses on this earth.»

«Gabriel (pbuh) calls to the inhabitants of the heavens: Indeed, Allah loves So-and-so, so love him. The inhabitants of heaven then love him, and an acceptance of him permeates the earth.»

A pleasant face, kind words, and good manners are the most powerful ways to ingratiate yourself into the hearts of people, yet even more powerful is gentleness. That is why the Prophet (bpuh) said:

«Anything that has gentleness in it is beautified by it, and anything that is bereft of it is stained.»

He also said:

«Whoever is bereft of gentleness has been precluded from a great deal of good.»

A wise man said, "Gentleness extricates a snake from its hole."

As they say in the West, "Gather the honey, but don't break the hive."

The Prophet (bpuh) said in an authentic hadith:

«The believer is like a bee that eats what is wholesome and produces what is wholesome, and when it lands on a (small) branch, it doesn't break it.»

Travel to different lands

As I mentioned in an earlier chapter, traveling and visiting various lands brings happiness to the soul.

{Say: Behold all that is in the heavens and the earth.}

(Qur'an 10: 101)

{Have they not traveled through the earth and seen...}

(Qur'an 12: 109)

{Say: Travel in the land and see...}

(Qur'an 29: 20)

Whoever reads Ibn Baṭoota's book of travels – exaggerations notwithstanding – will be amazed with Allah's creation. Traveling and reading the open book of creation are means by which the believer grasps many morals and lessons.

{So travel freely...}

(Qur'an 9: 2)

{Until, when he reached the setting place of the sun...}

(Qur'an 18: 86)

{I will not give up [traveling] until I reach the junction of the two seas or [until] I spend years and years in traveling.}

(Qur'an 18: 60)

Perform the late-night voluntary prayers

To stand for prayer late at night, when no human can see you, gives tranquility and serenity to the heart. In an authentic hadith, the Prophet (bpuh) said that waking up late at night, remembering Allah, making ablution, and then standing for prayer makes one active and joyful.

{They used to sleep but little by night [invoking their Lord and praying, with fear and hope].}

(Qur'an 51: 17)

{And from [part of] the night, pray with it as an additional [worship] for you...}

(Qur'an 17: 79)

An authentic hadith in Abu Dâwood indicates that performing the late-night prayer removes sickness from the body. The Prophet (bpuh) said:

«Don't be like So-and-so. He used to stand at night (for prayer), and then he abandoned doing so.»

The following is related in a narration from 'Abdullâh ibn 'Umar (may Allah be pleased with him):

«'Abdullâh is a good man, but would that he stood at night (for prayer).»

Don't grieve over things that are fleeting; everything in this universe will perish except Allah.

{Everything will perish save His face.}

(Qur'an 28: 88)

{Whatsoever is on it [the earth] will perish, and the face of your Lord, full of majesty and honor, will abide forever.} (Qur'an 55: 26-27)

Your reward is paradise

My soul that owns things is itself departing,

Then why should I cry when something leaves me?

The whole world, with all its gold, silver, and mansions does not deserve even a teardrop. In a hadith related by Tirmidhi, the Prophet (bpuh) said:

«The world is cursed, and what is in it is cursed, except the remembrance of Allah, what follows it (such as other good deeds that Allah loves), the scholar, and the student.»

An Arab poet said:

Wealth and family are only a loan,

And the day must come when the loan is returned.

All of the wealth in the world cannot postpone death when its appointed time comes.

{And this worldly life is not but diversion and amusement.}

(Qur'an 29: 64)

Ḥasan al-Baṣri said, "Do not seek any remuneration other than paradise, especially since the value of a believer's soul is so expensive."

Yet some people sell theirs for a base value. Those who mourn over bankruptcy or the destruction of a house or car, and do not grieve over a low level of faith and over their sins, will soon come to realize the absurdity of their outlook on life. That realization, teamed with regret, will be augmented according to the degree of their particular delusions. It is an issue that strikes deep because it is one of values, morals, and priorities.

{Verily! These [disbelievers] love the present life of this world, and put behind them a heavy day [that will be hard].}

(Qur'an 76: 27)

True love

To find true happiness, you must be from those who love Allah. The most prosperous person is the one whose mission in life is to achieve the love of Allah, a love that Allah refers to in this verse:

{Allah will bring a people whom He will love and they will love Him...}

(Qur'an 5: 54)

{Say. [O Muhammad]: If you should love Allah, then follow me, [so] Allah will love you and forgive you your sins.}

(Qur'an 3: 31)

The Prophet (bpuh) announced, for all to know, a superior characteristic of 'Ali (may Allah be pleased with him) – a merit that was like a crown upon his head. The Prophet (bpuh) described him as a man

«...who loves Allah and His Messenger, and whom Allah and His Messenger love.»

One of the Prophet's Companions loved the chapter of the Qur'an that begins:

{Say [O Muhammad]: He is Allah, [the] One.}

(Qur'an 112: 1)

He would repeat it in each unit of the prayer, and he would constantly read it at other times as well, to give solace to his heart and spirit. The Prophet (bpuh) said to him:

«Your love for it is what has made you enter paradise.»

I found the following lines in a biography of a Muslim scholar:

If the love of the roaming one for Layla, takes away one's mind and one's faculty of reasoning, Then what do you suppose will be the case for he whose heart throbs for the higher world?

{And [both] the Jews and the Christians say: We are the children of Allah and His loved ones. Say: Why then does He punish you for your sins?}

(Qur'an 5: 18)

The story of Majnoon's love for Layla is well known. His extreme love for her killed him, whereas for Qâroon it was the love of wealth, and for Pharaoh it was the love of position and power. On the other hand, there were Ḥamzah, Ja'far, and Ḥandhalah (may Allah be pleased with them all), who all died for their love of Allah and His Messenger (bpuh). Vast is the distance that separates these three noble Companions in their love – and those believers who are like them -from the rest.

The Sharia is made easy for you

Ease and facilitation – these are two qualities of the Sharia that give comfort to the believer.

{We have not sent down the Qur'an unto you [O Muhammad] to cause you distress.}

(Qur'an 20: 2)

{And We shall make easy for you [O Muhammad] the easy way [that is, the doing of righteous deeds].}

(Qur'an 87: 8)

{Allah burdens not a person beyond his scope.}

(Qur'an 2: 286)

{Allah puts no burden on any person beyond what He has given him.}

(Qur'an 65: 7)

{And He has not laid upon you in religion any hardship...}

(Qur'an 22: 78)

{He releases them from their heavy burdens [of Allah's covenant] and from the fetters [bindings] that were upon them.}

(Qur'an 7: 157)

{So verily, with the hardship, there is relief. Verily, with the hardship, there is relief.}

(Qur'an 94: 5-6)

{Our Lord, do not impose blame upon us if we have forgotten or erred. Our Lord, and lay not upon us a burden like that which You laid upon those before us. Our Lord, and burden us not with that which we have no ability to bear. And pardon us; and forgive us; and have mercy upon us. You are our protector, so give us victory over the disbelieving people.}

(Qur'an 2: 286)

The Prophet (bpuh) said:

«My nation will not be held accountable for mistakes, for forgetfulness, and for what they were forced to do (sins that were committed under duress).»

He also said:

«Verily, this religion is easy; when one makes the religion too harsh, one will become overcome by it.»

Tranquility and peace

In a 1994 issue of the magazine Ahlan wa sahlan, I read an article by Dr. Hassan Shamsi Basha entitled, Twenty Ways to Avoid Anxiety. The following points are summarized from the article:

1. The length of your life has already been decided upon, for everything takes place according to preordainment and decree. So there is no need to feel anxious in that regard.
2. The decision of how much sustenance any one of us receives is with Allah alone: no one else owns that sustenance or has the power to take it from you.
3. The past is gone and has taken with it its woes and miseries. It could not return even if the whole of mankind worked as one unit to bring it back.
4. The future is from the unseen world and has not yet arrived. It brings with it matters, showing no regard for your permission or feelings, so do not call it forth until it actually arrives.
5. Doing good to others brings happiness to both the heart and the soul. A good deed provides greater benefits to the benefactor -in terms of blessings and recompense and peace -than it does to the receiver.
6. Among the noble qualities of the believers is that they do not concern themselves with spurious criticism. No one has been spared from curses and criticism, not even Allah, the Lord of all that exists, Who is Perfect and Exalted.

Beware of ardent love

Beware of falling in love with appearances; such love is beset with anxiety and perpetual misery. It is a blessing for Muslims that they stay away from messages found in lyrics and music -messages about ardent love, unrequited love, or separation from the beloved.

{Have you seen him who takes his own lust [vain desires] as his [god], and Allah knowing [him as such], left him astray, and sealed his hearing and his heart, and put a cover on his sight.}

(Qur'an 45: 23)

In reproaching himself, an Arab poet wrote the following:

I am the one who has brought death a knocking,

Then who is to blame when the murdered is the murderer?

He is blaming himself for the perpetual pain and misery that he experienced, finally recognizing that by falling passionately in love –and then by not being able to fall out of it – he alone was to blame for his woes.

{And if an evil whisper comes to you from Satan, seek refuge with Allah.}

(Qur'an 7: 200)

{Indeed, those who fear Allah – when an impulse touches them from Satan, they remember [Him] and at once they have insight.}

(Qur'an 7: 201)

Ibn al-Qayyim expounded on this topic in his book The Disease and the Cure. He mentioned a number of factors that contribute to one's falling hopelessly and uncontrollably in love. Among them are the following:

1. An empty heart that is bereft of love for Allah, remembrance of Him, and fear of Him.

2. Allowing one's eyes to wander and stare. The eye is a scout that can bring back misery to the heart.

    {Tell the believing men to lower their gaze [from looking at forbidden things]...}

    (Qur'an 24: 30)

    A look is an arrow from the arrows of the devil. An Arab poet said:

    When you allow your eyes to wander ahead as a scout,

    Looking at all eyes and stares will then follow,

    Seeing what you are not capable of embracing completely,

    While not being patient for getting something partially.

3. Being negligent in worship – especially in remembrance, supplication, and prayer.

> {Indeed, prayer prohibits immorality and wrongdoing...}
>
> *(Qur'an 29: 45)*

Some cures for ardent, unbridled love

> {Thus it was, that We might turn away from him evil and illegal sexual intercourse. Surely, he was one of Our chosen, guided slaves.}
>
> *(Qur'an 12: 24)*

1. Strive to improve your worship by being more sincere, and invoke Allah to cure you.

2. Lower your gaze.

    > {And protect their private parts [from illegal sexual acts, et cetera].}
    >
    > *(Qur'an 24: 30)*

    > {And those who guard their chastity [that is, private parts, from illegal sexual acts].}
    >
    > *(Qur'an 23: 5)*

3. Travel away from the object of your passion.

4. Keep yourself busy in doing good deeds.

    > {Verily, they used to hasten to do good deeds, and they used to call on Us with hope and fear...}
    >
    > *(Qur'an 21: 90)*

5. Marry lawfully, in accordance with the Sharia.

    > {...Then marry women of your choice...}
    >
    > *(Qur'an 4: 3)*

    > {And among His signs is this, that He created for you wives from among yourselves, that you may find repose in them...}
    >
    > *(Qur'an 30: 21)*

The Prophet (bpuh) said:

«O group of young men, whoever from you is capable of (paying) the dowry (and taking care of all necessary expenses related to marriage), then let him marry.»

The rights of brotherhood

Upon meeting your Muslim brothers and sisters, call them by names they love, and greet them with a smiling face.

«To smile at your brother is charity.»

Encourage them to speak with you; give them an opportunity to talk to you about themselves and about their lives. Ask them about their affairs, but only about those things that will not cause them embarrassment.

«Whoever is unconcerned with the affairs of the Muslims is not from them.»

{The believers, men and women, are Awliyâ' [helpers, supporters, friends, protectors] of one another...}

(Qur'an 9: 71)

Don't blame them for, or remind them of, their past errors, and don't cause them discomfort by making fun of them.

«Do not dispute with your brother, don't make fun of him, and don't make an appointment with him and then not show up.»

Two secrets regarding sinning (even if you know them, don't sin)

Some of the people of knowledge mentioned that:

1. After repenting from a sin, one's feelings of self-importance and sanctimoniousness are quelled.
2. Allah's names and attributes, such as 'Most Merciful' and 'Oft-Forgiving', bear a greater meaning to the one who sins and then repents than they do to others.

Seek out sustenance, but don't be covetous

All glory and praise is for the Creator and Provider. He gives sustenance to the worm in the ground, the fish in the water, the bird in the air, the ant in the dark, and the snake within the crevice of a rock.

Ibn al-Jawzi mentioned something he witnessed that was wonderful yet strange. A blind snake lived on a branch at the top of a tree. A bird would come to it with food in its mouth. It would chirp a signal to the snake, which in return would open its mouth and allow the bird to insert the food. All praise and glory belongs to Allah, Who caused this one to help the other.

{Nor a bird that flies with its two wings, but are communities like you.}

(Qur'an 6: 38)

Provision came to Mary, the mother of Prophet Jesus (pbuh), day and night. She was asked, "How does this come to you?" She replied, "It is from Allah. Verily, Allah provides for whom He wishes without reckoning." So don't worry, for your sustenance is guaranteed.

{And kill not your children for fear of poverty. We provide for them and for you.}

(Qur'an 17: 31)

People must realize that the Provider for both father and son is the One Who begets not, nor is He begotten.

The proprietor of infinite treasures has guaranteed your sustenance.

{So seek your provision from Allah [alone], and worship Him [alone], and be grateful to Him.}

(Qur'an 29: 17)

{And it is He Who feeds me and gives me to drink.}

(Qur'an 26: 79)

Pause to reflect

As for the prayer, its significance – or rather part of its significance – is that it empties the heart from bad feelings and fills it with strength and pleasure. During prayer, one's heart and soul are in communication with Allah. Closeness to Him, the comfort realized from asking of Him, and the spirituality felt from standing in front of Him – these are all realized during the prayer. Every limb is used in the prayer, but what is more important is that the heart must be wakeful as well. When one prays, tranquility and peace are achieved as one travels away, at least spiritually, from enemies and troubles. Thus the prayer is one of the most potent of remedies for the diseases of the heart. Yet only the worthy heart benefits from prayer; the weak heart, on the other hand, is like the body, in that it seeks its sustenance from material matter.

Therefore prayer is the greatest way to help us achieve the blessings of both this world and the hereafter. The prayer precludes one from sins, defends against diseases, illuminates both heart and face, makes one active, and in general, brings good upon the person who performs it sincerely.

A religion that is full of benefits

Islam offers the believers a broad range of benefits and rewards, benefits that encourage them to continue upon the true path and rewards that boost their hopes for the hereafter. Deeds that wipe out sins – such as prayer – are many in Islam. For example, a good deed is multiplied ten times in reward, or seven hundred times, or even much, much more. Another example is hardship, because any time the believers are afflicted with hardship, some of their sins are atoned for. (Also, during times of affliction, one benefits from the supplications of other believers).

{And if you would count the graces of Allah, never would you be able to count them.}

(Qur'an 16: 18)

{...amply bestowed upon you His favors, [both] apparent and unapparent...?}

(Qur'an 31: 20)

Fear not! Surely, you will have the upper hand

{Fear not! Surely, you will have the upper hand.}

(Qur'an 20: 68)

Prophet Moses (pbuh) was especially in trouble on three occasions:

1. When he entered the council of the evil Pharaoh, he said:

   {Our Lord! Verily! We fear lest he should hasten to punish us or lest he should transgress [all bounds against us].}

   (Qur'an 20: 45)

   {He [Allah] said: Fear not, verily! I am with you both, hearing and seeing.}

   (Qur'an 20: 46)

   The phrase, "I am with you... hearing and seeing" should always be in the mind of the Muslim.

2. When the sorcerers threw their rods, Allah (the Exalted) said:

   {Fear not! Surely, you will have the upper hand.}

   (Qur'an 20: 68)

3. When Pharaoh and his army were catching up with Moses, Allah (the Exalted) said:

   {Strike the sea with your stick.}

   (Qur'an 26: 63)

   When his companions despaired, Moses (pbuh) said:

   {Nay, verily! With me is my Lord, He will guide me.}

   (Qur'an 26: 62)

Stay away from these four...

The following four deeds bring misery to a person's heart, so avoid them:

1. Complaining and being angry with what Allah (the Exalted) has decreed.

2. Committing sins without repenting afterwards.

> {Say [to them]: It is from yourselves [because of your evil deeds].}
>
> *(Qur'an 3: 165)*

> {It is because of what your hands have earned.}
>
> *(Qur'an 42: 30)*

3. Hating people for the blessings that Allah (the Exalted) has bestowed upon them.

> {Or do they envy men for what Allah has given them of His bounty?}
>
> *(Qur'an 4: 54)*

4. Turning away from the remembrance of Allah (the Exalted):

> {... Verily, for him is a life of hardship...}
>
> *(Qur'an 20: 124)*

To find peace, turn to your Lord

Allah's slaves – meaning every one of us – can find comfort only by turning to Allah (the Exalted), Who mentioned tranquility in many verses of the Qur'an:

> {Then Allah sent down His Sakeenah [calmness and tranquility] upon His Messenger and upon the believers.}
>
> *(Qur'an 48: 26)*

> {... He sent down calmness and tranquility upon them...}
>
> *(Qur'an 48: 18)*

> {Then Allah did send down His Sakeenah [calmness, tranquility and reassurance, et cetera] on the Messenger [Muhammad]...}
>
> *(Qur'an 9: 26)*

Tranquility means having a heart that is at peace and that has a sound trust in Allah. Tranquility is a state of calm enjoyed by those believers who have been saved from doubt. It is according to one's closeness to Allah (the Exalted) and steadfastness in following the Messenger's way that one will achieve tranquility and peace.

{Allah keeps firm those who believe, with the firm word, in worldly life and the hereafter.}

(Qur'an 14: 27)

Two great words of solace

Imam Aḥmad related two phrases that were said to him during the difficult times in which he was being punished and tortured. A man who was imprisoned for drinking alcohol spoke first, when he met Imam Aḥmad and said, O Aḥmad, be steadfast, for you are about to be whipped for the truth that you are upon. I have been whipped many times for drinking, and even I was patient."

{So be patient [O Muhammad]. Verily, the promise of Allah is true, and let not those who have no certainty of faith discourage you from conveying Allah's Message [which you are obliged to convey].}

(Qur'an 30: 60)

{...If you are suffering [hardships] then surely, they [too] are suffering [hardships] as you are suffering, but you have a hope from Allah [for the reward, that is, paradise] that for which they hope not...}

(Qur'an 4: 104)

A desert Arab, seeing Imam Aḥmad in chains as he was being taken to prison, said the second phrase, "O Aḥmad, be patient, for verily, if this is the spot from which you will be killed, it will also be the spot from which you will enter paradise."

{Their Lord gives them glad tidings of a mercy from Him, and that He is pleased [with them], and of gardens [paradise] for them wherein are everlasting delights.}

(Qur'an 9: 21)

Some positive effects of hardships

Hardship makes one turn humbly toward one's Lord. Someone once said, "How Perfect is Allah, Who has elicited supplication through hardship."

It has been related that Allah tested one of His slaves in a matter and then said to His angels that He had done so, in order to hear his voice, meaning the man's supplications and invocations.

Hardship instills humility in the heart of the afflicted:

﴾Nay! Verily, man does transgress all bounds [in disbelief and evil deeds, et cetera], because he considers himself self-sufficient.﴿

(Qur'an 96: 6-7)

People give comfort to, and pray for, the afflicted. Thus during times of hardship, the believers come together in a spirit of brotherhood and sisterhood.

Hardship should make one grateful for having been saved from an even greater hardship. Furthermore, hardship atones for sins. When the slaves of Allah gain an appreciation of these facts, they become thankful.

﴾Only those who are patient shall receive their rewards in full, without reckoning.﴿

(Qur'an 39: 10)

Knowledge

Ibn Ḥazm mentioned that from the benefits of knowledge are that it repels evil whispers from the soul and that it rids one of worries and troubles.

This is especially true for those who love knowledge, who study constantly, and who put into practice what they learn. Students of knowledge should distribute their time among memorizing, reading, revising, researching, and reflecting.

Happiness is a divine gift that does not distinguish between the rich and the poor

It is not uncommon to see laborers who are so poor that whatever they earn on any given day is spent on that same day. Yet many of them are happy and peaceful, with strong hearts and tranquil souls. This is because they are too busy to think about yesterday or tomorrow. Their lifestyle has given them an appreciation of today, since they have not been afforded the opportunity of thinking about anything else.

Compare these people to those who live in mansions. Inactivity and free time have afforded them ample time to think about their problems and their lack of purpose in life. Thus misery and worry afflict many of them day and night.

Being remembered after death is a second life

Being given a second life is a great blessing. Many are those who have purchased this life not with wealth or position, but with deeds. Prophet Abraham (pbuh) supplicated to His Lord to be remembered well by others and to be prayed for. 'Umar (may Allah be pleased with him) asked the children of Harim ibn Sinân, "What has Zuhayr given you, and what have you given him?" They said, "He gave us good compliments, and we gave him wealth." 'Umar said, "By Allah, what you have given him has perished, and what he has given you has remained."

Invoke Allah with the following

O Allah, give us a good share of piety, which will serve as a barrier between us and our disobeying You. Give us that share of obedience to You with which You make us enter paradise, and a share of the faith that serves to make the calamities of this world seem easy for us. Make us enjoy the blessings of our hearing, sight, and strength as long as You give us life... Grant us revenge against those who have wronged us, and help us against those who have transgressed against us. Do not cause our calamity to be in our religion; do not make the world the most important matter with us, nor make it the extent of our knowledge. Do not give those who show us no mercy the power to subjugate us on account of our sins.

A Lord Who wrongs not

You should feel reassured because you have a Lord Who is just.

Allah (the Exalted) admitted a woman into paradise because of a dog and sent another to the hellfire because of a cat. The first was a prostitute from the children of Israel; because she once gave drink to a thirsty dog, Allah forgave her and admitted her into paradise. This was a just recompense for her sincerity in doing a good deed – for her sincerity to Allah. The second was a woman who confined a cat to a room. She neither fed it nor gave it drink; by confining the cat, she prevented it from eating insects in the fields, and so Allah (the Exalted) made her enter the hellfire.

The story of the first woman is one that brings coolness to the heart, because it lets us know that Allah (the Exalted) gives great rewards for small deeds.

{So whosoever does good equal to the weight of an atom [or a small ant] shall see it. And whosoever does evil equal to the weight of an atom [or a small ant] shall see it.}

(Qur'an 99: 7-8)

{Verily, the good deeds remove the evil deeds [that is, small sins].}

(Qur'an 11: 114)

So help the grief-stricken, give to the poor, aid the oppressed, visit the sick, pray over the dead, lead the blind, give comfort to the afflicted, guide the misguided, and be generous to both guest and neighbor. All of these are deeds of charity, deeds that not only help the receiver of your kind acts, but also help you by giving you comfort and peace.

Write your own history

One day, I was sitting in the Sacred Mosque in Makkah; it was a sultry day and the noon prayer was about to begin when I noticed an old man distributing Zamzam water. He would fill a few cups and give them out to people, and then he would return and repeat the process. He continued doing this for some time and became soaked in sweat. I was amazed at the fortitude of this old man and at his love for doing kind deeds. He would give a smile and a cup of water to as many people as he was able to serve. It made me appreciate that, if Allah (the Exalted) guides one to doing a good deed, one will do it with a smile, even when it involves hard work.

Abu Bakr (may Allah be pleased with him) put his own life at risk on the road to Madinah in order to protect the Messenger of Allah (the Exalted). In order to feed his guests, Ḥâtim would sleep on a hungry stomach.

Abu 'Ubaydah would stand guard at night in order to allow the Muslim army to rest.

'Umar (may Allah be pleased with him) would walk through the streets at night, while people were asleep, in order to ensure their safety. In the year of the great famine, he went hungry in order to feed the people.

Abu Talhah (may Allah be pleased with him) used his body as a shield, protecting the Prophet (bpuh) from arrows during the battle of Uhud. Ibn Mubârak would distribute food while he himself was fasting.

{And they give food in spite of love for it to the needy, the orphan, and the captive.}

(Qur'an 76: 8)

Listen attentively to the words of Allah

Recite the Qur'an and listen to it being recited – in doing so, you will find happiness, peace, and tranquility. The Messenger of Allah (bpuh) used to love to hear the Qur'an being recited by one of his noble Companions.

You should allot a few minutes of every day to listen to a tape of Qur'anic recitation. The noises you hear in the streets, at work, or in the office are sure to aggravate you, so take time out to give yourself comfort by reading your Lord's Book:

{Those who believe [in the Oneness of Allah – Islamic monotheism], and whose hearts find rest in the remembrance of Allah, verily, in the remembrance of Allah do hearts find rest.}

(Qur'an 13: 28)

The following is related in an authentic hadith:

«The Messenger of Allah (bpuh) ordered Ibn Mas'ood to recite from the Qur'an. He recited verses from the chapter named 'Women', until the Prophet's tears began rolling down his cheeks. The Prophet then said: This is sufficient for you (in other words, you can stop reading now).»

{Say: If humankind and the jinn were together to produce the like of this Qur'an, they could not produce the like thereof, even if they helped one another.}

(Qur'an 17: 88)

Be Happy

{Had We sent down this Qur'an on a mountain, you would surely have seen it humbling itself and rending asunder by the fear of Allah.}

(Qur'an 59: 21)

The everyday routine of life often leads people to the road of apathy, whereby they care for nothing but eating and sleeping, thus descending to the level of animals. But when they return to the words of their Lord, they feel comfort and peace.

It is important to note here that it is the words of Allah, not music, that bring peace to a person. Music is a cheap and forbidden substitute. We have with us something better, that with which the Messenger of Allah (bpuh) came:

{Falsehood cannot come to it from before it or behind it [; it is] sent down by the All-Wise, Worthy of all praise [Allah].}

(Qur'an 41: 42)

{... you see their eyes overflowing with tears because of the truth they have recognized.}

(Qur'an 5: 83)

As for music, only fools find peace in it:

{And of humankind is he who purchases idle talks [that is, music, singing, et cetera] to mislead [men] from the path of Allah without knowledge...}

(Qur'an 31: 6)

Everyone is searching for happiness, but...

Few are those who are guided to the path that truly leads to happiness. Regarding that and other paths, here are three points for you to reflect upon:

1. Those who do not make the pleasure of Allah their main concern in life will end up losing in the end.

    {We shall gradually seize them with punishment in ways they perceive not.}

    (Qur'an 7: 182)

2. In order to achieve happiness, people attempt to follow many complicated and tricky paths. Little do they know that an easier path is ready for them in the religion of Islam – a path that will bring them the best of this life and the hereafter.

{...but if they had done what they were told, it would have been better for them, and would have strengthened their [faith].}

(Qur'an 4: 66)

3. There are too many people in this world who think they are doing well, but who, in reality, are losing out on this life and the hereafter, simply because they turn their backs on the true religion.

{And the word of your Lord has been fulfilled in truth and injustice.} *(Qur'an 6: 115)*

Prepare for bad times by being thankful when all is well

Supplicate often in times of comfort, peace, and wellbeing. Among the characteristics of the believers are that they are thankful and resolute: they sharpen the arrow before releasing it from the bow, and they turn to Allah before they are afflicted. The opposites of the believers in this regard are both the disbelievers and the injudicious Muslims.

{And when some hurt touches man, he cries to his Lord [Allah alone], turning to Him in repentance, but when He bestows a favor upon him from Himself, he forgets that for which he cried before, and he sets up rivals to Allah...}

(Qur'an 39: 8)

Therefore if you truly want to be saved, you must remain steadfast in supplicating and praising Allah (the Exalted). The purpose of supplicating to Allah during times of ease, as has been mentioned by Imam al-Ḥaleemi, is to praise Allah, to thank Him, and to recognize His many favors, and at the same time, to ask for guidance and help. It is also important to seek forgiveness for your shortcomings, for no matter how hard you try, you cannot completely fulfill the rights that Allah has upon you. If you remain heedless of those rights at a time when you have no worries or feel secure, then you fall under the category of those mentioned in the verse:

{And when they embark on a ship, they invoke Allah, making their faith pure for Him only, but when He brings them safely to land, behold, they give a share of their worship to others.}

(Qur'an 29: 65)

Bliss versus the fire

News agencies around the world reported the death by suicide of a French minister during the rule of Mitterand. The reason behind the suicide was that French newspapers waged an unmitigated war against the minister, besmirching his name and reputation. Having found no faith or sanctuary to resort to, or in which to seek support, he took his own life.

This wretched man, who sought refuge in self-destruction, was not guided by the divine guidance that is epitomized in the following verses:

{And be not distressed because of what they plot.}

(Qur'an 16: 127)

{They will do you no harm, barring a trifling annoyance...}

(Qur'an 3: 111)

{And be patient with what they say, and keep away from them in a good way.}

(Qur'an 73: 10)

It was because he was lost and was far away from the path of truth.

{Whosoever Allah sends astray, none can guide him...}

(Qur'an 7: 186)

There are some who suggest that every person who is downtrodden or who is in a hapless situation should go on a nature expedition, listen to music, go skiing, or play chess or backgammon.

The adherents of Islam lay claim to a cure that is more effective: it is to sit in the mosque between the call to prayer and the actual commencement of prayer, in order to remember Allah and to submit to and be contented with His divine decree. It is of equal importance that one places his total trust in Allah.

Have We not opened your breast for you [O Muhammad]?

{Have We not opened your breast for you [O Muhammad]?}

(Qur'an 94: 1)

These were the words that descended upon the Prophet (bpuh), and they became manifest in his character. His mind was at ease and he was in high spirits; he was optimistic and easygoing in his affairs. He was close to the hearts of the people in a venerable way; though he was close to them and was always smiling, there was always with him a sense of dignity and honor. In terms of character, his was complete and unparalleled. Maintaining his ample modesty, he would play with children and would openly welcome the visitor. Because he remained happy with Allah's favors and blessings, hopelessness and failure were concepts that were absolutely foreign to him. Instead he favored optimism of the promising kind. Hateful to him were ostentation, affectedness, and extravagance. It can easily be said that the Prophet (bpuh) was the epitome of all of the above-mentioned characteristics. He was noble, in the true sense of the word, because he was the conveyer of a true message, the proprietor of honorable principles, the example and teacher for an entire nation, the man of family and society, and the bearer of many virtues.

He was, in short, someone who was guided to all that is good.

{... He releases them from their heavy burdens [of Allah's covenant], and from the fetters [bindings] that were upon them.}

(Qur'an 7: 157)

Or in other words, he was:

{...a mercy to the worlds.}

(Qur'an 21: 107)

{As witness, and a bearer of glad tidings, and a warner – and as one who invites to Allah by His leave, and as a lamp spreading light.}

(Qur'an 33: 46)

Among that which goes against Islam and its message, which is easy to follow, is the extravagance of the Kharijites, the foolishness and extremes of Sufism, the passionate love of the poets, and the vainglory of those who worship this life.

{Then Allah by His leave guided those who believed to the truth of that wherein they differed. And Allah guides whom He wills to a straight path.}

(Qur'an 2: 213)

A good life

A Western thinker said:

> It is most possible for you, while you are behind steel bars, to look out upon the horizon and to smell roses. It is also extremely plausible for you to be in a castle replete with opulence and comfort, and yet be angry and discontented with your family and wealth.

Happiness is not determined by time or by place, but instead by faith in Allah (the Exalted) and obedience to Him, matters that are rooted in a person's heart. The heart has a far-reaching significance in that it is the place that Allah looks at and scrutinizes. If faith settles itself in the heart, happiness and tranquility will pervade both the heart and the soul.

Aḥmad ibn Ḥanbal was a venerable scholar and a prolific compiler of hadiths. He lived a productive life, yet he was not rich; his garment was patched in many places and every time it tore again, he would sew it himself. He lived in a three-room structure made of mud. Often, all that he could find to eat was a piece of bread. His biographers mention that he had the same shoes for seventeen years, and he would often patch them up or sew them if there was a tear. Meat would find its way to his plate only once a month, and on most days he fasted. He journeyed throughout the lands seeking out hadiths. Yet despite all of the hardships he had to bear, he was contented, comfortable, serene, and unworried. These qualities can be attributed to his fortitude, to his knowing his goal and final destination, to his seeking reward from Allah, and to his striving after the hereafter and paradise.

On the other hand, the rulers of his time, such as al-Ma'moon, al-Wathiq, al-Mu'taṣm and al-Mutawakkil, all lived in castles. They owned hoards of gold and silver, and they had entire armies at their disposal; they had all that they desired. In spite of all their material wealth, they lived in turmoil, and they spent their lives in anxiety and worry. Wars, uprisings, and insurgencies brought them misery. In the records of history, we even find that on their death beds many of them would renounce the world bitterly, feeling regretful for their extravagances on the one hand and for their shortcomings on the other. Shaykh al-Islam Ibn Taymiyah is another example. He spent his time on this earth with no family, no place to call home, no wealth, and no position. He had a room adjoining the central mosque, a slice of bread to keep him going for the day, and two garments. Sometimes he would sleep in the mosque. But, as he said about his situation, his paradise was in his breast, his execution meant martyrdom, imprisonment was peaceful seclusion, and being exiled from his country meant traveling abroad as a tourist. Such sentiments could come from him only because the tree of faith in his heart had firm and solid roots.

{...Whose oil would almost glow forth [of itself], though no fire touched it. Light upon light! Allah guides to His light whom He wills.}

(Qur'an 24: 35)

{He will expiate from them their sins, and will make good their state.}

(Qur'an 47: 2)

{While as for those who accept guidance, He increases their guidance and bestows on them their piety.}

(Qur'an 47: 17)

{You will recognize in their faces the brightness of delight.}

(Qur'an 83: 24)

Abu Dharr (may Allah be pleased with him) was a Companion known for his frugal lifestyle. Taking with him his wife and children, he left the city and settled in an isolated location. After setting up his tent, he spent most of his days chiefly in worship, recitation of the Qur'an, and reflection. Most days he fasted. His worldly possessions were limited to a tent, some sheep, and a few other small things. Some friends visited him once and asked, "Where is the world (referring to the material things that others have)?" He said:

In my house is all that I need from this world. The Prophet (bpuh) informed us that in front of us is an insurmountable obstacle (the Day of Judgment), and no one will pass it (safely) except for the one who has a light load.

Despite living a life of poverty, he had all that he needed from this world. As for superfluous possessions, he felt that they would divert him from his main purpose and would only cause him worry.

What then is happiness?

«Live in this world as if you are a stranger or a traveler who is just passing through.»

Happiness is not in the castle of 'Abdul-Malik ibn Marwân, in the army of Haroon ar-Rasheed, in the mansions of Ibn Jaṣṣaṣ, in the treasures of Qâroon, or in gardens of roses. Bliss and happiness were the lot of the Prophet's Companions (may Allah be pleased with them all) even though they were poor and led harsh lives.

Be Happy

Happiness was with Imam Bukhari in his collection of hadiths, with Ḥasan al-Baṣri in his truthfulness, with Shâfi'i in his deductions, with Imams Mâlik and Aḥmad in their introspection and self-denial, and with Thâbit al-Bannâni in his worship.

{That is because they suffer neither thirst, nor fatigue, nor hunger in the cause of Allah, nor they take any step to raise the anger of disbelievers nor inflict any injury upon an enemy but is written to their credit as a deed of righteousness. Surely, Allah wastes not the reward of the doers of good.}

(Qur'an 9: 120)

Happiness is not a check cashed, a car bought, or oil pumped.

Happiness is the solace that is derived from being upon the truth, the peace of mind that is achieved by living according to sound principles, and the calmness that is brought about by living a life of goodness.

We used to think that if we bought a bigger house, had more things, and purchased the latest appliances and machines that make life easier, we would be happy and joyful. We were surprised when we found that these very things were the cause of worry, anxiety, and trouble in our lives.

{And strain not your eyes in longing for the things We have given for enjoyment to various groups of them [polytheists and disbelievers in the Oneness of Allah], the splendor of the life of this world that We may test them thereby.}

(Qur'an 20: 131)

The greatest reformer in the world was the Messenger of guidance, Muhammad (bpuh). In terms of material wealth he was poor; at times, he wasn't even able to find the pit of a date with which to satisfy his hunger. Notwithstanding these difficulties, he lived a life of bliss and inner peace to an unparalleled degree, the extent of which no one knows except Allah (the Exalted).

{And removed from you your burden, which weighed down your back?}

(Qur'an 94: 2-3)

{And Ever Great is the grace of Allah unto you [O Muhammad].}

(Qur'an 4: 113)

{Allah knows best with whom to place His Message.}

(Qur'an 6: 124)

The Prophet (bpuh) said in an authentic hadith:

«Sin is what affects (and lingers in) the heart and what you hate for people to find out about; performing good deeds is what the heart and soul feel tranquil (and satisfied) with.»

Uprightness calms both conscience and soul. The Prophet (bpuh) said:

«Performing good deeds is tranquility, while performing sins is uncertainty.»

The doers of good are always at peace, but the sinners are always wary and suspicious of what goes on around them.

{They think that every cry is against them.}

(Qur'an 63: 4)

The wrongdoer goes from anxiety to suspicion and then finally to paranoia.

If one does ill, he will feel suspicious,

And he will believe whatever he imagines and fancies.

The solution for anyone who seeks happiness clearly lies in doing well and avoiding evil.

{They who believe and do not mix their belief with injustice – those will have security, and they are [rightly] guided.}

(Qur'an 6: 82)

Being a Muslim who is spiritually healthy is better than achieving the kingdoms of Khosrau and Caesar, since your religion is what will remain with you until you settle in the gardens of paradise. As for power and position, they are but momentary and fleeting.

{Verily! We will inherit the earth and whatsoever is thereon. And to Us they all shall be returned.}

(Qur'an 19: 40)

Good words ascend to Him

The Messenger of Allah (bpuh) taught his Companions a number of beautiful invocations that were brief in length but far-reaching in their implications.

Abu Bakr (may Allah be pleased with him) asked the Prophet (bpuh) to teach him a supplication, and he answered:

«Say: O my Lord, verily, I have greatly wronged myself, and no one forgives sins except You. So forgive me with Your forgiveness, and have mercy on me, since verily, You are the Oft-Forgiving, the Most Merciful.»

The Prophet (bpuh) said to 'Abbâs (may Allah be pleased with him):

«Ask Allah for pardon and good health.»

He told 'Ali (may Allah be pleased with him):

«Say: O Allah, guide me and direct me (to the right path).»

He said to 'Ubayd ibn Ḥusayn (may Allah be pleased with him):

«Say: O Allah, Inspire me to the right guidance and protect me from the evil of my own self.»

He taught Shaddâd ibn Aws (may Allah be pleased with him) to say:

«O Allah, I ask You to make me steadfast in the matter (of religion), resolute upon right guidance, thankful for Your blessing, and diligent in Your worship. I ask You, O Allah, to make my heart sound and my tongue truthful; I ask You from the good that You know. I seek refuge in You from the evil that You have full knowledge about, and I ask Your forgiveness for that which You (completely) know of. Truly, You are the Knower of all things unseen.»

He taught Mu'âdh (may Allah be pleased with him) to say:

«O Allah, help me to remember You, to thank You, and to worship You excellently.»

That we should ask for Allah's pleasure and for His mercy in the hereafter, that we invoke Allah to save us from His anger and punishment, and that we ask Him for help in worshipping Him and thanking Him – these are some of the more salient themes that are stressed in the previous supplications. Regarding these themes, there is one uniting or common factor: that we should seek what is with Allah and turn away from what is in this world; in other words, that we must not be covetous of material things that are, by their very nature, short–lived.

Such is the seizure of your Lord

{Such is the seizure of your Lord when He seizes the [population of] towns while they are doing wrong.}

(Qur'an 11: 102)

One can become sad and wretched for different reasons, including: doing wrong to others, usurping their rights, and hurting the meek among the people. Some of the wise used to say, "Fear the one who finds no helper against you (in your wrongdoing) except Allah."

The history of nations has left us with poignant examples of what lies in store for the oppressor. 'Âmir ibn at-Tufayl plotted to assassinate the Prophet (bpuh), who in turn supplicated against him. 'Âmir immediately became afflicted with an enlarged gland; after an hour of screaming and writhing from pain, he died a most painful death.

Arbad ibn Qays was wretched enough to have similar plans, and the Prophet (bpuh) supplicated against him as well. Allah sent lightning down on Arbad, scorching both him and his mount.

Shortly before al-Hajjâj executed Sa'eed ibn Jubayr (may Allah be pleased with him), the latter supplicated, "O Allah, do not empower him over anybody after me." Al-Hajjâj was struck by an abscess in his hand, which quickly spread throughout his body. He experienced so much pain that he began to moan and moo like a cow, until finally, he died in a pitiable state.

Sufyân ath-Thawri was in hiding for a period of time because of threats from Abu Ja'far al-Mansoor. Abu Ja'far was heading for the Kaaba in Makkah while Sufyân was already there. He clung to the curtain of the edifice and fervently prayed to Allah not to allow Abu Ja'far to enter His house. Abu Ja'far died just before reaching the outer limits of Makkah.

Ahmad ibn Abi Du'âd al-Qadi al-Mu'tazili took part in inflicting harm upon Imam Ahmad ibn Hanbal. Imam Ahmad prayed against him, and so Allah punished Ibn Abi Du'âd by making him paralyzed on one side of his body. He was heard to have said afterwards:

> As for half of my body, if a fly were to land on any part of it, I would feel that the Day of Judgment had commenced. As for the other half, if it were to be cut up into pieces by a pair of scissors, I would not feel anything.

Imam Aḥmad, who was greatly wronged and harmed for a period of time, also prayed against another of his transgressors, 'Ali ibn Zayyat. Only a short period of time passed before someone tortured and killed Ibn Zayyat by putting him into an oven and hammering nails into his head.

During the reign of Jamal 'Abdul–Nâṣir, Ḥamzah al–Basyuni tortured many Muslims in prison. He wickedly scoffed, "Where is your Lord so that I can put him in steel?" Allah is far above what the oppressors say! A truck smashed into Ḥamzah's car, killing him, and appropriately, the truck was transporting rods of steel. One rod of steel entered his body from the top of his head until it made its way down to his bowels. The rescue team was unable to extract him from the car except in pieces.

{And he and his hosts were arrogant in the land, without right, and they thought that they would never return to Us.}

(Qur'an 28: 39)

{And they said: Who is mightier than us in strength? See they not that Allah, Who created them, was mightier in strength than them?}

(Qur'an 41: 15)

Similar is the case of Sâlaḥ Naṣr, a general under 'Abdul–Nâṣir who was known for perpetrating evil and oppression throughout the land. He became sick with ten painful and chronic diseases. He lived for many years in misery, and the doctors could find no cure for him. In the end, he died a humiliating death as a prisoner in the jails of those very leaders whom he used to serve.

{And those who did transgress beyond bounds in the lands [in the disobedience of Allah] and made therein much mischief. So your Lord poured on them different kinds of severe torment.}

(Qur'an 89: 11–13)

The Prophet (bpuh) said:

«Verily, Allah prolongs the life of the oppressor until when He takes him, there is no escape.»

He also said:

«Beware of the supplication of the oppressed one, for verily, between it and Allah, there is no veil (or barrier).»

The supplication of the wronged

Ibrâheem at–Tamimi once said, "When a man wrongs me, I pay him back with an act of mercy."

When some money was stolen from a righteous man who lived in Khorasan, he began to weep. Fu'dayl, who saw him in that state, asked, "Why are you crying?" He answered, "I remembered that Allah shall gather me and the thief together on the Day of Judgment, and I cried, feeling pity for him."

A man slandered a scholar from the early generations of Islam; in return, the scholar gave him a gift of dates. When asked later about the gifts, he said, "Because he did good to me." He meant that on the Day of Judgment, the man would have to give him some of his good deeds or take from him some of his bad ones.

The importance of having a good friend

Every Muslim needs a helpful, loving friend – to turn to, to share joys and hardships with, and to reciprocate affection.

{And appoint for me a helper from my family: Aaron, my brother. Increase my strength with him, and let him share my task [of conveying Allah's message and prophethood] that we may glorify You much and remember You much.}

(Qur'an 20: 29–34)

{They are but Awliyâ' [friends, protectors, helpers, et cetera] to one another.}

(Qur'an 5: 51)

{Verily, Allah loves those who fight in His cause in rows [ranks] as if they were a solid structure.}

(Qur'an 61: 4)

{And He has united their [the believers'] hearts.}

(Qur'an 8: 63)

{The believers are nothing else than brothers [in Islamic religion].}

(Qur'an 49: 10)

The topic we are now discussing is pertinent to the subject matter of this book because having a good and worthy companion brings joy to the heart. The Prophet (bpuh) related that Allah (the Exalted) said:

> «Where are the ones who love each other because of My Exaltedness (that is, who love each other for the sake of Allah)? Today I will provide shade for them in My shade – a day wherein there is no shade except for My shade.»

In Islam, security is a must

{For them [only] there is security and they are the guided.}

(Qur'an 6: 82)

{[He] Who has fed them against hunger, and has made them safe from fear.}

(Qur'an 106: 4)

{Have We not established for them a secure sanctuary [Makkah]...}

(Qur'an 28: 57)

{...Whosoever enters it, he attains security.}

(Qur'an 3: 97)

{...Then grant him protection...}

(Qur'an 9: 6)

The Prophet (bpuh) said:

> «Whoever spends his night safely in his home, with a healthy body and enough provision for his day, it is as if he has gained the world in its entirety.»

Security of the heart is the faith and sureness of knowing the truth. Security of the home is its freedom from shame and deviation and its being replete with tranquility and divine guidance. Security of our nation is its being united with love, its being founded upon justice, and in its application of the Sharia. The enemy of security is fear:

{So he escaped from there, looking about in a state of fear.}

(Qur'an 28: 21)

{...So fear them not, but fear Me.}

(Qur'an 5: 3)

Based on the above–mentioned categories of security, there is no true peace and security for the frightened one or for the disbeliever.

By Allah, how pitiable is the life of this world! If you are prosperous in one facet of your life, you are sure to be miserable in another. If wealth comes on the one hand, sickness arrives on the other. If your body is healthy, some other form of difficulty will arise. Finally, when everything seems to be going well and you at last feel a sense of stability, you are ready to be put into a coffin.

A poet named al-A'shat, from Najd, was heading toward the Prophet (bpuh) to laud him in verses of poetry and to accept Islam. Abu Sufyân met him on his way and offered him one hundred camels to give up his mission and go back home. He accepted the offer and set off with the camels. To make the return journey, he mounted one of the camels, but it soon turned wild and threw him off, causing him to land on his head; upon impact, his neck snapped and he died. He parted from this world without having achieved either religious or worldly gain.

Fleeting glory

Happiness, if it is of the true kind, must be perpetual in its presence and complete in its magnitude. In terms of always being present, I mean that it should never be interrupted by worry and that it should exist for a person both in this world and in the hereafter. Its completeness is realized when it is neither spoiled nor diminished by troubles or worries.

An-Nu'mân ibn al-Mundhir, who was the king of Iraq, sat under a tree to relax and to drink alcohol. He called 'Adee ibn Zayd, a wise man, to come and advise him. 'Adee said, "O King, do you know what this tree says?" The king said, "No, what does it say?" 'Adee replied:

Many people sought rest around me,

To drink wine mixed with pure water,

Soon after, time began to play with them

(that is, some harm befell them),

Time is like that: always changing from one state to another.

Tormented by the eventuality described to him, the king became embittered. He stopped drinking, but he remained miserable until he died.

As the Shah of Iran celebrated the passing of 2500 years since the establishment of the Persian Empire, he began to make plans for expanding the scope of his power to lands outside of his reign. Then, in the blink of an eye, he was toppled from power:

﴿You give the kingdom to whom You will, and You take the kingdom from whom You will.﴾

(Qur'an 3: 26)

Chased from his castle and his world, he died in exile as a poor man in a far-off country. No one shed tears for him:

﴿How many of gardens and springs have they [Pharaoh's people] left? And green crops [fields, et cetera] and goodly places, and comforts of life wherein they used to take delight!﴾

(Qur'an 44: 25-27)

A similar case is that of Ceausescu, the former president of Romania. He ruled for twenty-two years, and he had 70,000 personal guards. In the end, though, it was his own people who surrounded his castle. He fled but was soon caught, given a brief trial, and executed by a firing squad.

﴿Then he had no group or party to help him against Allah, nor was he one of those who could save themselves.﴾

(Qur'an 28: 81)

Thus he died without anything to show for his long reign: no worldly goods did he take with him and no prospect of prosperity in the hereafter.

Another example is the former leader of the Philippines, Ferdinand Marcos. He gathered wealth and power for himself while heaping misery upon his people. In turn, Allah made him feel that same misery as he was driven away from his country, his family, and his power. With no sanctuary to turn to, he died ignominiously: his own people even refused to allow him to be buried in the Philippines.

﴿Did He not make their plot go astray?﴾

(Qur'an 105: 2)

{And Allah seized him in exemplary punishment for the last and the first [transgression].}
(Qur'an 79: 25)
{And We punished each [of them] for his sins.}

(Qur'an 29: 40)

Virtuous deeds are the crown on the head of a happy life

To attain happiness and peace, you must be one of those who hasten to do virtuous and beautiful deeds. The Prophet (bpuh) said:

> «Strive toward that which benefits you, and seek help from Allah.»

A Companion of the Prophet Muhammad (bpuh) asked to be one of his Companions in paradise. He replied:

> «Help me to help you by prostrating often, for Allah will raise you by one degree for every prostration that you make for Him.»

Another Companion asked the Prophet (bpuh) to inform him of one deed that encompassed much good. He told him:

> «That your tongue should remain moist with the remembrance of Allah.»

In response to a third such seeker of good, the Prophet (bpuh) said:

> «Don't curse others, and don't hit others with your hand. If someone curses you regarding something that he knows about you, don't curse him regarding something that you know about him. Don't disparage any kind of good deed, even if that deed consists of pouring some water from your bucket into the container of the one who seeks drink.»

{And march forth in the way [which leads to] forgiveness from your Lord, and for paradise...}

(Qur'an 3: 133)

{Verily, they used to hasten on to do good deeds...}

(Qur'an 21: 90)

{And the forerunners, the forerunners –} (Qur'an 56: 10)

Do not delay when it comes to doing good and righteous deeds.

{So for this let the competitors compete.}

(Qur'an 83: 26)

After being stabbed, and while his blood was gushing out, 'Umar (may Allah be pleased with him) said to a young man who was dragging his lower garment on the ground, "O son of my brother, lift up your garment, for to do so is more righteous and purer for your clothes." Even during the pangs of death, he invited others to do good!

{To any of you that chooses to go forward [by working righteous deeds], or to remain behind [by committing sins].}

(Qur'an 74: 37)

Verily, happiness is not achieved by sleeping much, by seeking comfort, or by being averse to doing good deeds.

{But Allah was averse to their being sent forth, so He made them lag behind, and it was said [to them]: Sit you among those who sit [at home].}

(Qur'an 9: 46)

The logic of downtrodden and lethargic souls is:

{And they said: Do not go forth in the heat.}

(Qur'an 9: 81)

{Who say to their brethren when they travel through the earth or go out to fight: If they had stayed with us, they would not have died or been killed.}

(Qur'an 3: 156)

We are prohibited from lagging behind when it comes to doing good deeds:

{What is the matter with you, that when you are asked to march forth in the cause of Allah [jihad] you cling heavily to the earth?}

(Qur'an 9: 38)

{There is certainly among you he who would linger behind [from fighting in Allah's cause].}

(Qur'an 4: 72)

{... But he clung to the earth...}

(Qur'an 7: 176)

{Am I not even able to be as this crow!}

(Qur'an 5: 31)

{That is because they loved and preferred the life of this world over that of the hereafter.}

(Qur'an 16: 107)

{And do not dispute [with one another] lest you lose courage and your strength departs.}

(Qur'an 8: 46)

{And when they stand up for the prayer, they stand with laziness...}

(Qur'an 4: 142)

The Prophet (bpuh) said:

«O Allah, I seek refuge in You from laziness.»

The wise people subdue themselves and work for what comes after death. Weak persons obey themselves in their desires, and though they perform no deeds that are worthy of reward, they keep vain and false hopes in Allah.

Everlasting life and paradise are there, not here!

Do you wish to stay young, healthy, rich, and immortal? If you desire these things, you will not find them in this world; however, you can find them in the hereafter. Allah (the Exalted) has decreed misery and impermanence for this world. He called this life a trifle and an enjoyment of deception.

There is a well–known poet from long ago, who for the greater part of his life lived a life of poverty. In the prime of his youth, he wanted money and could not get it. He wanted a wife too, but he failed in that pursuit as well. When he became old, with white hair and brittle bones, he became rich. Many women were now willing to marry him, and he lived a comfortable life. The irony of his story is that he was poor when he was able to enjoy all comforts, but he became rich when he could no longer enjoy the pleasures of life. He composed these verses in the latter part of his life:

What I desired to own when I was only twenty,

Came into my possession after turning eighty.

Be Happy

Young Turkish girls now surround me,

Singing and wearing silks and jewels.

They say: Your moans keep us awake all night long,

So what is it that you complain of?

I said: Of being an octogenarian.

{Did We not give you lives long enough, so that whosoever would receive admonition could receive it? And the warner came to you...}

(Qur'an 35: 37)

{...And they thought that they would never return to Us.}

(Qur'an 28: 39)

{And this life of the world is only amusement and play!}

(Qur'an 29: 64)

«The example of this world is that of a rider who seeks shade under a tree – to rest for a short period of time – and then gets up and leaves.»

Enemies of the divine way

As I was reading material written by proponents of atheism, it became clear to me that those writers blatantly showed enmity toward the principles of the true religion. Based on what I read, and on what I perceived in terms of their ill manners and lack of humility, I feel shy even to relate what they said and wrote.

Suffice it to say that I realized that a person who does not have principles, and who does not attribute a correct meaning to life, becomes transformed into an animal, possessing only the shape and appearance of a human being.

{Or do you think that most of them hear or understand? They are only like cattle – nay, they are even farther astray from the path [that is, even worse than cattle].}

(Qur'an 25: 44)

I asked myself how it is possible for them to be happy despite their having turned away from Allah, Who owns happiness and gives it to whomever He pleases. How could they be happy after having severed the rope between them and their Lord, and after having shut the doors of Allah's vast mercy upon their own weak selves? How could they find happiness and comfort after having earned His anger and after having waged war upon Him?

I grasped that the first punishment they receive is one that is inflicted upon them in this life, as an introduction, or prelude, to the greater punishment of the hereafter (if they fail to repent). This harbinger of punishment includes misery, general apathy, a feeling of being constricted, and a sense of hopelessness.

{But whosoever turns away from My reminder [that is, neither believes in this Qur'an nor acts on its orders, et cetera], verily for him is a life of hardship...}

(Qur'an 20: 124)

Many people who are in this category wish that their life would end. Some common factors between atheists of old and present–day atheists are: a lack of appropriate manners with Allah, an arbitrary approach to deciding upon values and principles, and a lack of knowledge – or a feigned lack of knowledge – of the evil end results of their actions. In addition, they share a general lack of concern for what they say, do, or write.

{Then is one who laid the foundation of his building on righteousness [with fear] from Allah and [seeking] His approval, better or one who laid the foundation of his building on the edge of a bank about to collapse, so it collapsed with him into the fire of hell? And Allah does not guide wrongdoing people.}

(Qur'an 9: 109)

The reality of this life

We will be happy to the degree that we remember Allah and recite His Book. After considering this principle, we may estimate our worth in this world and in the hereafter.

{And if it were not that the people would become one community [of disbelievers], We would have made for those who disbelieve in the Most Merciful – for their houses – ceilings and stairways of silver upon which to mount, and for their houses – doors and couches [of silver] upon which to recline, and gold ornament. But all that is not but the enjoyment of worldly life. And the hereafter with your Lord is for the righteous.}

(Qur'an 43: 33–35)

These verses proclaim in clear terms the temporary, and therefore insignificant, worth of material possessions and social status.

We should realize that this life is not the yardstick of success when we see that the disbeliever often lives a life of opulence, while the believer is often precluded from many worldly pleasures, a phenomenon that merely indicates the paltry value of this world.

While giving a sermon on a Friday, 'Utbah ibn Ghazwân, a well-known Companion of the Prophet (bpuh) was reminiscing out loud about what the days were like when he lived with the Prophet (bpuh). 'Utbah would fight with him in the way of Allah, and to avoid starvation, they would eat the leaves of a tree. Yet he remembered those days to be the happiest of his life. Then he recalled how he departed from the Prophet (bpuh), becoming a governor of a province. Despite this rise in worldly status, he felt wonder at how much lower the true quality of life became after the death of the Prophet (bpuh).

After the death of the Prophet (bpuh), Sa'd ibn Abi Waqqâs (may Allah be pleased with him) felt bewildered and confused when he became governor of Kufa. During the Prophet's lifetime, he too would eat tree leaves or the skin of a carcass. He could not bear the castles of his new life after having tasted the pleasure of his old life in the company of the Prophet (bpuh).

{And indeed the hereafter is better for you than the present [life of this world].}

(Qur'an 93: 4)

Therefore there is a secret to guide you in this life – and that is to know the triviality of this world.

{Do they think that We enlarge them in wealth and children, We hasten unto them with good things [in this worldly life, so that they will have no share of good things in the hereafter]? Nay, but they perceive not.}

(Qur'an 23: 55–56)

Once when he entered the house of the Prophet (bpuh), 'Umar (may Allah be pleased with him) saw marks on the Prophet's side, the result of his always lying down on straw, and he also noticed the bareness of the room. His eyes swelled with tears after seeing such a moving sight. The Messenger of Allah (bpuh), the example and leader of all, in such a situation! It was too much for him.

{And they say: Why does this Messenger [Muhammad] eat food, and walk about in the markets [like ourselves]?}

(Qur'an 25: 7)

'Umar (may Allah be pleased with him) said, "You know, O Messenger of Allah, of the lifestyle of Khosrau and Caesar!" The Prophet (bpuh) replied:

«O son of Khaṭṭâb, are you in doubt? Are you not pleased that for us is the hereafter, and for them is this world?»

It is a just balance and a fair distribution. So let them try to find their happiness in dollars, gold, silver, mansions, and cars. Verily, by Allah (the Exalted) they will never find it in those things.

{Whosoever desires the life of the world and its glitter; to them We shall pay in full [the wages of] their deeds therein, and they will have no diminution therein. They are those for whom there is nothing in the hereafter but fire; and vain are the deeds they did therein. And of no effect is that which they used to do.} (Qur'an 11: 15–16)

The key to happiness

If you know Allah and worship Him, you will have found happiness and peace, even if you are living in a hut made of mud.

In contrast, if you deviate from the true path, your life will truly be wretched, even if you are living a life of luxury and comfort in a large mansion. If this latter case applies to you, then you do not have with you the key to happiness.

{And We gave him of the treasures, that of which the keys would have been a burden to a body of strong men.} (Qur'an 28: 76)

Pause to reflect

{Truly, Allah defends those who believe.} (Qur'an 22: 38)

In other words, He protects them from evil, both in this world and in the hereafter. In this verse, Allah enlightens us, warns us, and gives us glad tidings. He repels evil from the believers in proportion to their faith. The evil of the disbelievers, the evil whispers of the devil, the evil in their own selves, and the evil of their deeds – all of these does Allah ward off from the true believers. When calamity falls, its burden will be lightened from them.

Every believer has a share in this divine protection, yet it varies according to one's level of faith: some will receive less, others more.

Among the fruits of faith is that it gives solace to the believer in times of hardship.

{...And whosoever believes in Allah, He guides his heart...}

(Qur'an 64: 11)

This refers to the believers who are afflicted with hardship, who know that it is from Allah and that it was decreed for them. They are satisfied and submit their will to what has been predestined for them. Thus, the fatal blow of hardship will lose its effect on them because they know that it came from Allah and that they will be rewarded for their patience.

How they used to live

Let us go back and take a glimpse at how one of the Prophet's Companions would spend his day. 'Ali ibn Abi Ṭâlib (may Allah be pleased with him), who was married to Fâṭimah (may Allah be pleased with her), the daughter of the Prophet (bpuh), woke up early one morning. He and his wife searched for food, but there was nothing to be found in their humble home. This occurred on a bitter cold day of winter, so 'Ali put on some warm clothes and went out. He searched through all of the precincts of the city and finally remembered a Jew who owned a garden. When 'Ali reached the garden, the Jew said, "O Arab, come and harvest the dates for me; for each large bucket that you fill, I will give you a single date." So he toiled for a period of time until his hands hurt and his body ached. He took the paltry number of dates that he earned and went to the Prophet (bpuh) to share them with him. With what was left over, he and Fâṭimah sustained themselves for the rest of the day.

This was their life, yet – in what may seem to be a contradiction to the material minded person – their homes were filled with illumination and happiness.

Their hearts were filled with the noble principles that were revealed to the Prophet (bpuh). Through the spiritual illumination of their hearts, they perceived the truth and accepted it, while they recognized falsehood and rejected it. They worked in the path of the former and they steered far away from the latter. They came to realize and grasp the true value and worth of things.

Where is the happiness of a man like Hâmân, the companion of Pharaoh, who is still cursed for his wrongdoing?

{As the likeness of vegetation after rain, thereof the growth is pleasing to the tiller; afterwards it dries up and you see it turning yellow; then it becomes straw.}

(Qur'an 57: 20)

True happiness is with Bilâl, Salmân, and 'Ammar; Bilâl was a caller to the truth, Salmân was truthful, and 'Ammar was faithful in fulfilling his obligations.

What the wise say about patience

The following words are ascribed to the Persian ruler Anushirwan:

Calamity in this life is of two kinds. The first kind allows for a way out; worrying is its remedy. The second kind permits for no solution or way out; patience is its cure.

It is also said that, "Whoever follows patience, success will follow him."

It has also been said:

Strive to remain alive by seeking out death. For how many have remained because they sought out death, and how many have perished who preferred to stay! Safety most often comes after treading the path of uncertainty.

The Arabs would say, "Verily, even in evil, there are degrees of better and worse." Abu 'Ubaydah explained the meaning of this expression, saying,

If you are afflicted with a hardship, know that you could have been hit with far worse. If you have such an outlook, you will be better able to deal with the hardship.

A way out of difficulty most often comes when hope is lost:

{They are those from whom We shall accept the best of their deeds and overlook their evil deeds. [They shall be] among the dwellers of paradise, a promise of truth, which they have been promised.}

(Qur'an 46: 16)

{[They were reprieved] until, when the Messengers gave up hope and thought that they were denied [by their people], then came to them Our help...}

(Qur'an 12: 110)

{Truly! Allah is with the patient ones.}

(Qur'an 2: 153)

{Only those who are patient shall receive their rewards in full, without reckoning.}

(Qur'an 39: 10)

Sometimes Allah brings success and relief when hope is lost and all seems dark. This is in order to encourage us to turn our hopes to Him, to trust completely in Him, and to never lose hope of His help at any time. When afflicted, we should be satisfied with the knowledge that we are suffering from something minor and were saved from what could have been worse. Is-ḥâq said, "Perhaps Allah tests a slave with a calamity but then saves him from destruction. Thus, the calamity is really a great blessing (in disguise)."

It has been said that if we endure hardship and show contentment with Allah's decree by being patient, some hidden benefit or blessing will come about through that experience.

It has been related from some Christians that one of their prophets said:

> Calamities are a means of discipline from Allah; disciplining is not something that is continuous. So glad tidings to whoever is patient when disciplined. Such a person should be crowned with the crown that symbolizes both overcoming and victory -the victory that Allah promised to the ones who love Him and obey Him.

Is-ḥâq also said, "Beware of complaining if you are caught in the sharp claws of a hardship, for the way to safety is a difficult path to tread."

The importance of a positive attitude

A writer justly said:

> Verily, hope encourages and steers one towards patience, hope arises from having a good opinion of Allah, and hope in Allah precludes the possibility of failure. But why should we be so confident that hope in Allah precludes the possibility of failure? If we were to study the characteristics of generous people, we would find that they take special care of those who think well enough of them to turn to them for help. They will also tend to eschew those who think ill of them. What is important here is that they refrain from hurting the hopes of those who single them out for help. Then what will be the case regarding the Most Generous

One, Whose kingdom is not decreased in the least when He gives even more than what the hopeful ones expected from Him in the first place?

A person who finds no way out of a difficult situation illustrates the most poignant example of Allah's generosity and guidance for His slaves. After losing all hope in everyone that he turned to for help, he is forced to remember that there is one door that remains open and that he should have hope in no one except Allah (the Exalted). Then he feels the chastisement for not having put his hope in Allah, the Exalted, the Almighty in the first place, and at that point, aid and relief arrive.

{Verily, those whom you call upon besides Allah are slaves like you. So call upon them and let them answer you if you are truthful.}

(Qur'an 7: 194)

A few words on patience

Ibn Mas'ood (may Allah be pleased with him) is reported to have said, "Relief and aid are from faith and contentment. Anxiety and grief are from doubt and anger."

He also used to say, "The patient one achieves the best of aims."

Abbân ibn Taghlab said:

I heard a desert Arab say: One of the noblest of characteristics becomes manifest when one is afflicted by a trial and then uses patience to overcome that trial. His patience and hope affect him positively; it is as if he constantly visualizes himself being saved from his problem. His state of mind is positive to such a high degree because of his trust in Allah and his good opinion of Him. Whenever one possesses these characteristics, he will never have to wait long for Allah to fulfill his needs and remove hardship from his life. He will be saved, and his religion and honor will remain safe.

Al–Asma'ee related that a desert Arab said:

Fear evil when you find yourself to be in a good situation; hope for good when you are in an evil situation. Many have lived who have sought death, and many have died who have sought life. Safety comes most often for a person after he has followed the path of fear.

Some of the wise would say:

> The wise person, when afflicted by hardship, consoles himself in two ways: the first is to be contented, and the second is in hoping for a way out of the difficulties that have befallen him. The ignorant person is shaken and nervous in situations of hardship in two ways: the first is in the number of people from whom he seeks aid, and the second is in his constant fears and apprehensions about that which is worse than what has already befallen him.

As I mentioned earlier, it has been said that Allah (the Exalted) disciplines us through trials, a form of education that opens hearts, ears, and eyes. Ḥasan ibn Sahl described trials as being a wake-up call for the forgetful ones, a means of achieving reward for the patient ones, and a reminder of blessings for everyone. The decree of Allah is always better, especially for those who, through their bravery, appear to be seeking out death – who are searching for a life of remembrance, and who are unlike those described in the following verse:

{[They are] the ones who said about their killed brethren while they themselves sat [at home]: If only they had listened to us, they would not have been killed. Say: Avert death from your own selves, if you speak the truth.}

(Qur'an 3: 168)

Pause to reflect

{If you are suffering [hardships] then surely, they [too] are suffering [hardships] as you are suffering, but you have a hope from Allah [for the reward, paradise] that for which they hope not...}

(Qur'an 4: 104)

For the reason mentioned in this verse, the true believers have a high level of tolerance when they are afflicted with calamity. Patience, steadfastness, serenity, and a sincere desire to fulfill one's duty as a slave of Allah – these are qualities that you can find in a true believer.

Ma'qil ibn Yasâr (may Allah be pleased with him) related that the Prophet (bpuh) said:

«Your Lord, Most Blessed and Most High, says: O son of Adam, dedicate your time to My worship, and I will fill your heart with wealth and your hands with sustenance. O son of Adam, don't distance yourself from Me, or I will fill your heart with poverty and your hands with problems that will preoccupy you.»

Don't grieve if you are poor, for your true value is not determined by your bank balance

'Ali (may Allah be pleased with him) said, "The (true) value of every person is weighed according to the good that he does."

Therefore the value of scholars is based on their knowledge, on whether it is limited or vast, and on the degree to which they disseminate their knowledge. Similarly, poets are appraised based on the quality of their poems. And so it goes for every person of every occupation: their worth with people is measured by their excellence in what they do. In terms not of occupation, but of religion and life in general, all of us should strive to increase our value and worth by performing good deeds, by increasing our knowledge and level of wisdom, by cultivating and polishing our minds, and by developing noble personality traits.

A word on reading

Reading opens the mind, guides one to correct morals, and sharpens one's ability to think. Reading is a comfort for the lonely, a stimulant for the thinker, and a lamp for the traveler.

To not read makes one limited in one's speech, thinking, and personality. Most books contain at least some benefit, whether it is in wise sayings, interesting stories, strange experiences, or new knowledge. It can even be said that the benefits of reading are beyond enumeration. We seek refuge in Allah from one of the greatest of calamities: to have weak determination and willpower.

Don't be sad, and study Allah's signs in the creation

If you study Allah's signs in the world and universe, you will find marvels that will remove your worries and anxieties; the soul finds delight in the strange, the wonderful, and the bizarre.

Bukhari and Muslim narrated a hadith from Jâbir ibn 'Abdullâh (may Allah be pleased with him), who said:

The Messenger of Allah sent us on a mission and appointed Abu 'Ubaydah to be our leader. We were to meet with a caravan from Quraysh. Since he could find nothing else, the Messenger of Allah (bpuh) provided us only with a container of dates for the journey. From the day we left onward, Abu 'Ubaydah would give us (each) one date for each day.

The narrator of the hadith asked Jâbir what they would do with the dates. He said:

We would suck on one of the dates the way a child does. Then we would drink water over it. This was enough for us until the night fell. We would then strike at the leaves of trees with our sticks, wet the leaves, and eat them. We were hiking on the shores of the sea when we saw something that looked like a huge sand-hill from a distance. As we came nearer, we realized that it was a large sea creature called a whale fish. Abu 'Ubaydah said that it was an animal that had died without being slaughtered (so it was not lawful to eat). He then said, No, we are the messengers of the Messenger of Allah, we are in the path of Allah, and now we are in a dire situation -so eat, all of you.

We, all three hundred of us, lived off of this creature for one month until we became fattened. I remember how we took spears and thrust them into the eye socket of the creature. From inside the socket we scooped out pieces of fat, with a piece being the size of a bull. So large was the creature that when Abu 'Ubaydah asked thirteen of our men to line up in the eye socket of the creature, there was enough space to accommodate them all. He also took one of its ribs and erected it on the ground. Then he found the tallest camel and made our tallest man ride on it, and they were able to pass underneath the rib. Finally, when we left the site, we took provisions from the meat for the return journey. When we arrived in Madinah, we went to the Messenger of Allah (the Exalted) and told him what happened, and he said:

«This is sustenance that Allah has taken out (of the sea) for you. Do you have any of its meat with you to feed us from it?»

We sent some to the Messenger of Allah, and he ate from it.

{Our Lord is He Who gave to each thing its form and nature, then guided it aright.}

(Qur'an 20: 50)

After a seed is placed in the ground, it will not grow until the ground shakes ever so slightly. The Richter scale picks up this minor jolt. The seed then splits and begins to grow:

{We send down water [rain] on it, it is stirred [to life], it swells and puts forth very lovely kind [of growth].}

(Qur'an 22: 5)

{Our Lord is He Who gave to each thing its form and nature, then guided it aright.}

(Qur'an 20: 50)

Dr. Zughlool an–Najjar, a researcher in cosmology, mentioned in one of his lectures that there is a comet that began its journey eons ago. Though it travels at a speed of up to 36,000 km/hr, it still has not reached the earth.

{So I swear by Mawaqi' [setting or the mansions, et cetera] of the stars [they traverse].}

(Qur'an 56: 75)

{Our Lord is He Who gave to each thing its form and nature, then guided it aright.}

(Qur'an 20: 50)

An amazing story was reported by the newspaper Recent Happenings in 1953. Ona, entering Paris guarded by many policemen, was a gigantic Norwegian stuffed whale that weighed more than 80,000 kilograms. Eight tractors carried the mammoth–sized monster, all tied together to a transport trailer. The whale was to be put on display for a period of one month, and visitors were going to be allowed to enter its electrically illuminated belly.

The organizers and police were unable to agree on a venue for the display, since the size and weight of the creature posed a threat to the structure of any building or street that it might be displayed in.

Despite the young age of this whale (eighteen months), it reached the remarkable length of twenty meters. Caught in Norwegian waters the previous year, it was to be transported via train from one city to another for display. Due to the problems of its size and weight, it had to be transported by a special trailer that was thirty meters in length.

{Our Lord is He Who gave to each thing its form and nature, then guided it aright.}

(Qur'an 20: 50)

Abdur-Razzâq aṣ-Ṣana'ni related that Ma'mar ibn Râshid al-Baṣri said, "I saw in Yemen a cluster of grapes that was the size of a full load that is placed on a mule."

{And tall date-palms, with ranged clusters.}

(Qur'an 50: 10)

All trees and plants are nourished by the same kind of water:

{Yet some of them We make more excellent than others to eat.}

(Qur'an 13: 4)

Every plant is endowed with a defense system that is specific to it. Some are strongly built, some have thorns with which they protect themselves, and yet others are bitter and sting.

{Our Lord is He Who gave to each thing its form and nature, then guided it aright.}

(Qur'an 20: 50)

Astronomers say that the universe is still expanding little by little, similar to the way that a balloon expands:

{With power did We construct the heaven. Verily, We are Able to extend the vastness of space thereof.}

(Qur'an 51: 47)

Others say that while dry land is constricting, the oceans are expanding.

{See they not that We gradually reduce the land [in their control] from its outlying borders?}

(Qur'an 21: 44)

{Our Lord is He Who gave to each thing its form and nature, then guided it aright.}

(Qur'an 20: 50)

In 1982, Faisal magazine reported the story of a cabbage that weighed 22 kgs (48.5 lbs) and was one meter (yard) in diameter, an onion that weighed 2.3 kgs (5 lbs) and was 30 cms (about one foot) in diameter, and a tomato that was 60 cms (about two feet) in circumference. All of these anomalies were found on the farm of a single Mexican farmer.

{Our Lord is He Who gave to each thing its form and nature, then guided it aright.}

(Qur'an 20: 50)

In the head are four liquids: sweetness in the mouth that mixes well with food and drink, stickiness in the nose that prevents dust from entering, saltiness in the eyes that prevents dryness, and sourness in the ears that protects one from insects and from harm in general.

{And also in your ownselves. Will you not then see?}

(Qur'an 51: 21)

{And [Allah] taught you that which you knew not.}

(Qur'an 4: 113)

{Allah Has taught man that which he knew not.}

(Qur'an 96: 5)

{And Allah has brought you out from the wombs of your mothers while you know nothing. And He gave you hearing, sight and hearts...}

(Qur'an 16: 78)

{And We taught him the making of metal coats of mail [for battles]...}

(Qur'an 21: 80)

{Rather, they have denied that which they encompass not in knowledge and whose interpretation has not yet come to them.}

(Qur'an 10: 39)

{And not an Âyâh [sign, et cetera] We showed them but it was greater than its fellow...}

(Qur'an 43: 48)

{Our Lord is He Who gave to each thing its form and nature, then guided it aright.}

(Qur'an 20: 50)

The heart does not feel deserted except when it disobeys its Lord. Ḥasan al-Baṣri said:

O son of Adam, after Prophet Moses objected to [the actions of] Khiḍr on three occasions, the latter said: This is the parting between you and me. Then how will it be with you, who disobey your Lord many times in a single day? Do you feel so secure (and sure) that He will not say to you: This is the parting between you and Me?

O Allah! O Allah!

{Nay [O Muhammad]: Allah rescues you from it and from all [other] distresses...}

(Qur'an 6: 64)

{Is not Allah Sufficient for His slave?}

(Qur'an 39: 36)

{Say [O Muhammad]: Who rescues you from the darkness of the land and the sea [dangers, like storms]...}

(Qur'an 6: 63)

{And We wished to do a favor to those who were weak [and oppressed] in the land...}

(Qur'an 28: 5)

Allah (the Exalted), said about Adam (pbuh):

{Then his Lord chose him, and turned to him with forgiveness, and gave him guidance.}

(Qur'an 20: 122)

And about Prophet Noah (pbuh):

{We listened to his invocation and saved him and his family from great distress.}

(Qur'an 21: 76)

And about Prophet Abraham (pbuh):

{We [Allah] said: O fire! Be you coolness and safety for Abraham!}

(Qur'an 21: 69)

And about Prophet Jacob (pbuh):

{It may be that Allah will bring them [back] all to me.}

(Qur'an 12: 83)

And about Prophet Joseph (pbuh):

{He [Allah] was indeed good to me, when He took me out of the prison, and brought you [all here] out of the Bedouin life...}

(Qur'an 12: 100)

And about Prophet David (pbuh):

{So We forgave him that, and verily, for him is a near access to Us, and a good place of [final] return [paradise]...}

(Qur'an 38: 25)

And about Prophet Job (pbuh):

{And We removed the distress that was on him...} *(Qur'an 21: 84)*

And about Prophet Jonah (pbuh):

{And [We] delivered him from the distress.}

(Qur'an 21: 88)

And about Prophet Moses (pbuh):

{But We saved you from great distress...}

(Qur'an 20: 40)

And about Prophet Muhammad (bpuh):

{If you help him [Muhammad] not [it does not matter], for Allah did indeed help him...}

(Qur'an 9: 40)

{Did He not find you [O Muhammad] an orphan and gave you refuge? And He found you unaware [of the Qur'an, its legal laws, and Prophethood, et cetera] and guided you? And He found you poor, and made you rich [self-sufficient with self-contentment, et cetera]?}

(Qur'an 93: 6-8)

{Every day He has a matter to bring forth [such as giving honor to some, disgrace to some, life to some, death to some, et cetera]!}

(Qur'an 55: 29)

Very often, a crisis is only a cloud that quickly disperses.

{None besides Allah can avert it, [or advance it, or delay it].}

(Qur'an 53: 58)

Don't grieve, for change must take place

When Muhammad ibn al-Ḥanafiyah was imprisoned in 'Ârim prison, Kuthay'ir said:

The beauty of the world will not last for the affluent,

The harshness of this world is not a fatal blow,

For this one and for that one is a period that will finish,

And what each has undergone will be the dream of a dreamer.

Now, centuries later, I reflect on what happened, and truly, Ibn al-Ḥanafiyah and the 'Ârim prison are both the dreams of a dreamer.

{And how many a generation before them have We destroyed! Can you find a single one of them or hear even a whisper of them?}

(Qur'an 19: 98)

In an authentic hadith, the Prophet (bpuh) said:

«The rights shall be paid back to all (on the Day of Judgment); even the sheep that has no horns will get its retribution from the horned (beast).»

Don't give pleasure to your enemy by displaying grief

By being sad, you give pleasure to your adversary, which is why our religion commands us to instill awe into the hearts of the enemy.

{... To threaten the enemy of Allah and your enemy...}

(Qur'an 8: 60)

On the day of Uḥud, when Abu Dujanah (may Allah be pleased with him) was strutting between the rows of the Muslim army, the Prophet (bpuh) said:

«Verily, it is a way of walking that Allah hates, except in this situation.»

When the disbelievers were observing the Muslims from hilltops, the Prophet (bpuh) ordered the Companions to jog around the Kaaba in order to display their strength and endurance.

{And on that day, the believers [Muslims] will rejoice [at the victory given by Allah to the Romans against the Persians].}

(Qur'an 30: 4)

The enemies of the truth feel pain when they find out that we are happy or joyful.

{Say: Perish in your rage.}

(Qur'an 3: 119)

{If good befalls you [O Muhammad], it grieves them...} (Qur'an 9: 50)

{They desire to harm you severely.}

(Qur'an 3: 118)

The Prophet (bpuh) said:

«O Allah, don't allow the enemy or the jealous one to rejoice at my misfortune.»

An Arab poet said:

A young man can forbear every kind of misfortune,

Except for the enemy's joy in his affliction.

Our pious Muslim predecessors would smile, be patient, and display tolerance in the face of hardship, in order to thwart the jealous one and the one who gloats over another's grief.

{But they never lost heart for that which did befall them in Allah's way, nor did they weaken nor degrade themselves.}

(Qur'an 3: 146)

Optimism versus skepticism

{As for those who believe, it has increased their faith, and they rejoice. But as for those in whose hearts is a disease [of doubt, disbelief and hypocrisy], it will add suspicion and doubt to their suspicion, disbelief, and doubt, and they die while they are disbelievers.}

(Qur'an 9: 124-125)

When faced with a difficult or harsh situation, the righteous Muslims from the early generations of Islam were positive in their attitude, positive that, though they were facing difficulties, there was benefit to be had, harm to be warded off, and ease to be met with when rounding the corner of time:

{... And it may be that you dislike a thing which is good for you and that you like a thing which is bad for you.}

(Qur'an 2: 216)

Abu ad–Dardâ' (may Allah be pleased with him) said:

I love three things that are hateful to people: poverty, sickness, and death. I love them because poverty is humility, sickness is expiation for sins, and death results in a meeting with Allah.

Some of the Arab poets were extreme in their hatred for poverty, as can be discerned from the following line, wherein the poet claims that even dogs hate poor people:

On a given day, if it sees the poor and indigent one,

It growls and shows its teeth in mocking.

Prophet Joseph (pbuh) said, concerning being imprisoned:

{O my Lord! Prison is more to my liking than that to which they invite me.}

(Qur'an 12: 33)

As for death, there were many among the righteous who welcomed it. Mu'âdh (may Allah be pleased with him) said, "Welcome death – a beloved one has come in time of need. And the one who regrets (his sins during his lifetime) is successful."

Others, though, fled from death and cursed its approach. The Jews, for example, are the most covetous of people when it comes to life. Allah (the Exalted) says:

{Say [to them]: Verily, the death from which you flee will surely meet you...}

(Qur'an 62: 8)

Being killed in the way of Allah is a dream and pleasant wish for the righteous:

{Some have fulfilled their obligations [been martyred], and some of them are still waiting...}

(Qur'an 33: 23)

Meanwhile others hated death and fled from it. A desert Arab said, "By Allah, I'd hate to die while being on my bed, so how can I be expected to seek death out in the frontlines?"

{Say: Avert death from your ownselves, if you speak the truth.}

(Qur'an 3: 168)

{Say: Even if you had remained in your homes, those for whom death was decreed would certainly have gone forth to the place of their death.}

(Qur'an 3: 154)

The story throughout history is one: it is merely the actors who change.

O son of Adam, don't despair

One who is bored with life, who finds it difficult to pass the days, and who has tasted the bitter vicissitudes of life, must remember that ease follows difficulty, that Allah's promise is true, and that, if we are true and sincere, victory is near.

{[It is] a promise of Allah, and Allah fails not in His promise, but most of men know not.}

(Qur'an 30: 6)

For your dilemma – whatever it may be – there is a cure, and for your difficulty – whatever it may be – there is a solution.

{All the praises and thanks be to Allah, Who has removed from us [all] grief.}

(Qur'an 35: 34)

O people: the time has come for you to remedy your doubts with faith and your deviant thoughts with guidance. You must remove the veil of darkness that covers you, so that you can see the brightness of a true sunrise; you must supplant the bitterness of sorrow with the sweetness of contentment.

O people: beyond the dry desert that you are crossing, you will find green pasture and fertile soil. The fruits therein grow profusely from all directions.

O people, who because of sleepless nights, scream in the late hours of the night, remember this:

{Is not the morning near?}

(Qur'an 11: 81)

O you whose mind has wandered in grief, move to action without haste, for upon the horizon of the unseen lies a solution and a way out of your difficulties. O you whose eyes are loaded with tears, repress your tears and give leisure to your eyelids. Relax and know that your Creator (Allah, the Exalted, the All-Powerful) protects and aids, and that His mercy for you will bring you peace. Be peaceful in mind, O slave of Allah, for the divine decree is written, and all matters have been decided upon. Know that your reward is secure with the one Who does not disappoint those who seek to please Him.

Be at peace, for after poverty comes wealth, after thirst comes drink, after separation comes a joyous meeting, and after sleeplessness comes sound rest.

{You know not; it may be that Allah will afterward bring some new thing to pass.}

(Qur'an 65: 1)

O you who are oppressed in the lands, who suffer from hunger, pain, sickness, and poverty: rejoice in the knowledge that you will soon be satisfied with food and that you will be happy and in good health.

{And by the night when it withdraws, and by the dawn when it brightens.}

(Qur'an 74: 33-34)

All Muslims must have good thoughts about their Lord and must wait patiently for His favor. The One Who has the power to say 'Be' to something and it is, is worthy to be trusted in regard to His promise. No one can bring about good except Him, and no one can ward off evil except Him. For every action, He has wisdom; after every hour, He brings ease. He made morning to follow the night and rain to follow dryness. He gives to be thanked and He puts to trial to know – and He has knowledge of all things – those who are patient. Therefore it is in the best interest of the Muslims to strengthen their relationship with their Lord and to ask of Him more frequently.

{...And ask Allah of His bounty.}

(Qur'an 4: 32)

{Invoke your Lord with humility and in secret.}

(Qur'an 7: 55)

Al-'Alâ' ibn al-Haḍrami and some Companions of the Messenger of Allah (bpuh) became stranded in the middle of the desert. Their water supply became depleted, and they were all on the verge of dying. Al-'Alâ' called out to His Lord, Who is All–Hearing and Who answers the prayer of the one who asks Him. He said, "O Most High, Most Great, O Most Wise and Most Benevolent." At that very moment, the rain started to pour down. They drank, made ablution, bathed, and gave drink to their animals.

{And He it is Who sends down the rain after they have despaired, and spreads abroad His mercy. And He is the Wali [Helper, Supporter, Protector, et cetera]. Worthy of all Praise.}

(Qur'an 42: 28)

Pause to reflect

Loving Allah, knowing Him, remembering Him, seeking peace in Him, singling Him out for complete love, fear, hope, and dependence – these are qualities that, when combined in a person, constitute a sort of heaven on earth. They are qualities that bring peace to those who love Allah, a sort of peace that has no comparison in this world.

If the heart is content and has a strong attachment to Allah, anxiety and grief will be removed from it. And vice versa: no one feels more constricted with grief than those whose hearts are attached to other than Allah – those who forget the remembrance of Allah and are not satisfied with what He has given them. We can verify this reality by studying the cases of some of those who have passed before us.

Blessings in disguise

{We have already destroyed what surrounds you of [those] cities.}

(Qur'an 46: 27)

There is the tragic example of the Barmak family, whose members lived a life of opulence, comfort, and extravagance. Their end, however, has served as a lesson and example for all Arabs who came after them. Haroon ar-Rasheed, the ruler during their period, ordered an unexpected attack on the Barmak family and on their possessions. Allah's decree came to pass over them in the morning, at the hands of the closest person to them; he destroyed their homes, took possession of their slaves, and shed their blood. Their loved ones and children wept at their disgrace. There is none worthy of worship except Allah, the Almighty, All-Merciful; those who know the story should especially appreciate the transitory nature of power and wealth in this world:

{Then take admonition, O you with eyes [to see].}

(Qur'an 59: 2)

Only one hour before their downfall, they were strutting in silks, full of joy and complacency, feeling secure from harm, unaware of the vicissitudes of life.

{And you dwelt in the dwellings of men who wronged themselves, and it was clear to you how We had dealt with them. And We put forth [many] parables for you.}

(Qur'an 14: 45)

They swaggered in their life of play; however, sadly for them, they mistook the mirage for water and this life for eternal existence. They wrongly thought that justice would not overtake them and that vindication would not come about for the wronged.

{...And they thought that they would never return to Us.}

(Qur'an 28: 39)

They woke up that morning in a state of joy, but by the time night had fallen, they were in their graves. In a moment of anger and caprice, Haroon ar-Rasheed unsheathed the sword of wrath upon them, killing Ja'far ibn Yaḥya al-Barmaki by hanging him on a cross and then burning his body. He imprisoned Ja'far's father Yaḥya and his brother al-Faḍl. Their wealth was confiscated. Their plight was mourned over by many Arab poets. One of them said:

When I saw the sword mixed in Ja'far,

And a caller announced the news of Yaḥya to the Caliph,

I mourned over this world and I came to truly believe

That in the near horizon is a day when a boy will depart from this world,

It is nothing but one country and ruler supplanted by another,

The event of misfortune follows the appointment of blessings.

If this one dwells in the high mansions of a king,

Then that one sinks to the lowest depths of misery.

But as for the present, where is Haroon ar–Rasheed and where is the Barmak family? Where is the murderer and where is the murdered? Where is the one who ordered the killing while he was lying down on a bed in his castle? And where is the one who was crucified? Yesterday and the actors of yesterday are both gone, but the Most Just will judge between them on a day about which there is no doubt, a day wherein there shall be neither wrongdoing nor injustice.

{The knowledge thereof is with my Lord, in a record. My Lord neither errs nor forgets.}

(Qur'an 20: 52)

{The Day when humankind will stand before the Lord of the worlds.}

(Qur'an 83: 6)

{That Day, you will be exhibited [for judgment]; not hidden among you is anything concealed.}

(Qur'an 69: 18)

Yaḥya ibn Khâlid al-Barmaki was asked concerning this calamity, "Do you know its cause?" He said, "Perhaps it was the supplication of someone whom we wronged, a prayer that traveled quickly through the night while we were unaware of it."

'Abdullâh ibn Mu'âwiyah ibn 'Abdullâh ibn Ja'far said in jail about his imprisonment:

We have departed from the world and we are still of its inhabitants,

We are neither from the dead nor from the living,

If the jail guard comes in for one reason or another,

We are astonished and say: This one has come from the world,

Overjoyed do we become after seeing a dream, because most of our talk

When we wake up is about the dreams we saw,

If it was a good one, ever so slowly it comes to pass,

And when it is bad, it waits not but comes with speed.

There is a good deal of cynicism in the last two lines; after reading them, I am reminded of the words of al-Jâḥidh:

When the mailman brings news to us,

Concerning some evil event, he loses no time and makes haste,

Thus, when evil, it arrives after a day and a night,

And when it is good, it takes its time and arrives after a week.

A Persian king once imprisoned a wise man, who wrote to him:

Every hour that I pass in here, I come closer to ease and you to wrath. So I wait for better times. Meanwhile, you are promised a bitter humiliation.

After reaching the summit of opulence and extravagance, Ibn 'Abbâd, the Sultan of Andalusia, faced a crisis. At a time when frivolity and musical instruments and dancers became prevalent in his castle, he was attacked, and so he sought aid from the Sultan of Morocco, Ibn Tâshfeen. The latter crossed the ocean with his army and brought with him victory. Ibn 'Abbâd treated him as an honored guest, allowing him to behave as if the castles and gardens were his own. But Ibn Tâshfeen was observing the situation like a lion, and he had other plans.

After only three days, Ibn Tâshfeen and his army attacked the weakened kingdom of Andalusia. Ibn 'Abbâd was taken captive, and his properties were seized. His castles and gardens were destroyed, and he was transported to his home province of Agmât as a prisoner.

{And so are the days [good and not so good], We give to men by turns.}

(Qur'an 3: 140)

The dominion of Andalusia fell into the hands of Ibn Tâshfeen. He claimed that the leadership was rightfully his, since it was the people of Andalusia who had summoned him from Morocco in the first place.

Much time passed, and then one day the daughters of Ibn 'Abbâd managed to visit him in prison. They came barefoot, hungry, wan, and in tears. When he witnessed their pathetic situation, he cried out:

In past days, I would rejoice on special occasions,

But what a miserable occasion is it in Agmât as a prisoner.

You see your daughters emaciated and hungry,

They stitch for people and they own nothing.

They come to see you fearful and weak,

With sad eyes and broken hearts,

Traveling on mud, barefoot,

As if those feet never trampled on precious perfume and roses.

{So when Our command came, We made the highest part [of the city] its lowest...}

(Qur'an 11: 82)

{The example of [this] worldly life is but like rain which We have sent down from the sky that the plants of the earth absorb – [those] from which men and livestock eat – until, when the earth has taken on its adornment and is beautified, and its people suppose that they have capability over it, there comes to it Our command by night or by day, and We make it as a harvest, as if it had not flourished yesterday.} (Qur'an 10: 24)

The fruits of contentment

{Allah is pleased with them, and they with Him.}

(Qur'an 5: 119)

Contentment bears many blessed fruits. More than anything else, by being contented with that which is decreed, one is able to soar to the highest levels of faith and truthfulness.

Some might wish for only good to befall them, for only pleasant things to occur in their lives, but that is not what being Allah's slave means. Many of the true believer's characteristics, which include patience, total dependence, contentment, humbleness, and submission of one's will, only become manifest when one is confronted with something that one dislikes. Being pleased with that which has been decreed does not mean being contented with only those things that suit one's disposition; the real gauges for true contentment are those times when one goes through a painful situation. It is not for the slaves to dictate the terms of preordainment; they can be happy or discontented, and it makes no difference except that by being discontented, they are sinning. Human beings do not have much of a choice in regard to the divine decree; the choices and decisions belong Only with Allah. He is All-Knowing and Most High.

Being pleased with Allah

We should know that if we are pleased with Allah, He is pleased with us. Therefore if you are pleased with a small amount of sustenance, He will be pleased with you for your small deeds. If you are pleased no matter what the situation, then you will find that you have earned your Lord's pleasure, and you will realize that Allah is most pleased with sincere people who are content. On the other hand, there are the hypocrites: Allah rejects their deeds, regardless of whether those deeds are many or few. They are displeased with what Allah (the Exalted) sends down, and they hate seeking His pleasure. Thus their deeds are performed in vain.

For the malcontented, there is wrath

By being dissatisfied with one's situation and thinking inappropriate thoughts about Allah, one opens the doors of anxiety and grief. On the other hand, contentment with one's situation and with Allah's decree opens the door to a paradise on earth even before that of the hereafter.

Questioning and complaining about what has been decreed cannot result in self-contentment and inner peace. Instead, it is by submission and acceptance that we can bring about favorable results, because the One Who sustains all things should never be accused concerning what He has decreed.

I still remember the story of Ibn ar-Rawandi, the well-known atheist philosopher. He saw a common ignorant man who lived in castles and who was very wealthy. Ibn ar-Rawandi turned to the sky and exclaimed, "I am the philosopher of my generation, yet I live in poverty, while this ignorant commoner is rich. This is a random and strange distribution."

Allah (the Exalted) then increased Ibn ar-Rawandi in his misery, humiliation, and poverty.

{...But surely the torment of the hereafter will be more disgracing, and they will never be helped.}

(Qur'an 41: 16)

The benefits one reaps by being contented

During hard times, if the believers remain contented with their situations, they are able to remain calm and composed; moreover, they demonstrate a true belief in the promise of Allah and His Messenger (bpuh). It is as if their hearts have voices saying:

{This is what Allah and His Messenger [Muhammad] had promised us, and Allah and His Messenger had spoken the truth, and it only added to their faith and to their submissiveness [to Allah].}

(Qur'an 33: 22)

In contrast, the malcontented heart is filled with sickness, doubt, and instability; such a heart remains rebellious and troubled. It is as if this heart too has a voice, but the words it speaks are ever so different:

{Allah and His Messenger promised us nothing but delusions!}

(Qur'an 33: 12)

The people who possess this kind of heart are contradictory in their dealings. If they have rights upon another, they hurry to claim their rights. Yet if they are sought after to fulfill their obligations, they turn away in disdain.

When good befalls them, they feel calm and complacent, but when they are put to the test, how sudden is their change for the worse! They are those who have lost not only this world, but also the hereafter.

{That is the evident loss.}

(Qur'an 22: 11)

So those are two opposites which yield results that are equally opposite in nature. Contentment leads to peace, which eventually leads to prosperity; resentment about Allah's decree leads to anxiety, which eventually leads to failure. You must remember that one of the greatest blessings that Allah (the Exalted) can give to His slaves is bestowing tranquility upon them, and one of the best ways of achieving tranquility is being contented and pleased with Allah at all times.

Do not challenge your Lord

By being contented, we are saved from being like those who challenge their Lord in His decrees and rulings. To understand this, we need only look at the case of Iblees (the devil). He argued and disputed with his Lord because he was displeased with His decree and ruling. Those who refuse to believe in Allah only do so because they seek to challenge Him in might and power instead of submitting to Him. Then they abandon His orders, perpetrate what is unlawful, and challenge His divine decree by showing resentment.

A just decree

Allah's ruling is binding upon His slaves: it will come to pass, and it is a just ruling, as mentioned in the hadith:

> «Your decree concerning me will be carried out, and You are Just with me in Your ruling.»

Allah (the Exalted) has forbidden Himself from being unjust with his slaves. Indeed it is people themselves who do wrong and are unjust.

The above-mentioned hadith, "And You are Just with Me in Your ruling" also includes the decree of sinning, in its effect and its punishment. Allah is the Most Just regarding His decree for sinning and for its punishment. He may have ordained a sin for one of His slaves for reasons that are beyond our grasp. There might be a purpose which, due to its being so profound in its ramifications, is known only to Him. That is the belief of the Muslim.

Resentment yields no return

Resentment about one's situation generally occurs for one of two reasons: either we fail to achieve our desires, or something occurs that we hate. Yet if we truly believe that whatever has passed us by was never meant for us, and that whatever afflicted us was always meant to be, then we have no reason to feel disgruntled. The Messenger of Allah, Muhammad (bpuh), said:

> «The pen has been lifted concerning what you will meet with, O Abu Hurayrah. The ordaining is finished with, the decree is completed, the measure of things has been written, the pens are raised, and the pages have dried.»

Safety is in contentment

Contentment offers safety in that the contented heart is healthy and free from deceit, corruption, and rancor. It is only a sound and healthy heart that will be saved from Allah's punishment, a heart that is safe and free from doubt, disbelief, and the various tricks of the devil. Such a heart is only concerned with how to please Allah (the Exalted).

{Say: Allah [sent it down]. Then leave them to play in their vain discussions.}

(Qur'an 6: 91)

Bitterness and resentfulness are concepts that are foreign to the healthy heart, so the more we are contented with Allah's decree, the more healthy and sound our hearts will be. Wickedness, corruption, and deceit accompany discontent, while a healthy heart, righteousness, and sincerity accompany contentment. Jealousy is another of the fruits of discontent.

Being pleased with Allah is a quality that is like a good tree that is nourished by the water of sincerity in the garden of pure Islamic monotheism. Its roots are faith, and its branches are good deeds. This tree bears fruit that is fresh and sweet. The Prophet (bpuh) said:

> «One has tasted the taste of faith if one is pleased with Allah as his Lord, with Islam as his religion, and with Muhammad as a Messenger.»

Dissatisfaction is the door to doubt

Dissatisfaction opens the door that leads to doubt in Allah -in His decree, in His wisdom, and in His knowledge. Rarely are the complainers free from these accompanying doubts that mix within their hearts and permeate their beings. If they were to delve deep into themselves with honest introspection, they would find their faith to be infirm and questionable. Contentment and faith are like brothers that accompany one another; meanwhile, doubt and discontentment have a similar fraternal relationship. Tirmidhi related that the Prophet (bpuh) said:

> «If you are able to show contentment with faith, then do so. If not, then verily there is much goodness in patience with what the self hates.»

So those who are dissatisfied are resentful on the inside, and also angry, even if their anger is not expressed in words. Inside them mingles an assortment of questions, such as: why has this happened, or how could this be?

Satisfaction is richness and safety

Whoever fills their hearts with satisfaction regarding the divine decree, Allah (the Exalted) in turn fills their hearts with richness, safety, and comfort. Whoever becomes dissatisfied, their hearts will be filled with the opposite and will be preoccupied with matters that clash with happiness and success.

Therefore contentment empties the heart of all superfluous emotions, leaving it entirely for Allah. Discontent removes from the heart all thoughts of Allah. So there is no real life for resentful, complaining people who always feel that they are shifting from one problem to the next.

They consider their sustenance to be insufficient, their luck poor, and their problems manifold; above all, they feel that they are deserving of more. Basically, they are discontented with what Allah (the Exalted) decreed for them. How then can such people find comfort, peace, and a good life?

{That is because they followed that which angered Allah, and hated that which pleased Him. So He made their deeds fruitless.} (Qur'an 47: 28)

The fruit of contentment is thankfulness

Contentment leads to thankfulness, which is among the highest levels of faith. In truth, it is the reality of faith. The epitome of all the differing levels of righteousness is thankfulness towards Allah, and the one who is not content with Allah's favors and rulings, and with His giving and His taking away, is not thankful to Him. Indeed, the thankful person is the most blessed.

The fruit of discontentment is disbelief

Resentment causes people to deny the favors of Allah (the Exalted). Eventually perhaps, it could even lead to disbelieving in Allah. If the slaves are pleased with their Lord in all circumstances, what follows necessarily is being thankful to Him. They therefore become among the pleased and thankful ones. If they are devoid of contentment, though, they join the resentful ones and follow the ways of the disbelievers. Falsehood and deviation in beliefs only occurred because many of Allah's slaves wanted to become their own gods, to the point that many of them attempted to dictate to their Lord their wants and desires.

{Do not put [yourselves] forward before Allah and His Messenger.} (Qur'an 49: 1)

Dissatisfaction is a trap of the devil

The devil prevails in his subjugation of human beings most often in two areas: dissatisfaction and desire. In these instances, he finds his prey to be extremely vulnerable, particularly when displeasure becomes deep-rooted. At this point, they say, do, and think that which displeases their Lord. For this explicit reason, the Prophet (bpuh) said upon the death of his infant son Ibrâheem:

«The heart is sad, the eye sheds tears, and yet we don't say anything except that which pleases our Lord.»

The death of one's child is something that might lead to resentment in a person's heart. Hence, the Prophet (bpuh) informed us that in such a situation – a situation in which most people are resentful and might say or do something displeasing to their Lord -they must not say anything except that which pleases their Lord. If individuals keep the following three points in mind when they are displeased and angry, then their burden will be lightened significantly:

1. Know and believe in the wisdom of Allah, and in the fact that He knows best what is good and beneficial for His slaves.

2. Be conscious of the great reward and recompense that Allah (the Exalted) promised to the slave who becomes afflicted and is then patient.

3. Know and accept that rulings and judgments are with Allah (the Exalted), while submission and obedience are for His slaves.

{Is it they who would portion out the mercy of your Lord?}

(Qur'an 43: 32)

Another word on contentment

The desires of those who are contented are subservient to what their Lord wants from them: that which Allah loves and what pleases Him. Hence, contentment and the blind following of one's own desires can never coexist in the same heart. If we have a share of the former and a share of the latter, our hearts will be conquered by the stronger of the two.

{And I hastened to You, O my Lord, that You might be pleased.}

(Qur'an 20: 84)

Contemplate this hadith:

«Become acquainted with Allah in good times, and He will know you in harsh (times).»

"Become acquainted with Allah" means that you should seek closeness to Him by being obedient to Him, by being thankful to Him for His blessings, and by turning to Him sincerely before hardship befalls you.

"In good times" refers to times of peace, safety, blessings, and good health.

"He will know you in harsh (times)" by alleviating your hardship and by giving you an exit from every difficult situation.

It is very important to maintain a special relationship in your heart between you and your Lord, a relationship that allows you to feel so close to your Lord that you require no other. Thus, you find company when you are alone, and you taste the sweetness of remembering Him and supplicating to Him. You will continually face hardship and difficulty until you die, but if you have a special relationship with your Lord – that of being an obedient slave – all of the hardships of life will become easy for you.

Overlooking the faults of your brothers and sisters

{Show forgiveness, enjoin what is good, and turn away from the foolish [that is, don't punish them].}

(Qur'an 7: 199)

It is not right for you to forsake your brothers and sisters because of one or two faults that you find in them, especially if the rest of their character is honorable. As we know, perfection for any one of us is unattainable. Al-Kindi said:

> How is it that you want your friend to possess a specific pattern of characteristics when your soul – which is the closest of souls to you – does not always obey your commands? What right do you then have to expect another person's soul to follow your orders?

{Even as he is now, so were you yourselves before until Allah conferred on you His favors [by guiding you to Islam]...}

(Qur'an 4: 94)

{So ascribe not purity to yourselves. He knows best him who fears Allah and keeps his duty to Him.}

(Qur'an: 53: 32)

It is enough for you that you are satisfied with the main part of another's character. Abu ad-Dardâ' (may Allah be pleased with him) said, "To reproach your brother for something is better than to lose him altogether."

Some of the wise said, "We are still not satisfied with ourselves, so how then can we expect ourselves to be satisfied with others?"

It has also been said:

If someone impresses you with a good character and sound judgment, don't remain aloof from him or her because of some minor fault that is surrounded by an ocean of virtues. You will not find, as long as you live, a person so cultivated that he or she is free from blemish and sin. Contemplate your own self and how it often errs and strays. This kind of introspection makes your demands on others more balanced and makes you more sympathetic to the sinner.

An Arab poet said:

Who is the one whose character is untainted?

Sufficient worthiness for someone is that his defects can be counted.

It has been said that one's suspicions concerning one's brother or sister should not ruin a good mutual trust that has been tested over time. Ja'far ibn Muhammad said to his son:

O my son, whoever among your brothers becomes angry with you three times, and on each occasion speaks only the truth about you, take him as a close friend.

Ḥasan ibn Wahb said, "From the rights of mutual love is to forgive and overlook shortcomings."

{So overlook their faults with gracious forgiveness.}

(Qur'an 15: 85)

Ibn Roomi said:

These are people and the world, and there is no doing away with dust that irritates the eyes or spoils the drink.

From the lack of fairness is to expect refinement

In the world, while you yourself are unrefined.

{And had it not been for the grace of Allah and His mercy on you, not one of you would ever have been pure from sins.}

(Qur'an 24: 21)

A poet said:

You seek a cultivated person who is free from defects,

But does the aloe exude a pleasant odor without smoke?

﴾So ascribe not purity to yourselves. He knows best him who fears Allah and keeps his duty to Him.﴿

(Qur'an 53: 32)

Take advantage of health and free time

You must not waste your health and free time. Do not become remiss in performing deeds of obedience to your Lord as a result of depending on past good actions. Take advantage of your health and free time by working and striving. Remember that you cannot always make up for lost time, and that sooner or later, you will rue those times that you wasted away in idleness. Bazrjamhar said, "If work causes one to tire, then inactivity causes one to decay." One of the wise said:

> Don't spend your day doing something that will not benefit you, and don't let your wealth remain idle by not investing it in some project. For there is too little time in one's life to throw it away on something useless, and one's supply of money is too small not to invest it. So the wise one is too judicious to waste his time in nonsense and to spend his money on something that will not bring a return.

More profound than that is the saying of Prophet Jesus (pbuh):

> Piety is in three: in speech, in sight, and in silence. Whoever's speech is not in remembrance (of Allah) has spoken nonsense. Whoever looks without trying to learn a lesson has forgotten (his true purpose). And whoever's silence is not accompanied by reflection has been heedless.

Allah protects those who believe

All of us, whether we admit it or not, are in need of a god, and it follows that this god must possess certain qualities, such as omnipotence, power, richness, and everlastingness. The One Who has all of these – and all other perfect qualities – is Allah, the Lord of all that exists.

Therefore the sincere seekers are drawn to, and then find comfort in, their belief in Allah (the Exalted). He is the sanctuary of the weak and of those who seek refuge.

{[Remember] when you sought the help of your Lord and He answered you.}

(Qur'an 8: 9)

{And He protects, while none can protect against Him...}

(Qur'an 23: 88)

{...When there will be neither a protector nor an intercessor for them besides Him...}

(Qur'an 6: 51)

Those who worship other than Allah, even if they love Him to a certain degree, are much worse off than those who enjoy eating poisoned food.

{Had there been therein [in the heavens and the earth] gods besides Allah, then verily both would have been ruined. Glorified be Allah, the Lord of the throne, [High is He] above what they attribute to Him!}

(Qur'an 21: 22)

The need we have for Allah is shown by the connection sought by us between the transient and the Everlasting, the weak and the Almighty, the poor and the All-Rich. Those who do not take Allah to be their Lord and God will positively take other than Him as a god. They will, for example, take pictures, objects of love, or their desires to be their deity, and then they become slaves and servants of that false deity. Of this there is no doubt.

{Have you seen him who has taken as his god his own desire?}

(Qur'an 25: 43)

{Yet they have taken besides Him other gods...}

(Qur'an 25: 3)

> «The Prophet (bpuh) asked someone: How many do you worship? The man answered: I worship seven: six on the earth and one in the heavens. The Prophet asked: Who of them do you hope from and fear? He replied: The One in the heavens. The Prophet said: Then abandon the ones on the earth, and worship the One in the heavens.»

Know that the need of the slave to worship Allah alone, without associating partners with Him, is more urgent than the need to breathe air.

Your reality resides in your heart and soul, and neither of them becomes healthy except by worshipping Allah.

Whoever craves for a meeting with Allah, loves Him,

And Allah will be for him stronger in love,

The opposite holds true for the one who hates. So ask Allah

For His mercy and favor, but don't depend

(on this alone, but perform good deeds also).

Even if you find pleasure in other than Allah (the Exalted), it is a condition that will not last, for when you become bored with one object or person, you immediately seek another. You will find blessings with this person one time, and find annoyance and vexation with the same person another time. Indeed, you might even come to hate a person whose company at one time had given you the utmost pleasure.

As for Allah, we are in constant need of Him, on all occasions and at all times.

I wish that You were pleased with me and every human was with me angry,

If You are pleased with me, that is the pinnacle of my hopes.

The Prophet (bpuh) said:

> «Whoever pleases Allah by making people angry, Allah will be pleased with him and He will make them pleased with him. Whoever angers Allah by pleasing the people, Allah will be angry with him and He will make the people angry with him also.»

{And thus We do make the wrong-doers supporters and helpers of one another [in committing crimes et cetera], because of that which they used to earn.}

(Qur'an 6: 129)

Signposts on the seeker's highway

If you want to know whether you are climbing upwards toward success, there are certain signs and indicators that can help you determine your progress.

1. As you become more knowledgeable, you become more humble and merciful to others. Think of an expensive pearl: the more heavy and valuable it is, the deeper it is in the ocean. A wise person knows that although knowledge is a gift, Allah tests the one whom He gives it to. When you are thankful for the gift of knowledge, you will be raised in rank.

   {Allah will exalt in degree those of you who believe and those who have been granted knowledge.}

   (Qur'an 58: 11)

2. The more you perform good deeds, the more cautious and fearful you become, in the sense that you do not feel secure from errors such as a slip of the tongue or a change of heart. You are always in a state of watching over yourself and of being wary, like a careful bird: each time it lands on a tree, it soon leaves it for another, afraid of the skilled hunter and his bullet.

3. The older you get, the less covetous you should be for this world, for you come to know with certainty that your time will soon be finished.

4. The wealthier you become, the more generous you should be towards others. You must understand that wealth is a trust given to you, and that Allah is testing you with wealth.

5. The higher your status becomes in society, the closer you should be to ordinary people, showing humility and fulfilling their needs.

But there are also signs that indicate wretchedness:

1. For some people, the more knowledge they attain, the more haughty and arrogant they become. Their knowledge is not beneficial; their hearts are empty, and their company is heavy to bear.

2. The more good deeds they perform, the prouder they become and the more contemptuous of others. They don't give the benefit of the doubt to anyone except themselves. Thus they deem that they are the only ones who will achieve salvation, while all others are bound for destruction.

3. The older they get, the more avarice and greed become part of their character. They gather but never share. Calamities and misfortune fail to move them into becoming benefactors to others.

4. The wealthier they become, the more miserly they become with their money.

5. The higher their position in society, the higher their level of arrogance and haughtiness. The Prophet (bpuh) said:

> «The arrogant ones will be gathered on the Day of Judgment in the form of small ants. People will trample on them with their feet.»

In each of the points discussed above, I mentioned some of Allah's favors, favors by which He tests His slaves; some of those slaves will pass the test, while others will fail it.

Being blessed with honor is also a test

Those who are endowed with power, honor, status, rank, or wealth must realize that they are being tested, too. When Prophet Solomon (pbuh) saw the throne of Bilqees (Queen of Sheba) brought before him, he said:

{This is by the grace of my Lord – to test me whether I am grateful or ungrateful!}

(Qur'an 27: 40)

Thus Allah (the Exalted) gives a blessing to see who accepts it properly – by being thankful for it, by preserving it, and by taking advantage of it in a good way; and who denies it – by not being thankful, by wasting away the favor, or even by using it to wage war against the One Who gave it to him in the first place!

We must understand, therefore, that blessings are trials from Allah (the Exalted). It is through trials that the gratitude of the grateful person is revealed while the ingrate is exposed. We also must remember that Allah tests us in good times as well as in bad times.

{As for man, when his Lord tries him by giving him honor and gifts, then he says [puffed up]: My Lord has honored me. But when He tries him, by straitening his means of life, he says: My Lord has humiliated me! Nay!...}

(Qur'an 89: 15-17)

The enduring treasures

The real treasures are those that we take with us to the hereafter. Islam, eemân (faith), righteous deeds, jihad (struggling or fighting in the cause of Allah), and repentance are all examples of such enduring treasures:

{Righteousness is not that you turn your faces toward the east or west, but [true] righteousness is [in] one who believes in Allah, the Last Day, the angels, the Book, and the Prophets and gives wealth, in spite of love for it, to relatives, orphans, the needy, the traveller, those who ask [for help], and for freeing slaves; [and who] establishes prayer and gives zakâh; [those who] fulfill their promise when they promise; and [those who] are patient in poverty and hardship and during battle. Those are the ones who have been true, and it is those who are the righteous.}

(Qur'an 2: 177)

Determination can overcome insurmountable barriers

Those who have great determination can, by the will of Allah (the Exalted), climb to great heights of virtue.

Among the characteristics of Muslims are that they not only have high and noble aims, but they also have strong determination, which is the fuel that propels us to higher virtues.

Determination – by the will of Allah – will bring great good to you. People will see you as one who is learning, doing good deeds, working for higher aims – basically, as one who is achieving.

Do not, however, fall into the error of confusing determination with arrogance. Between the two lies a distance as great as that between the sky and earth. When you have strong determination, you regret every missed opportunity, and therefore you are constantly goading yourself to reach your goal.

Strong determination is a characteristic of those who are righteous, just, and sincere, while arrogance is a sickness that is predominant among tyrants and wretched people.

Determination carries you upwards, while arrogance makes you fall; it drags its victim down to the depths of ignominy. O students of knowledge, remain steadfast and resolute in the path that you are upon, and do not falter.

Read to gain wisdom

An activity that brings joy to the soul is reading and contemplating the sayings of wise persons, the foremost of them being Prophet Muhammad (bpuh). Others can in no way be compared to him, for he was supported by revelation, confirmed by miracles, and sent to us with clear signs.

When I am ill, it is He Who cures me

{And when I am ill, it is He Who cures me.}

(Qur'an 26: 80)

Here are some bits of advice, regarding various issues, which have been passed down to us from the wise. Abqarât said, "Stay healthy longer by working hard, avoiding laziness, giving up drinking, and refraining from eating too much."

Some of the wise said:

Whoever wants health should eat properly and well and drink water moderately. Lying down after eating lunch and walking after dinner are recommended and one should be wary about taking a shower right after filling oneself with food.

Al-Hârith said, "Whoever wants to stay – and there is no true stay (meaning that life is transient and will come to an end) – should eat lunch and dinner early."

Plato said:

Five things weaken the body, and at times can even prove to be fatal: to be poor, to part with loved ones, to drink sour things, to refuse advice, and to not only be ignorant, but to also laugh at the wise.

It is also said that these four things weaken the body: talking too much, sleeping too much, eating too much, and engaging in sexual intercourse too frequently. Talking too much weakens the strength and sharpness of the mind and makes one age faster. Sleeping too much blinds the heart, making one lazy and callous.

Having intercourse too often weakens one's strength and has harmful effects upon the body in general. Four things destroy the body: anxiety, grief, hunger, and sleeplessness.

Four things bring serenity to the heart: looking at greenery, looking at flowing water, seeing a loved one, and gazing at fruits upon the trees.

Four things weaken one's eyesight: walking barefoot, having a frown on one's face early in the morning and before going to sleep, crying frequently, and reading words in small print.

Four things strengthen the body: wearing soft clothing, taking a shower using water of a moderate temperature, eating sweet and rich foods, and smelling pleasant odors.

Four things take the mirth and freshness out of one's face: lying, insolence, asking too many questions imprudently, and perpetrating evil deeds frequently.

Four things bring light and mirth to one's face: a sense of honor, fulfilling one's commitments, generosity, and piety. Four things make others abhor and loathe a person: arrogance, jealousy, lying, and spreading false rumors about others.

Four things make sustenance come to a person freely: standing up at night to pray, making repentance late in the night, giving charity habitually, and remembering Allah, the Almighty, in the first and last parts of the day.

Four things prevent sustenance from coming to a person: sleeping in the morning, not praying frequently, laziness, and treachery.

Four things weaken one's mind and understanding: constantly eating sour foods and fruit, sleeping on one's back, worrying, and feeling anxious.

Four things help one to improve one's understanding: having a light heart, not overfilling oneself with food and drink, adding sweet and rich foods in moderation to one's diet, and getting rid of extra body fat.

Take precautions

In all facets of life, you should take precautions and study the possible outcomes of every action, because by being careful, you will have no cause for future self-recrimination. If the results of your endeavors are good, you should thank and praise Allah. If the results are not so good, you should say, "Allah has made His decree, and whatever He pleases, He does."

Verify the facts yourself

The judicious person is one who, when hearing some news, does not rush to judgment based merely on hearsay. Instead, he or she verifies and authenticates the report, thinking things over and consulting with wiser and more experienced people. It has been rightly said that to err on the side of forgiveness is better than to err on the side of punishment.

{And afterwards you become regretful for what you have done.}

(Qur'an 49: 6)

Resolve to do something, then do it

Everything I have written in this book – including verses from the Qur'an, sayings from the Prophet (bpuh), verses of poetry, stories, and sayings of the wise – calls you to start a new life, a life filled with hope of a good and blessed ending. However, you will not be able to benefit from this book without true determination, strong resolve, and a sincere desire to rid yourself of sadness, anxiety, and nervousness. You will do well to remember that Allah singled out those Messengers who had a strong will:

{Therefore be patient [O Muhammad] as were the Messengers of strong will...}

(Qur'an 46: 35)

Adam (pbuh) was not from them.

{...But he forgot, and We found not in him determination.}

(Qur'an 20: 115)

And so is the case with his descendants. Imitating one's father is not wrong, but one should not follow him into sin on the one hand, without following him in repentance on the other. And it is Allah (the Exalted) alone Who helps us.

The life of this world

One's welfare in the hereafter hinges upon how one conducts oneself in this life.

It is imperative for every person to bear in mind the link between this life and the next, for some have wrongly thought that there is only this world; they spend their time gathering things and becoming attached to this life, a life that is fleeting. Then they die with their wishes and aspirations in their chests, unfulfilled and forgotten.

Sometimes I am amazed at our long-term hopes in this world -at our future expectations for a life which might end at any moment:

{No person knows what he will earn tomorrow, and no person knows in what land he will die.}

(Qur'an 31: 34)

Ask yourself these questions:

1. Do you really suppose that you will find peace and tranquility while you are not pleased with your Lord or with His decree, and while you are discontented with your sustenance and your talents?

2. Have you thanked your Lord properly for His blessings and favors, to the point that you deserve to ask for other favors? Whoever is incapable of handling a little is more than likely unable to handle a lot.

3. Why do we not benefit from those talents that Allah has given us, failing as we do to develop and cultivate them? Had we used those talents, we could have given to others and contributed to society.

Positive qualities and talents are often buried deep within us. Yet in so many of us, these talents are buried like expensive minerals underground – minerals that only the expert can mine, wash, and polish, making them shine. Therefore, our task lies in mining for our talents and then developing them.

Hiding from evil is a temporary solution

I read the book al-Mutawâreen, by 'Abdul-Ghani al-Azdi. An interesting book, it relates the stories of those who went into hiding because they feared being captured and taken to al-Ḥajjâj ibn Yusuf, the ruthless despot of his time.

Be Happy

Abu 'Umar ibn al–'Ulâ said of his difficulties:

When al-Ḥajjâj threatened me, I fled to Yemen and stayed in a house in Sanaa. At night, I would sit on the roof; during the day I remained concealed inside.

One night, while on the roof, he heard a man recite:

Perhaps the soul is terrified and troubled by a matter,

For which there is a solution like the untying of a knot.

Abu 'Umar further said:

When the man said 'solution', I felt a spark of hope and became happy. Then I heard another man explain the words of the first by announcing that al-Ḥajjâj had died. By Allah, I don't know which of the two things made me joyful: the word 'solution' or the words, 'al–Ḥajjâj has died'.

There is only one decision that is binding and must come forth into existence, and that is the decision of the One in Whose Hand is the control of the heavens and the earth.

﴾Every day He has a matter to bring forth [such as giving honor to some, disgrace to some, life to some, death to some, et cetera]!﴿

(Qur'an 55: 29)

Ḥasan al-Baṣri also had to hide from al-Ḥajjâj. When the news came of the latter's death, Ḥasan thanked Allah (the Exalted) by prostrating to Him.

﴾And the heavens and the earth wept not for them, nor were they given a respite.﴿

(Qur'an 44: 29)

Ibrâheem an-Nakha'ee was yet another who went into hiding because of al-Ḥajjâj. When the news of al-Ḥajjâj's death came to him, he wept tears of joy and said:

Joy has overcome me to the point that from

The greatness of what caused me joy, I was made to cry.

﴾And We have made some of you as a trial for others; will you have patience? And your Lord is Ever All-Seer [of everything].﴿

(Qur'an 25: 20)

On one occasion, a bird called al-Ḥummarah flapped its wings and flew over the head of the Messenger of Allah (bpuh). It was complaining against someone; the Messenger of Allah (bpuh) said:

«Who has tormented this one by (taking her) chicks? Return her chicks to her.»

Commenting on this, someone said:

A pigeon came to you with hope in you,

Complaining with a disturbed and trembling heart,

Who was it that informed it that your place

Is a sanctuary, and that you are a shelter for the wronged?

Sa'eed ibn Jubayr said, "By Allah, I continued to flee from al-Ḥajjâj for a period of time until I felt ashamed." Shortly after saying this, he was brought before al-Ḥajjâj. When the sword was unsheathed and was raised over his head, he smiled. Al-Ḥajjâj asked, "Why are you smiling?" He answered, "While I was in (deep) reflection, a thought entered my mind: I became amazed at your impudence towards Allah and at His mercy towards you." To put things in that light while being in those circumstances showed a great deal of fortitude, faith, and trust in Allah's promise!

Remember that you are dealing with the Most Merciful

The following hadith moved me deeply when I read it, and I should not be surprised if it has the same effect upon you. Aḥmad, Abu Ya'la, al-Bazzâr, and aṭ-Ṭabarâni all related the following:

«Leaning on a cane, an old man came to the Prophet (bpuh) and said: O Messenger of Allah, I have perpetrated treacherous and wicked deeds. Will I be forgiven? The Messenger of Allah said: Do you bear witness that none has the right to be worshipped except Allah and that Muhammad is the Messenger of Allah? The man said: Yes, O Messenger of Allah. The Prophet said: Verily, Allah has forgiven you for your treacherous and wicked deeds. The man departed, saying: Allah is the Greatest, Allah is the Greatest.»

There are certain conclusions, or facts if you will, that one should take away from this hadith. One of them is the vastness of Allah's mercy. Another is that accepting Islam or making repentance wipes out past sins. Yet another is that mountains of sins are nothing compared to the forgiveness of the One Who knows everything. And finally, it is imperative for you to have a good opinion of your Lord along with being hopeful of His comprehensive generosity and His far-reaching mercy.

Optimism

Ibn Abi Dunya's book Ḥusn adh-Dhan Billah contains more than 150 texts from the Qur'an and the Sunnah which entreat the believer to be optimistic, to repudiate hopelessness, and to strive towards betterment through work. Here is a promising fact: those revealed texts that promise good for doing righteous deeds far outnumber those that warn of impending punishment for perpetrating evil deeds. Allah (the Exalted) has given to everything its measure.

Life is toil

Don't grieve over the vicissitudes of your existence – you cannot escape hardship.

Life, for the most part, involves work and responsibilities. Happiness is an exception or only a fleeting phase that comes and goes sporadically. You long for this life, yet Allah does not want it to be a permanent abode for His righteous slaves.

If this world were not a place of trial, it would have been free from disease and hardship; it would have been a comfortable abode for the best of men – the Messengers and Prophets. Adam (pbuh) faced difficulties and troubles until the day he left this world. Prophet Noah's own people scoffed at and ridiculed him. Prophet Abraham was tested by the fire and by the command to sacrifice his son. Prophet Jacob was separated from his son and wept until he lost his sight. Prophet Moses endured the tyranny of Pharaoh and afterwards the disobedience of his own people. Prophet Jesus was poor. Prophet Muhammad (bpuh) patiently endured poverty and the impudence of his people, and he poignantly felt the loss of one of his favorite uncles, Ḥamzah.

The Prophet (bpuh) said:

«This world is a prison for the believer and a paradise for the disbeliever.»

In a literal sense, there are countless examples of the righteous, the scholars, and the truthful being imprisoned for their beliefs.

Pause to reflect

Zayd ibn Thâbit (may Allah be pleased with him) reported that he heard the Messenger of Allah (bpuh) say:

«Whoever's main concern is this world, Allah will scatter his affairs and afflict him with poverty between his eyes; moreover, nothing will come to him from this world except what was written for him. As for those who long for the hereafter, Allah will unite (and make smooth) their affairs. He will instill richness in their hearts and the world will come to them, though it might do so unwillingly.»

'Abdullâh ibn Mas'ood (may Allah be pleased with him) reported that he heard the Messenger of Allah (bpuh) say:

«Whoever transforms all of his concerns into one concern only – concern for the hereafter – Allah will satisfy his demands and needs in this life. As for he who devotes his concerns to worldly matters, Allah will not care in which valley he perishes.»

Treading the middle path saves you from destruction

There are two factors that help one lead a happy life:

1. Moderation in anger.

2. Moderation in fulfilling one's desires.

We have to be moderate in fulfilling our desires, lest our desires and lusts increase to the point of constantly seeking to be satisfied, an outcome that will lead to our destruction. The same can be said about anger, for it too can lead to destruction.

What is required in all affairs is moderation. Strength, when in excess, makes violence and killing easy; if there is a shortage of it, though, we will not be able to defend ourselves against transgressors. When we use strength moderately, we can display the qualities of patience, bravery, and wisdom, each in its proper place and time. The same goes for desire; if there is too much of it, then wickedness and licentiousness will prevail, but if there is too little of it, we will become weak. However, if it is present in due moderation, we will achieve both chastity and satisfaction.

Upon you is to follow the guidance of moderation.

{Thus We have made you [real believers of Islamic monotheism] a just [and the best] nation...}

(Qur'an 2: 143)

You are judged by your dominant characteristics

To be successful means that your good qualities outnumber and overshadow your bad qualities. When this becomes a reality in your life, you will find that people will shower compliments upon you, even for qualities that you do not possess. People will not accept criticism of you either, even if it is true – a mountain is not increased in worthiness by an extra rock, nor is it diminished by one less rock.

Although here and there I have read criticism of Qays ibn 'Âṣim, the generous one of the Arabs, and of the famous leader Qutaybah ibn Muslim, I have found that criticism and censure of such people is neither prevalent in books nor accepted by the masses. The reason for this is that their bad qualities were lost and drowned in an ocean of their goodness. On the other hand, I have read some good things about al-Ḥajjâj, Abu Muslim al-Khurasâni, and al-'Ubaydi, but nobody remembers such praise, nor would anybody believe that any good qualities were present in the likes of such men. This is because these qualities are lost in the mass of their evil and wicked deeds. How perfect and how just Allah is in managing the affairs of His creation!

Your inborn character

The Prophet (bpuh) said:

«Made easy for everything is that for which it was created.»

Why then are talents neglected and discarded? The person who wishes to be somebody else is among the most miserable and wretched of people. The intelligent and wise persons are those who study themselves and then fulfill the purpose for which they were created. If it is to be a driver, they will drive, and if it is to be a farmer, they will farm. Sibawayḫ', the scholar of Arabic grammar, studied the science of Hadith but found it to be too difficult. He moved on to grammar, and he became not only an expert but one of the foremost grammarians in history. A wise person once said:

> The person who pursues a line that is not suited to him is like the one who plants a date-palm tree in Damascus, or like the one who plants a citron in the Arabian Peninsula.

Consider this: Ḥassân ibn Thâbit did not have a voice suited for being the caller to prayer because he was not Bilâl. Khâlid ibn al-Waleed did not distribute the estate of the deceased because he was not Zayd ibn Thâbit, who was well versed in Islamic inheritance law (may Allah be pleased with them). So seek out and determine your place in the scheme of things. An Arab poet said:

> For battles are warriors that were created for them,
>
> And for books are writers and poets.

It's not enough to be merely intelligent: You need true guidance as well

While listening to the news, I heard of the attempted assassination of playwright Najeeb Maḥfoodh, a Nobel laureate in literature. As I was listening to the report, my thoughts returned to those books of his that I had read, and I asked myself this question: In spite of his obvious cleverness, how did he remain ignorant of the truth – the truth that reality transcends imagination, that everlastingness is greater than this transient life, and that divine principles are more important and higher than human ones?

{Is then He Who gives guidance to the truth more worthy to be followed, or he who finds not guidance [himself] unless he is guided?}

(Qur'an 10: 35)

He wrote his plays from his imagination, using his prodigious ability to visualize, present, and inspire. In the end, however, he produced nothing but stories that have no basis in truth.

After reading his biography, I grasped an important principle: you cannot succeed by making others happy at the expense of your own happiness. It cannot be considered correct, never mind sane, to make others pleased with you while you yourself are sad and miserable. Some writers have praised men of genius, not because they realized happiness and peace, but because they allowed themselves to burn on the inside in order to bring illumination to others. True geniuses, however, are illuminated on the inside first, and then they show others the way. They build a foundation of guidance and goodness first of all for themselves, and then for others.

The hereafter and the world of the unseen – you will not find these themes in Najeeb Maḥfoodh's writings. What you will find, though, is a world of imagination, dreams, and emotion; his works are alluring, and so they became popular and successful. But where are the higher aims and noble messages one finds in great works? Truth be told, you will not find these themes discussed in his books.

{To each [category] We extend – to these and to those – from the gift of your Lord. And never has the gift of your Lord been restricted.}

(Qur'an 17: 20)

I concede that Najeeb Maḥfoodh accomplished what he had set out to do, but it is not enough to accomplish what you always wanted; what is required is to fulfill what Allah (the Exalted) wants.

{Allah wishes to make clear [what is lawful and what is unlawful] to you, and to show you the ways of those before you, and accept your repentance, and Allah is All-Knower, All-Wise. Allah wishes to accept your repentance, but those who follow their lusts wish that you [believers] should deviate tremendously away from the right path.}

(Qur'an 4: 26-27)

I cannot say for certain who will enter paradise and who will enter the fire, except for those individuals who have been identified through revelation as heading towards one or the other. That being the case, I can only judge people by their sayings and deeds.

{But surely, you will know them by the tone of their speech!}

(Qur'an 47: 30)

As an afterthought on the subject, what benefit will one receive if he becomes a king while his heart is perverse and full of falsehood? If talent and success do not lead one to salvation, what then are they good for?

If you have inner beauty, you will discern beauty in the universe

To be truly happy, we should enjoy the beauty and splendor of life, an enjoyment that is limited only by the boundaries set forth by Islam. Allah has created for us beautiful gardens because He is Beautiful and He loves beauty, and in order for us to study His signs that are present in His wonderful creation.

{He it is Who created for you all that is on the earth.}

(Qur'an 2: 29)

The sweet-smelling odor, the delicious meal, and the awe-inspiring vista – these all bring lightness and happiness to the soul.

{Eat of that which is lawful and good on the earth...}

(Qur'an 2: 168)

The Prophet (bpuh) said:

«What has been made beloved to me from your world are perfume and women. And the delight of my eye is in the prayer.»

For some people, extremes of self-denial and rigid austerity have clouded and distorted the wonders of life. They live a life of celibacy, they purposely live in a state of poverty, and they deprive themselves of food. The Messenger of Allah (bpuh) said:

«But I fast sometimes and eat (without fasting) at other times; I stand (for prayer at night) and I relax; I marry women; I eat meat. So whoever deviates from my way, is not from me.»

It is strange and confusing to see what the adherents of some sects have subjected themselves to: some have abstained from certain foods, others have given up laughing, and yet others have forbidden themselves from drinking cool water. It is as though they do not realize that these actions are tantamount to torturing oneself and to extinguishing the light of one's soul.

{Say: Who has forbidden the adornment of Allah which He has produced for His servants and the good [lawful] things of provision?}

(Qur'an 7: 32)

The Messenger of Allah (the Exalted) ate honey, and he is the most pious and righteous human being. This is because Allah (the Exalted) created honey to be eaten:

{There comes forth from their bellies a drink of varying color wherein is healing for men.}

(Qur'an 16: 69)

The Messenger of Allah (bpuh) married a virgin, and he also married women who had been either widowed or divorced.

{Then marry [other] women of your choice, two or three, or four…}

(Qur'an 4: 3)

He wore the best of clothes on religious holidays and on other occasions as well.

{Take your adornment at every mosque…}

(Qur'an 7: 31)

The Prophet (bpuh) – whom we must follow and who was sent with the true religion – fulfilled the rights of both body and soul.

Relief after hardship

Hardship, no matter how great and far-reaching it becomes, never endures or lasts. Rather, the harsher and more difficult one's circumstances become, the closer one comes to ease, comfort, and relief. Then help and aid are forthcoming from Allah. Is not the end of every dark night a bright morning?

You are above jealousy

The most blessed of people are those who desire the hereafter and are not jealous of other people for what Allah has given them. They carry with them a message of higher principles, and they wish to impart that message to others. If they are unable to help others, then at least they cause them no harm.

Take the 'Ocean of Knowledge' and the interpreter of the Qur'an, Ibn 'Abbâs (may Allah be pleased with him) as an example. He managed, through his lofty manners and his generous soul, to transform enemies (Banu 'Umayyah, Banu Marwân, and their supporters) into friends. As a consequence, more people were able to benefit from his knowledge and understanding. He filled gatherings with knowledge and the remembrance of Allah. He forgot the days of the Battle of the Camel and of Şiffeen, and he left behind what came before and after those battles. He proceeded to build, to unite and to repair differences. Everybody came to love him and he became the 'Eminent Scholar' of the Islamic nation.

On the other hand, there is Ibn Zubayr), who was the epitome of nobleness, generosity, and sincere worship. He, however, preferred confrontation rather than giving up personal rights, so much so that he became preoccupied in this pursuit and consequently many Muslims were lost. Then the worst of it happened. The Kaaba became a place of fighting because his enemies found him in its precincts, and many were slaughtered. Finally, he himself was killed and then crucified. May Allah be pleased with him and with all of the Prophet's noble Companions.

{And Allah's command must be fulfilled.}

(Qur'an 33: 38)

I do not mean to disparage some and to praise others; I am merely attempting to study history with an eye for seeking out morals and lessons. Gentleness, compromise, and forgiveness – these qualities are present only in a minority of people. This is because, to achieve them and to incorporate them into one's character, one must repress and even subjugate oneself, forgetting lofty desires and ambitions.

Pause to reflect

The Messenger of Allah (bpuh) said:

«Acquaint yourself with Allah in good times, and He will know you in bad times.»

If you fear Allah (the Exalted) and observe His commands in times of ease, then you have acquainted yourself with Allah. In addition, a special link or relation will develop between you and Allah. Allah will then know you during bad times, meaning that He will help you because of your obedience to Him during good times.

"Acquaint yourself" and "He will know you" suggest a special kind of knowledge, one that points to closeness between Allah, the Almighty and His believing slave and to the love of Allah for that slave.

Patience, when truly applied, has the effect of changing misfortune into a blessing. It is all a matter of one's perspective and frame of mind. Allah does not test us in order to destroy us, but rather to assess our patience and degree of faith. This is because Allah has a right to be worshipped in bad times, just as He has the right to be worshipped during times of ease and wellbeing. Most people are faithful in their duties and responsive to commands when things are going well and are in accordance with their inclinations. A crucial point to understand is that the true test is often to worship and follow commandments that are contrary to one's liking, and in this regard, people differ in their faith. How they perform in those situations will determine their ranking with Allah.

Knowledge is the key to serenity and ease

Knowledge and an easygoing nature are like two inseparable companions; if the first is present, the other can be counted upon to accompany it. If you study the lives of Islam's greatest scholars, you will find that they led simple lives and that they were easy to deal with. They understood the purpose of life and knew which issues were paramount and which were less important. Meanwhile, you will find that the most obstinate of people are those who, without having knowledge, are ascetics. They misunderstand revealed texts and are ignorant of religious issues. The calamity of the Kharijites (a deviant sect) stemmed from a paucity of knowledge and understanding. They were not guided to understand that there are issues which are paramount in our religion, and which take precedence over other issues. As a result, they excelled in insignificant matters while failing miserably in lofty matters, not to mention the mere basics.

The wrong way to go about things...

I recently read two famous books, both of which are deprived of that ease and simplicity that the Sharia intends for us.

The first is Iḥyâ 'Uloom ad-Deen (Revival of the Religious Sciences) by al-Ghazâli. He gathered in it a number of hadiths, many of which are either weak or fabricated. He built upon them rules and principles that he thought were the greatest means of bringing a slave closer to his or her Lord.

Comparing this book to the hadith collections of Bukhari and Muslim, I noticed a clear difference. Al-Ghazâli's book consists of exaggeration, harshness, and affectation, while the latter two books consist of ease and moderation, perhaps because they only relate for us the authentic Sunnah. By comparing these books, I found a deeper meaning of the following verse:

{And We will ease you toward ease.}

(Qur'an 87: 8)

The second book is Qoot al-Quloob (Sustenance of the Hearts), written by Abu Ṭâlib al-Makkee. In it, the author encourages the reader to forsake this life, to renounce work, to refrain from even lawful pleasures, and to strive towards austerity and sternness.

The two authors, Abu Ḥamid al-Ghazâli and Abu Ṭâlib al-Makkee, had good intentions. The problem, though, was that their knowledge of the Sunnah was confused and weak. For this reason, errors crept into their way of thinking. We should learn this lesson from their mistakes: the guide must be skilled in the way; he or she must have an accurate map which shows the different paths that lead to one's goal.

{Be pious scholars of the Lord because of what you have taught of the Scripture and because of what you have studied.} (Qur'an 3: 79)

The noblest human being

Some salient features of the Messenger of Allah's character were contentment, optimism, and a generous heart. He was a bearer of glad tidings. He forbade people from extremes of austerity and asceticism, because these lead to deterring people from the truth. Hopelessness and failure were not in his dictionary. A smile was always on his face, and his heart was content. Furthermore, his commands were easy to follow, for his mission was to alleviate hardship and to remove the shackles of falsehood that hold people down.

One step at a time

When addressing the masses in a sermon, an orator must take a step-by-step, systematic approach. Systematic, in this instance, means that more important issues should be dealt with first. This principle is corroborated by the advice of the Messenger of Allah (bpuh) to Mu'âdh (may Allah be pleased with him), when he dispatched him to Yemen:

> «The first thing that you should call them to is to bear witness that none has the right to be worshipped except Allah and that I am the Messenger of Allah...»

In our personal endeavors, many of us realize that we should seek gradual development. Why then, when dealing with others, do we hurl everything down their throats at once?

{And those who disbelieve say: 'Why was the Qur'an not revealed to him all at once?' Thus [it is] that We may strengthen thereby your heart. And We have spaced it distinctly.}

(Qur'an 25: 32)

Muslims should feel a sense of comfort and ease in learning the teachings of Islam, especially since Islam came to save people from inner strife.

The term takleef, which literally means 'a burden' (at least in one of its connotations) was mentioned in the Qur'an only in the negative.

{Allah burdens not a person beyond his scope.}

(Qur'an 2: 286)

When the Prophet's Companions would come to him asking for general counsel or instruction, he would advise them with succinct and concise words, which were easily memorized. After understanding the questioner's situation, the Prophet of Allah (bpuh) always gave a practical and simple response.

We err greatly when we try to present to an audience all of the advice, teachings, manners, and wisdom that we have at our disposal.

{And [it is] a Qur'an which We have divided [into parts], in order that you might recite it to men at intervals.}

(Qur'an 17: 106)

Whether you have a little or a lot, learn to be thankful

The person who is not thankful to Allah for cold, pure water will not be thankful to Him for a mansion or a luxury car.

The person who is not thankful for warm bread will not be grateful if he suddenly becomes blessed with luxury food items, because an ingrate sees a little and a lot to be the same thing. Many before us have made binding promises to Allah that, if He were to give them blessings, they would in turn be grateful and give charity.

{And among them are those who made a covenant with Allah, [saying:] If He should bestow on us from His bounty, we will surely spend in charity, and we will surely be among the righteous. But when He gave them from His bounty, they were stingy with it and turned away while they refused.}

(Qur'an 9: 75–76)

Every day we see people of this sort, people who are mentally distressed, empty on the inside, and bitter towards their Lord because He did not give them more. They feel this way despite their good state of health and in spite of the nourishing food that sustains them daily, not to mention all of the basic necessities that they have. They are not thankful for these things, nor are they thankful for the free time that they have. What would then be the case if they were given castles or mansions? Indeed they would deviate even further from the path of their Lord, and they would increase in haughtiness and disdain.

The one who walks barefooted says, "I will be thankful to my Lord when he blesses me with shoes," and the one with shoes postpones being grateful until he gets an expensive car. We take blessings cash down and are thankful on credit. Our wishes from Allah are never-ending, yet we are slow and lethargic in applying His commandments.

Three plaques

A wise person hung up in his office three plaques, which he would read daily. Written on the first was, "Your today, your today!" Meaning: live within the boundaries of today, working and striving.

The second said, "Reflect and be thankful." Meaning: contemplate Allah's blessings upon you and then be grateful. "Don't be angry," was written on the third.

Pause to reflect

There are two points we should bear in mind when we think about the issues of hardship and relief:

First, when we can no longer bear a hardship, we will lose all hope in human beings, and as a result, our hearts will depend upon Allah (the Exalted) alone.

Secondly, as true believers, whenever we feel that relief is slow in coming, or that our prayers are not answered, we will blame no one but ourselves. We will say to ourselves, "I am in this situation only because of you. Had you been worth anything, your prayers would have been answered." Such self-reproach is more beloved to Allah than many good deeds. When the slaves of Allah go through this process of introspection and self-reproach, they break down before their Lord, admit their shortcomings, and confess that they deserve the calamity that befell them and that they don't deserve to have their prayers answered. At this point, their prayers are answered quickly, and the black clouds above them dissipate.

Ibraheem ibn Adham said, "If the kings knew our quality of life, they would fight us over it with swords."

Ibn Taymiyah said:

> My heart sometimes experiences a kind of inexpressible feeling for a number of hours, and I say: If the people of paradise are in a state similar to mine (right now), they are living a good life.

Be free from worry and fear

More than thirty chapters of the book al-Faraju B'ada ash-Shiddah deal with the topic of ease and relief after difficulty. The book stresses the point that the more severely we become engrossed in hardship, the closer we are to ease and relief. The book has more than two hundred stories, all of which revolve around this theme. Whatever the hardship may be, it is only a matter of days before better times arrive. At-Tanookhi said, "Be calm, for many have come before you who have trodden upon this path."

{And certainly, We shall test you with something of fear, hunger, loss of wealth, lives and fruits...} (Qur'an 2: 155)

{And We indeed tested those who were before them.}

(Qur'an 29: 3)

It is truly just that in this period of examination – which continues until we die – we are expected to worship Allah in bad times just as we are expected to do so in good times. Allah (the Exalted) changes our situations similar to the changing of night and day. Why then the anger, why the disobedience, and why the complaining?

{And if We had ordered them [saying]: Kill yourselves [that is, the innocent ones kill the guilty ones] or leave your homes, very few of them would have done it...}

(Qur'an 4: 66)

Deeds of charity

Abu Bakr (may Allah be pleased with him) succinctly said, "Deeds of charity protect one from life's ups and downs."

This statement is attested to by both revelation and sound logic.

{And had he not been of those who exalt Allah, He would have remained inside its belly [the fish] until the day they are resurrected.}

(Qur'an 37: 143-144)

Khadeejah (may Allah be pleased with her) said to the Prophet (bpuh):

Nay, by Allah, Allah will never forsake you. Verily, you are good to relatives, you carry the burdens of others, you provide for the needy, and you help people who are going through hard times.

Observe how she understood that good deeds necessarily lead to good results and that a triumphant ending follows a noble beginning.

Al-Wuzarâ by aṣ-Ṣabâbi, al-Muntadhim by Ibn al-Jawzi, and al-Faraju B'ada ash-Shiddah by at-Tanookhi: all of these books relate the following incident. A governor named Ibn al-Furât used to constantly seek to inflict harm upon Abu Ja'far ibn Bisṭâm. The latter went through much hardship because of this.

When Abu Ja'far was a child, his mother used to place a piece of bread beneath his pillow. On the following morning, she would give it to a needy person on her son's behalf. Later on in life, Abu Ja'far went to Ibn al-Furât for some purpose or another. Ibn al-Furât immediately said, "Is there a matter between you and your mother concerning bread?" He answered, "No." "You must be truthful with me," Ibn al-Furât insisted. Abu Ja'far, perhaps somewhat embarrassed, recounted the story of his mother in a manner that poked fun at her and at women in general. Ibn al-Furât said, "Do not speak in such a (joking) tone, for before sleeping last night, I prepared a plan that would have destroyed you, if it had succeeded. When I fell asleep, I saw a vision: it was as if my hands were raised with an unsheathed sword and I rushed towards you to kill you. Your mother blocked my way, and in her hand was a piece of bread that she used as a shield to protect you from me. As a result, I couldn't reach you. Then I woke up." Abu Ja'far gently reproached him for the animosity that had gradually been built up between them, and this incident opened the way for a truce between them. Ibn al-Furât generously helped Abu Ja'far in his affairs, and they soon became close friends. Ibn al-Furât was heard to have said after the incident, "By Allah, You will not see from me any evil after this."

Recreation and relaxation

Two salient and established characteristics of the Sharia are flexibility and simplicity. These two qualities help the Muslims in their worship and dealings.

{And that it is He [Allah] Who makes [whom He wills] laugh, and makes [whom He wills] weep.} (Qur'an 53: 43)

The Messenger of Allah (bpuh) would both laugh and joke, but he would speak nothing but truth. He ran races against 'Â'ishah (may Allah be pleased with her), and he explicitly forbade affectation, artificiality, and rigidity. He warned us that when we make the religion too stringent and harsh, it will overwhelm us. In another hadith, we are informed that the religion is solid and that we should delve into it gently. We are also told that every worshipper has a level of vitality, and that those who are too harsh will inevitably and eventually snap. They snap because they only look at present circumstances and are blind to the different situations that they might find themselves in at a future time. They forget about the long-term effects of this attitude and about the boredom caused by over-rigidity. Wiser are they who have a minimum level of deeds that they perform continually no matter what the circumstances.

If they happen to be more enthusiastic on any given day, they do more. But if they weaken, they at least still perform those deeds that are a part of their daily routine. Perhaps this is the meaning of the saying that is attributed to some of the Companions:

The soul comes forth at times and draws back at other times.

Take advantage of the times when it draws forth, and leave it alone when it draws back.

I have seen many people who had good intentions when they performed an inordinate amount of voluntary prayers and when they went to extremes in their application of the religion. Eventually, however, they returned to a weaker state than the one they were in prior to the surge of enthusiasm they experienced.

What many overlook is that the religion primarily came to bring prosperity and happiness to people.

{We have not sent down the Qur'an unto you [O Muhammad] to cause you distress.}

(Qur'an 20: 2)

Allah reproached those who overtaxed themselves by doing more than they were capable of – those who, as a result of withdrawing themselves from the real world, ended up reneging on their previously made commitments.

{But the monasticism which they invented for themselves, We did not prescribe for them, but [they sought it] only to please Allah therewith, but that they did not observe it with the right observance.}

(Qur'an 57: 27)

Islam distinguishes itself from other religions by being moderate, by being easy to follow, by caring for the soul and the body, by catering for this life and the hereafter, by consisting of beliefs that are innately acceptable to all.

{That is the right religion...}

(Qur'an 9: 36)

Abu Sa'eed al–Khudri (may Allah be pleased with him) related the following:

«A desert Arab came to the Messenger of Allah (bpuh) and asked: O Messenger of Allah, who is the best of the people? He replied: The believer who struggles with himself and his wealth in the way of Allah. Next is the man who isolates himself in a valley in order to worship his Lord.»

In another narration, he said:

«The one who fears Allah and leaves people to be safe from his harm.»

Abu Sa'eed (may Allah be pleased with him) also narrated the following hadith, which was recorded by Bukhari:

«The time is near when the most valuable property of the Muslim will be sheep, with which he will follow pastures in mountains and places of rain; he will be fleeing with his religion from trials.»

'Umar (may Allah be pleased with him) said, "Take your fair share of isolation." And in the well-put words of al-Junayd, "Enduring isolation is easier than enduring the whims and flattery involved in mixing with others." Al-Khaṭṭâbi said:

If isolation only meant being safe from backbiting and away from seeing evil that is beyond your ability to change, then it would still be something that had great benefits.

This last saying is similar in meaning to the hadith recorded by al-Ḥâkim and narrated by Abu Dharr (may Allah be pleased with him):

«Seclusion is better than sitting with someone who is a bad influence.»

This hadith has a good chain. Al-Khaṭṭâbi explained that in our religion, the ruling for seclusion and socializing depends upon the circumstances. In the revealed texts, we are encouraged to mix and gather with others for specific purposes: to follow the people of knowledge and to unite with the community for religious matters. As for other gatherings, those who are self-sufficient in preserving their religion and in earning their wealth are better off mixing with others only when necessary or when good deeds are involved. Nevertheless, they must still fulfill their obligations, such as praying with the community, returning greetings of peace, visiting the sick, attending funerals, and so on. What is required, then, is to refrain from socializing excessively, since that results in wasting time and neglecting more important matters. Mixing with others is akin to the body's need for food and drink. In both cases, you should limit your intake to only what is needed. This is purer for the body and the heart, and Allah (the Exalted) knows best.

In his dissertation on the topic of isolation, al-Qushayri said that those who seek seclusion should feel that they are doing so in order to protect people from their evil, not the opposite. This is because the former attitude breeds a modest opinion of themselves, which is required in the religion. The latter thinking, however, means that such people are attesting to their superiority over others, which is not acceptable in the character of a believer.

In this matter, people can be classified into three groups; two of them are opposites, while the third is at a middle point between them. Members of the first group isolate themselves from people to the extent of not attending Friday prayers, other congregational prayers, and gatherings that spread goodness; the people from this group have obviously erred. Those from the second group are social to the point that they even participate in evil or wasteful gatherings, where falsehood, rumors, and wastage of time prevail; they too have erred. Those from the middle group associate with others in matters of worship that must be carried out in congregation. They participate with others in spreading righteousness, in earning rewards, and more generally, in pleasing Allah. They avoid those gatherings that are dominated by evil, falsehood, and extravagance.

{Thus We have made [true believers], a just [and the best] nation.}

(Qur'an 2: 143)

Pause to reflect

'Ubâdah ibn Sâmit related that he heard the Messenger of Allah (bpuh) say:

«Persist in fighting in the way of Allah, for it is among the doors of paradise. Through it, Allah removes anxiety and worry.»

The effect that fighting in the way of Allah has upon a person is something that we might not accept, but it is something that our conscience accepts. Whenever the soul avoids combating evil, its level of fear and anxiety increases. But if it fights for the sake of Allah, Allah (the Exalted) will transform fear and anxiety into happiness, strength, and vigor:

{Fight against them so that Allah will punish them by your hands and disgrace them and give you victory over them and heal the breasts of a believing people, and remove the anger of their [believers'] hearts.}

(Qur'an 9: 14-15)

Therefore fighting in the way of Allah is one of the most potent remedies for combating anxiety, grief and worry; and to Allah do we turn for help.

Contemplate the universe

Look around and contemplate the signs that are present in the creation. The brook, the tree, the flower, the mountain, the earth and the sky, the sun and the moon, the day and the night – they will all remind you of the Creator of all things. Thus your faith will increase and so will your degree of righteousness:

{Then take admonition, O you with eyes [to see].}

(Qur'an 59: 2)

> A philosopher who embraced Islam said:

> Whenever I was beset by doubts, I would look at the book of creation, the letters of which spoke of miracles and ultimate skill. Then my faith would not only return to normal, but it would increase as well.

Follow a studied plan

Ash-Shawkâni said:

> Some scholars advised me that I should never give up writing, even if that meant writing only two lines every day. I acted in accordance with this advice, and I reaped its fruits.

> This is the meaning of the hadith:

> «The best deed is the one that a person continues to do, even if it is something small.»

> It is said that if you add enough drops of water, a flood will be the result.

When we try to do everything all at once, confusion results. What follow is boredom, fatigue, and worst of all, abandonment of action. If we do our work one step at a time, dividing it into stages, we will achieve so much more. Contemplate the prayer. We are ordered to perform it at five different times during the course of any given day. The intervals between the prayers allow for other activities, and there is just sufficient time between one prayer and the next so that the worshipper returns enthusiastically for another prayer. However, if the prayers had been combined all at one time, the worshipper would have become bored. The meaning of one particular hadith is that a person who pushes his horse to sprint during the course of a long journey will not only waste away his mount, but also will not arrive at his destination. Through the experiences of many, the following holds true: the one who works consistently for set periods of time achieves more than the one who tries to do everything at once.

That the prayer makes us organize our time is a lesson that I learned from the people of knowledge and that has benefited me in my life. It is a lesson that is inferred from the verse:

{Verily, the prayer is enjoined on the believers at fixed hours.}

(Qur'an 4: 103)

If we were to distribute our worldly and religious duties around the prayers, we would find our time to be blessed.

For example, if students of Islam were to allot the time after the morning prayer for memorizing, the time after the noon prayer for reading or attending study circles, the time after the afternoon prayer for researching issues, the time after the sunset prayer for visiting people or relaxing, and the time after the evening prayer for reading up on contemporary issues and for sitting with family, they would achieve much:

{O you who have believed, if you fear Allah, He will grant you a criterion and will remove from you your misdeeds and forgive you. And Allah is the possessor of great bounty.}

(Qur'an 8: 29)

Do not be disorderly in your affairs

Debt, financial responsibilities, and bills to pay can play a major role in causing sadness and anxiety. There are three principles regarding this issue that we must both understand and apply:

1. The one who is prudent will not become dependent upon others. Whoever spends prudently, by spending only when necessary and not wasting, will find help from Allah (the Exalted):

   {Verily, spendthrifts are brothers of the devils.}

   (Qur'an 17: 27)

   {And [they are] those who, when they spend, do so not excessively or sparingly but are ever, between that, [justly] moderate.}

   (Qur'an 25: 67)

2. Seek to derive your sustenance through lawful means, for Allah (the Exalted) is aṭ-Ṭayyib (noble, pure, and good) and does not accept other than what is noble, pure and good. He does not bless an income that is earned through unlawful means.

{...Even though the abundance of evil may please you.}

(Qur'an 5: 100)

3. Work diligently to earn wealth lawfully, and stop being inactive and lazy. When Ibn 'Awf migrated to Madinah, he took nothing with him. One of the helpers from Madinah offered him half of his wealth because the Prophet (bpuh) had established a brotherly bond between him and Ibn 'Awf. Ibn 'Awf declined the generous offer and simply replied, "Direct me to the marketplace."

{Then when the [Friday] prayer is finished, you may disperse through the land, and seek the bounty of Allah [by working, et cetera], and remember Allah much, that you may be successful.}

(Qur'an 62: 10)

Your value is determined by your faith and character

He was poor and wan and weak. He wore a torn garment with many patches on it. He was barefoot and hungry. Along with his having an obscure lineage, he possessed neither status nor wealth nor family. Without a roof to shelter him, he would sleep in the mosque and drink from public fountains. His pillow was his own arm, and his mattress was the uneven, rough ground beneath him. Yet he always remembered his Lord, and he would constantly recite the verses of Allah's Book. He would not be absent from the first row in prayer or from the front lines of battle.

«One day he met the Messenger of Allah (bpuh), who upon seeing him, called: O Julaybeeb, will you not marry?

He replied, meekly: Who would give me their daughter?»

He passed by two others who asked the same question, to which he gave a similar reply. The Messenger of Allah (bpuh) said to him:

«O Julaybeeb, go to So-and-so, the Anṣâri, and say to him: The Messenger of Allah sends his greetings of peace to you, and he requests that you marry me to your daughter.»

This particular Anṣâri was from a noble and esteemed household. When Julaybeeb carried out the Prophet's order, the Anṣâri replied, "And peace be upon the Messenger of Allah. O Julaybeeb, how can I marry my daughter to you when you have neither wealth nor status?" His wife heard of the news, and she exclaimed in astonishment, "Julaybeeb! He who has neither wealth nor status!" But their believing daughter heard the words of Julaybeeb, words that, to her, contained the message of the Messenger of Allah (bpuh). She said to her parents, "Do you turn down the request of the Messenger of Allah? By Allah, no!"

Forthwith, the blessed wedding took place. When their first night came, a caller was in the streets announcing a forthcoming battle. Julaybeeb responded without delay and set out for the battleground. With his own hands, he managed to kill seven disbelievers, and then he himself became martyred. He embraced death pleased with Allah and His Messenger (bpuh), and pleased with the morals for which he sacrificed his own life.

After the battle, the Messenger of Allah (bpuh) was asking about those who were martyred. The people began to inform him of those who had died, but they forgot to mention Julaybeeb because of his obscurity. Nevertheless, the Messenger of Allah (bpuh) remembered him, and he said:

«But I have lost Julaybeeb.»

He then found Julaybeeb's corpse, the face covered in dust. He shook off the dust from his face and said:

«You killed seven, and then you were killed! You are from me, and I am from you...»

The Messenger of Allah (bpuh) repeated the second part of that statement three times. This medal of distinction from the Messenger of Allah (bpuh) is by itself an ample reward and prize.

The value of Julaybeeb was his faith and his love for the Messenger of Allah (bpuh), along with the principles for which he died. His humble circumstances and obscure family name did not prevent him from the great honor that was bestowed upon him. With his meager resources, he achieved martyrdom, contentment, and happiness for this world and the hereafter.

{They rejoice in what Allah has bestowed upon them of His bounty, rejoicing for the sake of those who have not yet joined them, but are left behind [not yet martyred] that on them no fear shall come, nor shall they grieve.} (Qur'an 3: 170)

So remember, it is your principles and your character that determine your value. Poverty has never stood immovable in the way of distinction and the achievement of higher aims.

The bliss of the Companions (may Allah be pleased with them)

Among the many ways in which they were blessed, the Companions (may Allah be pleased with them all) were informed of their ranking through revelation. This verse was revealed about Abu Bakr (may Allah be pleased with him):

{But the righteous one will avoid it [hell] – [He] who gives [from] his wealth to purify himself.}
(Qur'an 92: 17-18)

'Umar (may Allah be pleased with him) was given glad tidings in this hadith:

«I saw a white castle in paradise. I asked who it belonged to, and I was told that it belonged to 'Umar ibn al-Khaṭṭâb.»

In the case of 'Uthmân (may Allah be pleased with him), the Messenger of Allah (bpuh) made this supplication:

«O Allah, forgive 'Uthmân for his past and future sins.»

The Messenger of Allah (bpuh) described 'Ali (may Allah be pleased with him) as:

«a man who loves Allah and His Messenger, and Allah and His Messenger love him.»

Concerning Sa'd ibn Mu'âdh (may Allah be pleased with him), the Messenger of Allah (bpuh) said:

«The throne of the Most Merciful quaked for him.»

And he said of Handhalah (may Allah be pleased with him) after he died:

«The angels of the Most Merciful washed him.»

The wretchedness of the disbelievers

As for Pharaoh:

{The fire: they are exposed to it, morning and afternoon...}

(Qur'an 40: 46)

As for Qâroon:

{We caused the earth to swallow him and his dwelling place.}

(Qur'an 28: 81)

As for al-Waleed ibn al-Mugheerah:

{I will cover him with arduous torment!}

(Qur'an 74: 17)

As for Umayyah ibn Khalaf:

{Woe to every slanderer and backbiter.}

(Qur'an 104: 1)

As for Abu Lahab:

{Perish the two hands of Abu Lahab [an uncle of the Prophet], and perish he!}

(Qur'an 111: 1)

And as for al-'Âṣ ibn Wâ'il:

{Nay! We shall record what he says, and We shall increase his torment [in hell].}

(Qur'an 19: 79)

Pause to reflect

Consider the following ill-effects of sinning and of being heedless to the remembrance of Allah: loneliness, not having your prayers answered, developing a hard heart, a lack of blessings in wealth and health, being prevented from knowledge, humiliation, anxiety, and being tested by evil companions who pollute your heart. The above-mentioned results follow sinning just as plants grow after being watered. If these then are the effects of sinning, the remedy lies only in repentance.

Be gentle with womenfolk

{And live with them honorably.}

(Qur'an 4: 19)

{And He has put between you affection and mercy.}

(Qur'an 30: 21)

The Messenger of Allah (bpuh) said:

«Take care of and be good to women, for they are restrained (and bound) to you.»

«The best of you is the one who is best with his family, and I am the best of you to his family.»

The happy family is replete with love, contentment, and the fear of Allah (the Exalted):

{Then is one who laid the foundation of his building on righteousness [with fear] from Allah and [seeking] His approval better or one who laid the foundation of his building on the edge of a bank about to collapse, so it collapsed with him into the fire of hell? And Allah does not guide the wrongdoing people.}

(Qur'an 9: 109)

A smile every morning

To get off to a good start every day, a husband should smile when he meets his wife, and vice versa. This smile is an introductory announcement of agreement and compromise.

«A smile in your brother's face is charity.»

The Messenger of Allah (bpuh) always wore a smile on his face.

{Give greetings of peace upon each other – a greeting from Allah, blessed and good.}

(Qur'an 24: 61)

{When you are greeted with a greeting, greet in return with what is better than it, or [at least] return it equally.}

(Qur'an 4: 86)

Upon entering one's home, one should always make the prescribed supplication:

«O Allah, I ask you for the best of entries and the best of exits. By Allah's name do we enter, and by Allah's name do we exit. And upon Allah, our Lord, do we place our trust.»

To speak in a friendly tone also breeds understanding in the home:

{And say to My slaves [that is, the true believers of Islamic monotheism] that they should [only] say those words that are the best.}

(Qur'an 17: 53)

Would that both husband and wife remember the other's good points and forget the negative ones. When a husband keeps the positive aspects of his wife in his mind, while forgetting (or at least blocking out) her defects, he will find peace and happiness.

An Arab poet said:

Who is the one who has never erred?

And who is the possessor of pure good?

{And had it not been for the grace of Allah and His mercy on you, not one of you would ever have been pure from sins. But Allah purifies [guides to Islam] whom He wills, and Allah is All-Hearer, All-Knower.}

(Qur'an 24: 21)

Minor and trifling matters are the causes of most domestic problems, and I myself have witnessed many marriages that ended in divorce, not because of irreconcilable differences, but because of something small and unimportant. One such domestic strife began because the house was not clean; another resulted because dinner was not cooked on time; the cause of yet another was the woman's objection to the inordinate number of guests coming to see her husband. A list of these and other problems can end up tearing a family apart, leaving children missing their father or mother.

It is incumbent upon us to live in a world of reality (especially as regards our spouses) and not to dream up a utopia, insisting that it be realized in the home. We as humans can become angry and irritable, weak and erring. Therefore, when we speak about or search for domestic bliss, we should keep in mind the concept of relative happiness, and not expect total happiness.

The agreeable nature and good companionship of Imam Aḥmad ibn Ḥanbal deserves mention here. He said after the death of his wife, "She has been my companion for forty years, and in that span of time, I never had a disagreement with her."

The husband must remain quiet when his wife becomes angry and vice versa, at least until the anger subsides and the storm abates. Ibn al-Jawzi said in Ṣayd al-Khâṭir:

> When your companion becomes angry and says something that is unwarranted, you should not take it too hard. His situation is that of a drunken person who is not aware of what is taking place. Instead, be patient, even if it means only for a little while. If you reciprocate his words with harsh words of your own, you become like the sane person who seeks revenge on a madman, or the conscious person who seeks retribution from an unconscious one. Look at him with a merciful eye and pity him for his actions.

Know that as soon as the person awakes from this state, he or she will regret what happened and will come to recognize your value because of your patience. You should especially be patient if the angry person is your parent or spouse. Let them say whatever they want until they calm down, and do not hold them accountable for their words. If those who are angry are met with anger, their own anger will fail to subside, even after they have revived from their drunken--like state.

An obsession for revenge is poison that flows through a diseased soul

The Crucified Ones in History is a book full of stories about revenge--seekers who inflicted harsh punishments on their enemies. What one realizes as one reads this book (which is probably what the author wants us to realize) is that killing their enemies was not enough to quench their thirst for revenge. The irony that the author conveys is that the crucified person actually ceases to feel pain after the soul departs from his or her body. Meanwhile, the revenge--seeking killer will never find peace or happiness because the fire of revenge has enveloped, or rather taken over, his entire being.

The book relates the lives of some of the leaders of the Abbasids; they missed the opportunity of killing their rivals from the Umayyads simply because the latter group died before the former group took office. Still enraged, one of them would remove the corpse of his enemy from the grave and whip it or crucify it and then burn it. So understand this: the seekers of revenge will always feel more pain and misery than the objects of their revenge because they have lost both peace and serenity.

Enemies do not afflict the ignorant person

Nearly as much as the ignorant person afflicts himself.

{And when they meet you, they say: We believe. But when they are alone, they bite the tips of their fingers at you in rage. Say: Perish in your rage...}

(Qur'an 3: 119)

Pause to reflect

When the believers are overcome by misfortune, only by repenting can they truly find a way out of their difficulties. Rather than looking outward, at extrinsic influences, the believers should search inward and recognize that they are blameworthy and deserve what has befallen them. Only when they reach this level of consciousness can they begin the process of correcting, or in some cases redressing, their errors, and repenting to Allah for past mistakes. When they take care of these inner matters, Allah will take care of their outer ones. These words might sound simple, but there are very few who put them into practice.

Do not melt into someone else's personality

The human being passes through three stages: 1) imitation, 2) selection and choice, 3) invention and creativeness. Imitation, the act of copying someone else's personality and mannerisms, is resorted to either because of a strong liking for, or an extreme attachment to, the person being copied. When practiced to extreme, as when the imitators copy someone else even in their tone of voice or bodily gestures, what they are really doing is burying their own personality. Though this might seem absurd to some, one need only look at the younger generation of today: you will find some teens imitating famous people in their walk, talk, and movements. All of their idiosyncrasies are abandoned for the sake of copying their idols. Had they been imitating noble traits and noble personalities, I would commend them, since imitating someone in seeking knowledge, in being generous, or in having good manners, is a truly noble action.

I feel compelled here to reiterate what I have said before: you are a unique entity, and from the time Allah (the Exalted) created Adam (pbuh) no two people have been exactly alike in appearance.

{...And the difference of your languages and colors.}

(Qur'an 30: 22)

Why then, do we wish to be exactly alike in other matters, such as characteristics and talents?

The beauty of your voice is in its uniqueness, and the beauty of your appearance is in its being specific to you.

{...And among the mountains are streaks white and red, of varying colors and [others] very black.}

(Qur'an 35: 27)

Waiting for relief from Allah

Thâbit ibn Qays (may Allah be pleased with him) was an eloquent orator who spoke on behalf of the Messenger of Allah (bpuh) and Islam. However, he would often raise his voice while giving a sermon, and sometimes this occurred in the presence of the Messenger of Allah (bpuh).

{O you who believe! Raise not your voices above the voice of the Prophet, nor speak aloud to him in talk as you speak to one another, lest your deeds may be rendered fruitless while you perceive not.}

(Qur'an 49: 2)

When this verse was revealed, Thâbit thought that it referred to him, and so he isolated himself in his home and wept continuously. The Messenger of Allah (bpuh) noticed that he was absent from a gathering and inquired about him. The Companions informed him of what had occurred, and the Messenger of Allah (bpuh) replied:

«Never! But he is from the inhabitants of paradise.»

In this way, the warning – in Thaibit's case it was merely a perceived warning – became transformed into a glad tiding.

'Â'ishah cried continuously for one month, day and night, because she was falsely accused of wrongdoing. She became wan and pale because of the serious nature of the accusations. Then, suddenly, relief came from Allah, and the Qur'an established her innocence:

{Verily, those who accuse chaste women, who never even think of anything touching their chastity and are good believers, are cursed in this life and in the hereafter.}

(Qur'an 24: 23)

She praised Allah, her reputation was restored, and the believers rejoiced with her.

When the call was made for the battle of Tabuk, three of the believers lagged behind. Allah (the Exalted) revealed verses in which those who remained behind were warned about an impending punishment. The three believers referred to above became miserable because of what they had done, and they repented sincerely. They believed that there was no sanctuary from Allah except with Him; after a short period, which seemed interminable to them, the verses of forgiveness were revealed.

Pursue work that you enjoy

Ibn Taymiyah said:

> I once became ill, and the physician told me that reading and giving talks on knowledge would only exacerbate my condition. I told him that I couldn't abandon those pursuits, and that I would, if possible, like to make his own knowledge a judge between us. Isn't it the case, I asked him, that if the soul feels happy and joyful, the body becomes stronger and sickness is repelled? The doctor replied in the affirmative. Therefore, I said to him, my soul finds joy, comfort, and strength in knowledge. The doctor yielded and admitted that my situation was beyond the pale of his science of medicine.

{Consider it not a bad thing for you. Nay, it is good for you.}

(Qur'an 24: 11)

Pause to reflect

Az–Zarkali's al-'Aylâm contains the biographies of Eastern and Western politicians, scholars, writers, and doctors. The common factor among them all – and the reason they were written about in the first place – is of course that each one of them had a profound effect upon others. After reading their biographies, I began to appreciate the promise and way of Allah: those who strive for something in this world will get their fair share of it by becoming famous, popular, powerful, or rich, depending in each case on what their goals are. Those who strive for the hereafter will find the results both here and there, by benefiting others and by receiving rewards from Allah (the Exalted).

{To each –these as well as those –We bestow from the bounties of your Lord. And the bounties of your Lord can never be forbidden.}

(Qur'an 17: 20)

As I read az-Zarkali's book, I noticed that the non-Muslim figures who contributed to humankind – especially those who strove in the arts – gave happiness to others instead of to themselves. Some of them led miserable personal lives, others were always unsatisfied, while some even went to the extreme of committing suicide.

I asked myself this: what is the benefit of pleasing others while being miserable oneself?

You gave happiness to many, and you are miserable,

You made people laugh, and you yourself cry!

I found that Allah (the Exalted) gave to each one of them according to what he or she wanted, in realization of His promise. Some of them won the Nobel Prize, because that is what they wanted and strived for; others became famous, because that was their higher goal; still others became wealthy because of their love of money and comfort. However, there were also those pious slaves of Allah who achieved both their reward in this life and the reward of the hereafter: people who strove to seek the favor and pleasure of Allah.

A simple shepherd in the Arabian Peninsula was happier on the inside than was Tolstoy. Why? The first led a simple unaffected life, knowing where he was going in this life and in the hereafter. The second never satisfied his desires fully and had no idea where he was going.

Muslims have what is the greatest remedy that humankind has ever known: the belief in what has been divinely preordained, a belief that I have discussed often throughout this book, and for a purpose. I know that I, and others like me, believe in the Islamic concept of preordainment when things go according to our liking, but we tend to complain when things go against our inclinations. This is why an article and condition of our faith is to believe in preordainment, the good of it and the bad of it –when it is sweet and when it is bitter.

Guidance: A natural consequence of belief

Here are some stories that pertain to preordainment. Colonel R. V. C. Bodley authored many books, including The Messenger: The Life of Mohammed. In 1918, he settled in northwest Africa among a group of nomadic desert people. These were Muslims who prayed, fasted, and remembered Allah. He later wrote about some of his experiences with them. This is how he begins one particular narrative:

> One day, a strong sandstorm began gathering force. The vicious winds destroyed much, and the heat was so intense that I felt the roots of my scalp burning. During this experience I felt that I was on the brink of madness. To my astonishment, though, the Arabs did not complain at all. They shook their shoulders with resignation and said that it was something that was written for them and was preordained. Forthwith, they returned to their daily labor with vigor. The head of the tribe said: We didn't lose much if you consider that we deserved to lose everything. But all praise and thanks are for Allah; we still have forty percent of our livestock and we are capable of starting afresh.

> He related the following about another incident:

> As we were traveling through the desert in a car, we had a flat tire, and to make things worse, the driver had forgotten to take along a spare one. I was overcome with both anger and worry. I asked my Arab companions what we were going to do. They calmly reminded me that anger was not going to help the situation, but rather was more likely to aggravate it. We were moving at an excruciatingly slow pace on three good tires and on one that was flat; it wasn't long before the car stopped altogether, and not because of the tire situation, but because we had also run out of fuel. Even when this happened, my traveling companions remained undisturbed. Furthermore, they cheerfully recommenced the journey on foot while singing in unison. After spending seven years in the desert with the Arab nomads, I became thoroughly convinced that the widespread European and American problems of drunkenness, mental sickness, and depression were the results of a fast--paced city life.

He also said:

> I never felt any stress at all while I was living in the desert. I felt that I was in God's paradise. I felt that I had discovered peace, tranquility, and contentment. Many people scoff at the fatalistic beliefs of the Arabs. But who knows? Maybe the Arabs have with them the truth after all, for as I reminisce about the past, it becomes clear to me that my life was composed of disjointed periods that were the results of events or happenings that were pushed onto me without my having any choice. The Arabs refer to these events as being 'Allah's Preordainment and Decree.' In summary, seventeen years have elapsed since I left the desert, and I still take the stance of the Arabs regarding 'Allah's Preordainment and Decree.' I respond to events that are out of my control with serenity, calmness, and composure. This quality that I learned from the Arabs has done more to calm my nerves and lower my level of stress than thousands of prescription sedative pills can do.

To comment on the words of Bodley, I would first like to mention that the source of truth with the desert Arabs was the Messenger of Allah, Muhammad (bpuh). The substance of his message was to save people from hopeless wandering – to take them out of darkness and bring them into light. His noble message contained the secret to peace and salvation: namely, to recognize that Allah predestined everything while at the same time all members of a community must work and do their best to reach their desired goals. The noble message of Islam came to show you your place in the universe, so that you can be the ideal person, who knows the secret and purpose of human existence.

The middle course

{Thus We have made you [true believers], a just [and the best] nation.}

(Qur'an 2: 143)

Happiness is found between two extremes: excess and negligence. The middle course is the divinely prescribed way that saves us from the clear falsehood of two extremes – for instance, the extremes of Judaism and Christianity. Jews had with them knowledge, but they discarded action; Christians worshipped excessively, but they abandoned the divine knowledge that was revealed to them. Islam came with both knowledge and action; it cared for the body and for the soul, and it recognized both revelation and the mind, with each given its rightful place.

When you are moderate in worship, you are following the middle path. What this means is that you should not be so excessive in performing acts of voluntary worship that you hurt and weaken your body; nor should you abandon voluntary deeds of worship altogether. In spending, you should not be extravagant, squandering away your resources, but neither should you be miserly. Moderation in character means finding a level between being harsh and overly lenient, between constantly frowning and constantly laughing, and between lonely isolation and excessive socializing.

Islam provides a middle and just way in all affairs.

{Then Allah by His leave guided those who believed to the truth of that wherein they differed. Allah guides whom He wills to a straight path.} (Qur'an 2: 213)

Avoiding extremes

Muṭarrif ibn 'Abdullâh said, "The worst journey is the haqhâqah."

Haqhâqah is a journey wherein the traveler is rash and hurried, exhausting both himself and his mount. The Messenger of Allah (bpuh) said that the worst leaders are the ones who are too severe with those under their authority.

Keep in mind that generosity comes between extravagance and meanness, and that courage comes between cowardliness and recklessness. A smile is between a frown and a laugh. Patience is between hardiness and squeamishness. Extravagance has a remedy: it is to put out a part of the flame. Meanwhile, the cure for negligence is to whip oneself into shape by developing a stronger level of determination.

{Guide us to the straight path –the path of those on whom You have bestowed favor, not of those who evoked [Your] anger or of those who are astray.}

(Qur'an 1: 6-7)

Pause to reflect

There is no quality that is harder to adopt than patience, regardless of whether patience is required after separation from a loved one or when unfavorable events occur. It is most difficult to be patient when the period of waiting is prolonged or when hopelessness takes over. During this period, one needs provisions, provisions that vary according to the situation:

1. Look at the level of hardship you are bearing, and appreciate that things could have been worse.
2. Hope that Allah compensates you for your sufferings in this world.
3. Keep in mind the reward of the hereafter.
4. Know that anxiety and restlessness are of no use.

Add to this list anything else that may help you be patient during a period of hardship.

Who are the righteous ones?

Waiting eagerly for the call to prayer, arriving at the mosque before the commencement of prayer, bearing no personal grudges against others, leaving alone other people's private affairs, being content with the basic necessities of life, studying the Qur'an and the Sunnah, feeling concern for the pains of other Muslims, and being charitable with one's wealth – these are all qualities of a righteous person.

A middle path with regard to wealth is highly recommended. You should seek neither the level of affluence that can entice you towards evil (unless, of course, you use your wealth wisely and spend it generously in the way of Allah), nor the level of poverty that causes you to forget about the hereafter. The best situation for many believers is to have just enough wealth to fulfill all of their needs in a lawful manner – not much more and not any less.

Basic needs may differ slightly from person to person, but in general, they include a house to live in, a spouse to seek comfort with, a suitable vehicle to move about in, and enough money to buy necessary provisions.

Allah is Most Kind to His slaves

A high-ranking member of the Riyadh community related to me that in 1376 AH, a group of fishermen from the town of Jubayl set out for the sea, and after spending three days and three nights fishing, they did not manage to catch even a single fish. Meanwhile, a group of nearby fishermen caught many fish. They were surprised, not merely at the disparity between their failure and the other group's success, but because they were performing the five daily prayers and failed, while the other group was not praying and succeeded. One of them said,

How perfect is Allah! We prayed to Allah every single prayer and we didn't get anything; the other group did not prostrate to Allah even once over the last few days, and look at all that they managed to get!

In this way, the devil whispered evil suggestions to them and advised them to abandon the prayer. The next day, they did not wake up for the dawn prayer. They also neglected to perform the noon and afternoon prayers. Before nightfall, they set out for the sea; they caught a fish and upon slitting it open they found a pearl in its stomach – a very expensive pearl. One of them took the pearl in his hand, stared at it, and said, after reflecting:

How perfect is Allah! When we obeyed Him we got nothing, and when we disobeyed Him this is what we got! Indeed, this sustenance before us is of a doubtful nature.

Then he took hold of the pearl and hurled it into the ocean, saying immediately afterwards:

Allah will recompense us with better than this. By Allah, I will not take it, for we acquired it after abandoning the prayer. Come with me, and let us leave this place wherein we disobeyed Allah.

They traveled three miles before camping for the night. Shortly afterwards they went fishing again, and they caught a fair--sized fish. When they slit it open, they found the same valuable pearl inside its stomach. They said, "All praise is due to Allah, Who has provided us with good sustenance." They had caught the fish after praying, remembering Allah, and asking for His forgiveness, so this time they kept it.

You should notice one important difference: the object was one and the same, but it was filthy when they acquired it while they were disobeying Allah, and it was pure when they acquired it while obeying Him.

{Would that they were contented with what Allah and His Messenger gave them and had said: Allah is Sufficient for us. Allah will give us of His bounty, and [also] His Messenger [from alms, et cetera]. We implore Allah [to enrich us].}

(Qur'an 9: 59)

Verily, it is Allah's kindness. So whenever somebody abandons something for Allah, Allah (the Exalted) provides him or her with something that is better.

This reminds me of a story about 'Ali (may Allah be pleased with him). One morning, he entered the mosque of Kufa to pray two voluntary units of prayer. Before entering, he found a boy standing at the door. He said to him, "O boy, hold my mule for me until I finish praying." As 'Ali was entering the mosque, he made an intention to reward the boy with a dirham for his services. Meanwhile, the boy removed the noseband from the mule and rushed off to the marketplace to sell it. When 'Ali came out of the mosque, he found no boy, but only his mule without its noseband. He commissioned a man to go after the boy, instructing him to go to the marketplace since the boy would probably go there to sell the noseband. The man found the boy auctioning it in the market, so he bought it from him for one dirham. He returned to 'Ali and informed him of what had happened. After hearing what occurred, 'Ali said, "How perfect Allah is! By Allah, I intended to give him a lawful dirham, but he refused to take it other than in an unlawful way."

{Whatever you [O Muhammad] may be doing, and whatever portion you may be reciting from the Qur'an, – and whatever deed you [mankind] may be doing [good or evil], We are Witness thereof, when you are doing it. And nothing is hidden from your Lord [so much as] the weight of an atom [or small ant] on the earth or in the heaven.}

(Qur'an 10: 61)

And [He] will provide for him from where he does not expect

{And [He] will provide for him from where he does not expect.}

(Qur'an 65: 3)

At-Tanookhi related in al-Faraju B'ada ash-Shiddah a story of a man who fell into a state of dire poverty. All doors of ease were shut tight before him. On one particular day, his situation became so frightful that he and his family had nothing whatsoever in the house to eat. He later said:

The first day, we went hungry. The second passed in a similar fashion, and when the sun was about to set, my wife said to me: Go out and find anything that you can for us to eat, for we are on the verge of dying. I remembered a female relative of mine and set out for her home. Upon meeting her, I informed her of our pathetic situation. She said that they had nothing in the house other than a rotten fish. I told her to give it to us anyway, since we were close to starving. I took it home with me and slit it open, and to my astonishment, I found a pearl lodged in its stomach. I sold it for thousands of dinars, and then I informed my relative of what happened. She said that she would only take a share of the proceeds, not all of it. My situation improved greatly after that, and I furnished my house from my share of the profits. I knew that it was the kindness of Allah, and nothing else.

{And whatever of blessings and good things you have, it is from Allah.}

(Qur'an 16: 53)

{[Remember] when you sought help of your Lord and he answered you.}   (Qur'an 8: 9)
{And He it is Who sends down the rain.}   (Qur'an 42: 28)

A virtuous worshipper recounted to me what happened to him when he was in the desert one day with his family. He said:

We were in the middle of the desert when we ran out of water. I set out to search for water, and I found that the small brook that was near us had gone dry. I continued to search for water in all directions but was unable to find even a drop. Soon afterwards we were overcome by thirst. My children desperately needed to drink something. I remembered my Lord, Who answers the prayer of the one who is in distress. I stood, made the alternate ablution (the dry ablution that is performed when one cannot use water) with sand, faced the Kaaba, and prayed two units of prayer. Then I raised my hands and cried. My tears flowed as I was ardently asking Allah for help. I remember now that the following verse repeatedly came to mind:

{Who responds to the distressed one, when he calls Him...}   (Qur'an 27: 62)

By Allah, immediately, as I stood from my place of prayer (and there had not been a cloud in the sky), a cloud approached our very spot in the desert. It stopped directly above us, and it started to rain generously. The brooks around us became replenished. We drank, washed, and made ablution. Then we praised and thanked Allah. Shortly afterwards, we traveled away from where it had rained, and I found that the surrounding area was dry and barren; it had only rained where we were. I realized that Allah brought for us the cloud in response to my prayer, and so I praised Him.

{And it is He Who sends down the rain after they had despaired and spreads His mercy. And He is the Protector, the Praiseworthy.}

(Qur'an 42: 28)

We have to be diligent in asking Allah (the Exalted), for only He can provide for, guide, and help His slaves. Allah mentioned one of His Messengers and said:

{And We cured his wife [to bear a child] for him. Verily, they used to hasten on to do good deeds, and they used to call on Us with hope and fear, and used to humble themselves before Us.}   (Qur'an 21: 90)

An early recompense

Ibn Rajab and others gave an account of a worshipper who ran out of resources while he was in Makkah. He became extremely hungry and was about to die from lack of nourishment. One day, as he was wandering in the precincts of Makkah, he found an expensive necklace. He put it into his sleeves and headed for the mosque. On his way, he came across a man announcing that he had lost a necklace. The poor man later said:

I asked him to describe it to me, and he did so perfectly, leaving no room for doubt. I gave him the necklace without taking any reward from him. I said: O Allah, I have given it up for you, so compensate me with what is better.

He then went to the sea and began a journey in a small boat. Only a brief period of time passed before a storm came, with heavy winds crashing into the boat. The boat smashed into pieces, and the man was forced to cling to apiece of wood. The violent winds propelled him to the left and to the right. Finally, he was washed ashore onto an island.

He found there a mosque filled with people who were praying, so he joined them. He found papers with parts of the Qur'an written on them, and he began to recite from them. The people of the island asked him, "Do you read the Qur'an?" He answered in the affirmative. They said, "Teach our children the Qur'an." So he began to teach them, and he took a salary for his services. One day, they saw him writing, and they asked, "Will you teach our children to write?" Again he answered in the affirmative and began teaching them for a salary.

A short time later they said to him, "There is an orphaned girl with us whose father was a good man. Will you marry her?" He agreed to the marriage and later related:

I married her, and when I saw her on the wedding night, I found that she was wearing that exact same necklace. I asked her to tell me the story of the necklace. She said that her father lost it in Makkah, and a man found it and returned it to him. She said that whenever her father prostrated, he would supplicate for his daughter to be blessed with a husband similar to that honest man. I then informed her that I was that man.

He abandoned something for the sake of Allah, so Allah compensated him with something that was better.

> «Verily, Allah is good and pure, and He does not accept other than what is good and pure.»

When you ask, ask Allah

Allah's kindness is very near to us. He hears all and answers our supplications. It is we who are full of shortcomings, and so we badly need to be persistent in our supplications. Boredom or hopelessness should never cause us to stop invoking Allah, nor should one of us say: I prayed, yet I have not been answered. Instead, we should press our heads humbly on the ground and beg for help from Allah. The best way to do this is to ask Him by His perfect names and attributes. But until we are answered, we must be persistent in asking Him.

{Invoke your Lord with humility and in secret.}

(Qur'an 7: 55)

A writer narrated this story:

> A Muslim went to a certain country as a refugee, and he implored the authorities there to grant him citizenship. All doors were shut before him. Despite his many efforts at asking help of others, all of his contacts failed. One day he met a righteous scholar, and he gave him an account of his predicament. The scholar said to him: Supplicate to your Lord, for He is the One Who makes things easy. The meaning of this advice is found in the hadith:

> «If you ask, then ask Allah; and if you seek help, seek help from Allah. And know that if the nation were to gather together in order to give you some benefit, they would not bring you any benefit, except with what Allah has written for you.»

The refugee later related: By Allah, I stopped going to people for help or for intercession, and instead, I began praying to Allah in the last third of the night, just as the scholar had told me to do. Just before the break of dawn, I would call to Allah and invoke Him for relief. Only a few days later, I submitted an application for citizenship without using any person of position to intercede for me. A few more days passed by, and then suddenly, to my astonishment, I was called to pick up my citizenship request papers. They were stamped: Approved.

{Allah is very Gracious and Kind to His slaves.}

(Qur'an 42: 19)

Precious moments

At-Tanookhi gave the account of a governor in Baghdad who usurped the wealth of an elderly woman in his province. He took away all of her rights and confiscated her property. She went to him, wept before him, and complained of his oppression and wrongdoing. He was neither regretful nor ashamed of what he had done. In a fit of anger, she said, "I will pray against you." He laughed at her in mockery and said, "Then you should pray in the last third of the night." His arrogance had made him say this to her. She went away, and in accordance with the governor's mock advice, she was steadfast in praying during the last third of the night. It was only a matter of days before he was violently removed from office. As a reward for his tyranny, his properties were seized, and he was publicly whipped. After the whipping, the woman passed by him and said, "You did well! You advised me to pray in the last third of the night, and I found the results to be most favorable."

The last third of the night is a very precious time in our lives. Why? During this time, Allah (the Exalted) says:

«Is there someone who is asking? I will give to him. Is there someone who is seeking forgiveness? I will forgive him. Is there someone who is supplicating? I will answer him.»

From childhood until now, I can recall a number of occasions on which it was clear that help comes only from Allah. Approximately ten years ago, I was on a flight from Abha to Riyadh. Shortly after takeoff, an announcement was made that the plane was returning to Abha due to a mechanical problem.

They then claimed to have fixed the problem, and we took off for a second time. Upon approaching the runway in Riyadh, the landing wheels would not open. We circled the city of Riyadh for a whole hour. The pilot made ten attempts to land, but on each occasion, the landing gear did not respond. Many people in the plane panicked, and tears were flowing profusely as we waited in the sky for death. At that moment, we saw how insignificant and fleeting this life is, and our hearts became attached to the hereafter. We began to repeat, "There is none worthy of worship except Allah alone, and He has no partners. The kingdom belongs to Him; all praise is due to Him, and He is upon all things capable." An old man stood and exhorted the people to turn to Allah, to supplicate to Him, to seek forgiveness, and to make repentance. And Allah said about people that:

{When they embark on a ship, they invoke Allah, making their faith pure for Him only...}

(Qur'an 29: 65)

We invoked the One Who answers the prayer of the one who is in distress. On the eleventh attempt, we descended safely, and when we landed, it was as if we were returning from our graves. Tears dried, smiles appeared, and our peace of mind returned. How merciful and kind is Allah! An Arab poet said:

How often do we ask Allah when we become afflicted?

But when our troubles leave us, we forget Him,

When in the ocean, we invoke Him to save our ship,

When we return safely to land, we disobey Him,

We fly in the sky in safety and comfort,

And we do not fall because our protector is Allah.

Divine preordainment

In al-Qaseem, a newspaper printed in Syria, an article was written about a young man who booked a flight to travel abroad. He informed his mother of the flight time and asked her to wake him up a short time before departure. After he fell asleep, his mother heard on the radio that the weather conditions were awful and that the wind was blowing violently. The compassion that she felt for her only child caused her to not wake him up, in the hope that he would miss the flight.

When she was sure that the flight had taken off, she went to wake up her son. Upon entering his room, she found that he was lying dead on his bed.

{Say [to them]: Verily, the death from which you flee will surely meet you, then you will be sent back to [Allah], the All-Knower of the unseen and the seen, and He will tell you what you used to do.}

(Qur'an 62: 8)

Death

Shaykh 'Ali aṭ-Ṭanṭawi related that a man who drove a truck in Syria once picked up a passenger to give him a lift. The passenger sat in the back, where there was neither a roof nor a cover. There was, however, a coffin that had been prepared for burial. It started to rain and the man, noticing that it was a large coffin, decided to seek shelter inside of it. Another passenger came onto the truck, and he also made his way to the back. He happened to choose a seat beside the coffin. While it continued to rain, the second passenger thought that he was alone in the truck. Without warning, the first passenger stuck his hand out of the coffin to see if the rain had subsided. On seeing the hand, the second passenger became terrified, thinking that a dead man in the coffin was rising to life. From the sheer terror and shock of the moment, the man stumbled backwards, fell out of the truck, and smashed his head on the pavement, dying instantaneously.

This unexpected way of dying is how Allah had written for this man to die.

«Everything happens according to a divine decree, and in the deaths of others are morals and lessons.»

We must realize that death is hovering above us. At any moment, day or night, death can come. 'Ali (may Allah be pleased with him) expressed in lucid terms the reality of our life:

The hereafter is traveling towards us, and this life is traveling away from us, so be from the children of the hereafter and not from the children of this world. For today is action without reckoning (Judgment), and tomorrow is reckoning without action.

From this saying, we can learn how imperative it is for us to improve ourselves, to renew our repentance, and to know that we are dealing with Allah, Who is Most Generous and All-Powerful. Death does not ask a person for permission prior to arrival, nor does it give one an early warning about its being on its way:

{No person knows what he will earn tomorrow, and no person knows in what land he will die.}
(Qur'an 31: 34)

{...For you is the appointment of a day [when] you will not remain thereafter an hour, nor will you precede [it].}
(Qur'an 34: 30)

At-Tantawi related another story that equally illustrates the unexpectedness of death. A bus full of people was moving when the driver suddenly pressed the brakes. The passengers asked him what was wrong. He said, "I am stopping for this old man who is waving so that he can get on the bus." They all said in wonder, "We don't see anyone." He said, "Look at him over there." They repeated that there was no one to be seen. He said confidently, "Now look, he is coming to get in." Now the situation was beyond wonder, and they exclaimed, "By Allah, we don't see anyone." Then, in an instant, the driver died in his seat. Thus death came to him in the most bizarre and unexpected of scenarios:

{When their term is reached, neither can they delay it nor can they advance it an hour [or a moment].}
(Qur'an 7: 34)

People are cowardly when they face danger; their hearts begin to thump when the possibility of death arises, and then, without prior warning, they die at a time when they feel most safe.

{[They are] the ones who said about their killed brethren while they themselves sat [at home]: If only they had listened to us, they would not have been killed. Say: Avert death from your ownselves, if you speak the truth.}
(Qur'an 3: 168)

The strange thing is that we do not think about meeting Allah or about the transient nature of this life.

Allah alone is All-Powerful

Sometimes it is a minor incident that wakes one up to the reality of life. In 1413 AH, I traveled to Riyadh in order to meet a friend of mine. He had to work late on the day of my arrival, so I went directly to my hotel. Since it was a quiet season, there were not many people in the hotel. The porter directed me to a room on the fourth floor, far away from the activities of the hotel staff.

After entering the room, I placed my briefcase on the bed and went to the washroom to make ablution. I closed the washroom door behind me, and after washing up, I went to the door to get out. To my vexation, the door was jammed; no matter how hard I tried, I couldn't open it. I tried many times using different techniques. Soon I realized that I was stuck in this constricted place with no window, no telephone, and worst of all, no one nearby to whom I could call for help. I remembered my Lord and supplicated to Him for assistance. I stood absolutely powerless for twenty minutes, though it seemed more like three days. For those twenty minutes I sweated, my heart rate increased alarmingly, and my body began to shake. The main cause of my high level of panic was that this had happened suddenly, without warning, and that I was in a strange place with no means of contacting anyone for help.

After what seemed like a lifetime, I decided to try and force the door open using bodily strength. I began to shake and jerk the door with my weak, skinny body. I continued to shake it until I got tired and needed to rest. I carried on in this manner for a while, taking rest whenever I became exhausted. Finally, the door gave in and I emerged with the sort of feeling that someone might have who has come out of his grave. I praised and thanked Allah. I remembered how weak human beings are and how helpless we can become in the passing of an instant. Then I remembered our shortcomings and our forgetfulness of the hereafter:

{And be afraid of the day when you shall be brought back to Allah.}

(Qur'an 2: 281)

{Wheresoever you may be, death will overtake you, even if you are in fortresses built up strong and high!}

(Qur'an 4: 78)

Death comes in ways that we do not expect. I have read and heard of people who go forth seeking death, and in the end, they are granted a long life. Meanwhile, there are others who go forth seeking safety, only to end up dying in the very place where they felt most secure. One person seeks treatment for a sickness and meets death this way, while another lives dangerously and remains safe. How perfect is Allah, the Most Wise; He has created everything and planned everything according to His divine wisdom.

Unexpected relief

I recently read of a story of a man who was paralyzed. He remained bedridden in his home for years, and eventually, boredom and a sense of failure overcame him. Doctors were unable to do anything for him. One day, he was alone at home when a scorpion descended from the ceiling of his room, and even though he saw it coming, he was unable to move. After landing on his head, the scorpion repeatedly stung him. His whole body, from head to toe, broke out into convulsions. Slowly, and to his astonishment, sensation returned to his limbs, and after a short period of time, he found himself walking about in the room. He then opened the door and went to his wife and children. They could not believe their eyes when they saw him standing before them. Only when they finally calmed down was he able to inform them of what had taken place.

How perfect is Allah, Who caused the scorpion to be a remedy for his ailment!

I mentioned this story to a doctor, and he accepted it as being plausible. He told me that there are kinds of poisonous serum that, when their toxicity is chemically reduced, are used by doctors to treat paralyzed patients.

And Allah (the Exalted) has not sent down a sickness, except that He has also sent down for it a cure.

Allah allows miracles to occur for His righteous slaves

Ṣilat ibn Ashyam, a pious Muslim of the second century AH, was traveling in the way of Allah, and when night fell, he decided to take shelter in a nearby forest. He entered it, made ablution, and then stood for prayer. Without warning, a lion rushed towards him; as it came dangerously near him, he continued to pray. It began to circle around Ṣilat, yet he did not break away from his prayer, instead remaining steadfast, beseeching Allah for help. He made the final salutation that one makes to exit the inviolable state of prayer, and he then said to the lion, "If you have been ordered to kill me, then do so. If you have not been ordered to do so, then leave me alone so that I may speak privately to my Lord." The lion departed quietly and left Ṣilat alone.

Ibn Katheer, in al-Bidâyah wan–Nihâyah, mentioned a story analogous to the one just related. Safeenah (may Allah be pleased with him), the freed slave of the Messenger of Allah (bpuh), was traveling with his Companions along the shore of the ocean. When they moved inland, a lion approached them menacingly. Safeenah said, "O lion, I am from the Companions of the Messenger of Allah, and I am his servant."

These are my companions, so there is nothing that you can do against us." The lion turned around and raced away as if it were fleeing from them.

Many such stories are true and have been related by reliable sources. What is important, though, is that you take away from them a realization that our Lord is Most Merciful and Most Wise, and that He is aware of all that takes place in the universe.

{There is no private conversation of three but that He is the fourth of them, nor are there five but that He is the sixth of them – and no less than that or no more except that He is with them [in knowledge] wherever they are.}

(Qur'an 58: 7)

Good Reads

* Don't Be Sad! Be Happy!   ISBN: 9781643544878
* Stories of the Prophets   ISBN: 9798774942602
* The Ideal Muslimah   ISBN: 9798834334422
* Hadiths on Good Moral   ISBN: 9781643544823
* Matters of the Heart   ISBN: 9781643544731
* The Battles of Prophet   ISBN: 9781643544724
* Stories of the Qur'an   ISBN: 9781643544700
* Timeless Seeds of Advice   ISBN: 9781643544694
* Tafsir Ibn Kathir   ISBN: 9781643544625
* The Lofty Virtues of   ISBN: 9781643544601
* Inner Dimensions of Salah   ISBN: 9781643544571
* The Journey of the Spirit   ISBN: 9781643544496
* Al-Husain Ibn Ali   ISBN: 9781643544328
* The Friends of Allah   ISBN: 9781643544236
* Gardens of Purification   ISBN: 9781643544229
* The Spiritual Cure   ISBN: 9781643544212
* Fleeing From the Fire   ISBN: 9781643544205
* The Journey of the Strangers ISBN: 9781643544175
* The Heavenly Dispute   ISBN: 9781643544168

* Disciplining the Soul	ISBN: 9781643544151
* Life in al-Barzakh	ISBN: 9781643544144
* Diseases of the Hearts	ISBN: 9781643544106
* The Path To Guidance	ISBN: 9781643544052
* Miracles of the Prophet	ISBN: 9781643544038
* Al-Fawaid: A Collection of	ISBN: 9781643543789
* Great Women	ISBN: 9781643543772
* The Story of Muhammad	ISBN: 9781643543635
* Thirty Lessons for those Fast	ISBN: 9781643543628
* Seerat of Prophet	ISBN: 9781643543611
* WhasWasa: The Whispering	ISBN: 9781643543499
*Khalid Bin Al-Waleed	ISBN: 9781643543444
* The Islamic Jesus	ISBN: 9781643543376
* The Spiritual Path to Allah	ISBN: 978164354488-5

www.ingramcontent.com/pod-product-compliance
Lightning Source LLC
Chambersburg PA
CBHW071949070526
44583CB00015B/1127